THE
SURVIVAL
HANDBOOK

D1102555

THE
SURVIVAL
HANDBOOK

JIM AITKEN

and

JOHN MUSTON

NEW
ORCHARD

This edition first published in Great Britain 1991
by New Orchard Editions
Villiers House, 41/47 Strand, London WC2N 5JE,
a Cassell Company.

The material in this volume was first published in *Survival
Training and Techniques* and *Take the Survival Challenge*.

ISBN 1-85079-171-6

Illustrations by Roy Carr

Printed and bound in Great Britain by
Mackays of Chatham PLC

PART ONE: TRAINING AND TECHNIQUES

CONTENTS

1. INTRODUCTION

This book is intended to cover the survival needs of people in the climatically temperate parts of the world, e.g., the United Kingdom and Europe. No attempt has been made to cover the specialized requirements of jungle or desert although some reference may be made to both. It does cover the problems of cold since arctic conditions can be found even in Great Britain.

With the increase in outdoor leisure pursuits such as hill-walking, sailing, camping, etc., a greater proportion of the population need to have some idea of basic survival techniques, and even those who have no intention of indulging in such activities could well find themselves in a survival situation with a broken-down car on a lonely stretch of high moorland road in the middle of winter. More than one family that has gone out onto the so-called gentle moors at the back of their home has been caught by the sudden onset of bad weather, or by a child breaking an ankle a long way from a road. No one can say 'It will never happen to me.'

This is the handbook for the ordinary person who wants to learn the basic skills needed to cope with the unexpected. The first part explains the techniques used by survival experts and some of the situations which may result in the knowledge you have gained being put into action. The second part, Take the Survival Challenge, assumes you would like to put your skills into practice and test yourself. We take you step by step through one man's survival challenge and explain how you can plan your own exercise.

No attempt has been made to cater for those who yearn for 'the good life' of self-sufficiency. There are no chapters on goat management or cabbage growing. The man (or woman) in a survival situation cannot wait for Nature to take its slow course with such matters. He or she is concerned with survival now.

A word of warning, especially to the younger readers. Any skill or technique needs to be practised in order to perfect it and we hope that readers will go out and do this. As a safeguard make sure your first attempt takes place within reach of civilized facilities so that you do not put yourself at risk if your first snowhole or your first attempt at improvised cooking is a disaster. If it is you will learn a lot and your next attempt will be much better. There are some things, however, you cannot practise fully. It is illegal to kill virtually all species of birds and small animals so you should not contemplate setting snares or other devices except in a real life or death situation. Only then will you have a possible excuse. Nevertheless, with the help of your friendly butcher you can certainly practise skinning and cooking a rabbit or a pigeon.

Finally, we have assumed that you have the basic knowledge to practise whatever activity you are involved in. For this reason you will not find information on how to use a compass or read a map if you are a hill-walker. Similarly, the motorist stranded on the lonely moor referred to above will not find instructions on how to change a wheel or diagnose an electrical fault. These are skills which are part of your activity interest; a lack of them may cause you to be precipitated into a survival situation so be well warned and make sure you are capable of being a safe hill-walker, competent motorist, etc.

2. A BIT OF PSYCHOLOGY:
Survival stresses

What is Survival? Before going any further it is possibly worth defining this. I suggest that the following sums it up in one not too lengthy sentence. *Survival is the art of remaining alive in and escaping from a hostile environment, without full facilities.* Something simple like that needs a bit of explanation. I, like many other mountain enthusiasts, have often camped high in some Scottish glen in the middle of winter and enjoyed it. However, I have been equipped with a good sleeping-bag, mountain tent, stove and plenty of food. That is not survival; it is winter mountain camping. At the other extreme, some backpackers and those who compete in mountain marathons and similar events pare their equipment and food down to the last fraction of an ounce – or gramme for the metrically minded – by careful selection of the lightest adequate tent, clothing, dehydrated food, etc. A total kit weight of 12lb per head is considered heavy by such people, and this includes everything needed for a weekend. Yet they will sleep warm at night and have an adequate amount of food, if not to gourmet standards. Again, that is not survival; it is lightweight camping.

In both these examples those concerned are equipped with full facilities for their chosen activity and they have planned for it. They have trained and practised, sometimes over many years, for these pastimes and have become very proficient as a result. To them the environment is not hostile; indeed, they probably gain aesthetic pleasure from being in a wild and beautiful area far from the madding crowd. To them there is no stress involved but possibly the opposite – peace and relaxation.

For another individual, clad only in a city suit and unversed in the skills of winter camping and with no specialized equipment, the same location could present a survival situation of great seriousness, in which death could well be the outcome.

WHO SURVIVES?

The answer is almost anyone. Success in a survival situation does not appear to be the preserve of any particular race, creed, sex, age group or other classification. As I write this new-born babies are being pulled out alive after being buried for nine days in the rubble of a Mexican hospital demolished by an earthquake. At the other extreme there is a well-documented case of an elderly man who broke his leg while walking alone in the Lake District but was found alive and well after 21 days. He had survived with no additional clothing or equipment other than what one might expect a hill-walker to carry for a day's walking. The babies probably survived because they were not old enough to be aware that being entombed in concrete normally causes stress. They were well wrapped in bedding and their cots protected them physically. The elderly man in the Lakes probably survived because his age brought a mature outlook to bear on the situation and because he did the maximum with the limited facilities available – a little food, a spare jersey and an understanding of the need to crawl to a sheltered spot.

Although **anyone can survive** there are indications that some qualities and characteristics will improve a person's chances of surviving. It is your mental attitude more than your ability to light a fire or carry out some other practical task which is most likely to ensure your ultimate survival. For this reason it is

FIG. 1. DETERMINATION

worth considering these qualities in some detail.

If I were allowed only one characteristic I would, without doubt, demand **determination**. This above all has kept men alive in heat, in cold, at sea, in the air, in concentration camps and in many other situations when every fibre in their body was telling them to 'Give up'. You cannot learn determination, it cannot be taken out of a bottle. It is an amalgam of your background, upbringing at home, training at school, in a youth organization or at work and, above all, what you decide to make it. It is the essential 'you' and only you can decide if, when faced with a problem, any problem, you will tackle it with everything you have got or if you will always take the easy way out and give up. In this sense, improving one's determination is easy since we can practise it every day by our approach to any problem – and life is not short of these!

Let me quote something I read in a book many years ago about a Mexican called Pablo, '. . . who survived for eight days in the desert on two gallons of water. The mean daily maximum temperature was 35°C and the mean daily minimum 28°C. Pablo's limit should have been about 50 miles; in fact, he travelled 35 miles in the saddle and at least 100 miles on foot. When Pablo was picked up his estimated weight loss

was 25 per cent. His flesh was black and dry, and his lips, nose and eyelids had shrunk to nothing; his skin was covered with cuts and scratches, none of which bled. He was deaf to all but loud sounds, and blind except to light and dark, but he had retained sufficient of his faculties to find his way back almost to the camp from which he had set out. He had a slow 'roaring' respiration and a slow pulse, which could not be detected below the knees and elbows. Bad though his condition seemed, he made a complete recovery, "soaking up water like a dry sponge", then after regurgitating it at first, drinking and retaining vast quantities of water. It was three days before his vision and hearing returned to normal. Four days later he was still "deliberately and methodically devouring water-melons". One week later, a fortnight after he had been picked up, he was well, cheerful and back to his old weight, but his hair had turned grey. Pablo had been determined to live, and he succeeded.' If you can emulate Pablo you will not be lacking in determination.

Wilfred Noyce, in his book *They Survived*, examined a number of case histories of people who had experienced a major survival incident to see if there was some common thread. He found no such link, but came up with a view that soldiers/mountaineers would probably prove to be very good survivors. I must immediately declare my partiality to this view since I qualify under both counts, but Noyce, although a great mountaineer, had pacifist leanings. Nevertheless, these did not prevent his making a scholar's assessment that **self-discipline**, a trait often found in both soldiers and mountaineers, was a worthwhile quality in survival. Self-discipline makes people adopt a well-ordered lifestyle, makes them do things now rather than later, makes them do things completely and properly rather than badly and inadequately, makes them neat and tidy rather than scruffy and unkempt. Much of the daily process of living can be an exercise in self-discipline if we choose to make it so.

To survive you must be **self-sufficient.** We live in a soft, easy world with warmth and comfort available at the touch of a switch. Some lean heavily on alcohol, nicotine or other drugs for constant support. They buy their food oven-ready and their entertainment video packaged. Suddenly all this is swept away as you crawl from the crashed light aircraft or find you are forced to spend a night on a bleak mountainside. Those who have no need of these so-called aids to modern living will probably cope a lot better.

An American publication, *The Survival Book*, contains the following quote: 'Rescue Service personnel say that country boys, or city boys who have had a lot of Boy Scout training are the best survivors.' Had I not been introduced to the wonders and delights of the great outdoors as a Scout at the age of eleven I would not be writing this book or have had half a lifetime of magnificent experiences. Familiarity with **outdoor living** will provide you with the best foundation of practical skills that you could possibly want should real survival be thrust upon you. This book will give you much of the theory of survival, but it will only be of full value if you go out and practise it by getting to know Nature in all her moods

as you walk, camp, climb, ski, fish, etc. In a book an igloo looks easy to build; so easy that there does not seem any point in going out to practise it on a freezing cold day when you could be watching Arsenal v. Manchester United on television. Anyway you have read somewhere that Eskimos can build one in twenty minutes so it must be easy. If you can build one in twenty minutes you should be writing this book because it takes me a lot longer – and I have practised the art.

There is no such thing as book or theoretical survival. It is an intensely practical affair when it happens. 'Knowledge Dispels Fear' is the motto of the RAF Parachute School and it is nice to remember this as you step out of the door of an aircraft 800 feet above the ground. Perhaps more importantly knowledge gives confidence. For the parachutist it is the knowledge that his parachute will open or, for the one in a million times when it does not, that he knows how to operate his reserve, which gives him the confidence to step out into space. **Confidence** in survival techniques will keep you alive for a very long time. Moreover it is the best antidote to the two great enemies of successful survival – fear and panic. More people die from wrong decisions taken as a result of panic than die from cold, heat, wild animals or other risks.

The survival of a group may well be helped by **good leadership.** This may not always come from the person with badges of rank on his arm. Some of the most unlikely people only really rise to the occasion when the need for them is totally real and vital. That rather quiet, shy person may have spent much of his life in pastimes which particularly fit him to take the lead in a survival incident. A gamekeeper or a poacher would be much more useful than a business executive if you wanted to know how to catch rabbits. It is in a survival situation that the artificial powers denoted by badges of rank or titles suddenly begin to have less impact; the leader then must lead by virtue of his personality and ability.

Physical and mental fitness will help in any survival situation. It is less likely that the overweight, out of condition man or woman will cope. There is no evidence that great bodily strength is an advantage, and there is no shortage of examples of slightly built women who have proved to be magnificent survivors. Indeed, there is a view that women, in general, will survive longer than men because of a deep-seated instinct that upon them depends the continuance of the human race. I would not dare to comment further on this theory! Mature persons, provided that they are fit, should survive more easily since they are better able to endure the sheer monotony and tedium which is part of survival. The young want to be up and doing actively when the best course of action is masterly inactivity.

MENTAL PROBLEMS OF SURVIVAL

A survival situation is a dramatic change. Very seldom indeed, does it gradually evolve. At the first hint that problems might arise in the next hour or two, people usually take avoiding action. The sailor seeing rough weather ahead sets course for a harbour or shelter. The motorist running low on fuel as he approaches a long stretch of lonely road looks for a garage and does not expect his engine to run on air when the fuel tank is empty. No one slowly breaks a leg over a number of hours. It happens in an instant, and then you are in trouble.

A sudden change of almost anything frightens people; not just the young or the old but anyone, because we all are doubtful about the unfamiliar. No one takes a large spoonful of some new foreign dish when it is first produced. We all take a small tentative taste to make sure we like it or at least can manage to get it down. If we are aware of these possible fears we will understand them when they occur and this

will immediately reduce their threat by about 90 per cent. So let us consider some of the possible causes of fear. These are the more general ones, but do not forget those which are peculiar to you; like my wife, who is panic-stricken at the sight of a moth and yet thinks mice are quite friendly little things.

As I have hinted above, anything **unknown** causes a degree of apprehension. You may be a mountaineer and know the hills in all their moods and weather. To a non-mountaineer a dark brooding crag with mist swirling about it can be very frightening. Remember the first day at school? All of us have been frightened then. So much was new and unknown. You may be very frightened by your first encounter with the jungle, but just stop and remember that thousands of people live all their lives in the jungle and do it very well. Thousands more from Western civilizations have, over the centuries, gone into the jungle, explored it, exploited it and survived quite happily – and so could you. You just stop, take a few deep breaths, then start thinking and planning. The unknown soon becomes the known and familiar. You were once new in the place where you live and it was all unknown. Now you probably know it like the proverbial back of your hand.

Few of us seek out **discomfort** for the sake of it. Some of us put up with it in order to enjoy some greater pleasure. To climb a high mountain will, almost certainly, involve some discomfort, but the reward in the view at the top or the sense of achievement makes the discomfort worth enduring. I am told (you will appreciate that this is something I cannot test for myself) that there is some discomfort in childbirth, but I have yet to meet a mother who counted it but a small thing in comparison with the wonder and thrill of the new-born baby. Despite these examples generally we do not enjoy discomfort and for some, especially those who take care never to stray far from soft beds, warm rooms and mechanized travel, it is a matter for real fear. The thought of being cold, wet, hungry, etc., is a major worry; yet one of the great sayings of the outdoorsman is 'any fool can be uncomfortable' implying that one can be comfortable with very little. An experienced camper will always make himself very comfortable. A little practise and experience of the outdoors will solve this problem for you for ever.

Most of us are with **people** every day and yet we can fear them especially in the unusual circumstances of survival. At arm's length in normal life we are happy with most people, but huddled together in a tiny snowhole is a different matter. You may think that you are God's gift to the opposite sex, but the reverse is probably much nearer the truth; so think about how you can minimize other people's fears of you. Kindness, courtesy and a caring attitude will go a long way to alleviate the fears of others, and what better place to start than in your everyday life. If you have fear of others you must hope that they will have read this book and be trying to help you. But look for their better qualities and try to see them as ordinary people like you despite the colour of their skin, their accent, their style of dress or whatever else it is that frightens you.

In a difficult situation we are often frightened that our **own weaknesses** will let us down. In an expensive restaurant we worry about which of the imposing array of knives, forks and spoons to use for which course. In a survival situation we will worry that we will not be able to keep up, or keep a fire going when it is our turn. The solution is to practise survival skills under controlled conditions so that you are familiar with them if you ever need them for real. If you have not trained yourself in this way beforehand, take heart from the fact that possibly most of those with you will not know any more than you. If any people in the group claim to be experts, let them show the

rest of you what to do. Remember, the one thing an expert likes to do is show how good an expert he really is. If he is only a 'mouth expert' his lack of ability will soon show up and that will put him right back along with the rest of you. No matter how inexpert you think you are you can do something, maybe only one thing, better than everyone else. Someone I know acted as leader to a party of people on a package tour to see some of the natural wonders of Iceland and this included travelling in a tracked vehicle over the snowfields. The weather got rough and my friend had finally to ski ahead to find the route. One of the party was an American lady of very ample proportions who was quite hopeless at everything. One night, however, when they camped it was very cold and the butter was rock-solid and difficult to use. This lady said, 'Give it to me,' and enfolded the block of butter somewhere in the inner recesses of her clothing and within a short time the butter was in a perfect state for spreading. Even she had one thing she could do well.

I have briefly mentioned **terrain and climate** in the introduction to this section. Most of us live in cities and we enjoy the temperate climate of Europe, but remember that people dwell all over the world in all sorts of environments and weather conditions. For some the starker places of the earth such as the desert or the Arctic are sought out as places of beauty. They feel wonderfully at home there and so can you if you realize that you can live anywhere if you make a few small adjustments to your style of living. In the tropics people get up early and take a rest in the middle part of the day, working again in the evening if necessary. If you are suddenly precipitated into a new environment, just stop, look around and take an interest in what is different about it. Then think and plan how you are going to cope.

If I were to ask you when you were last completely **alone** for a period of more than 24 hours I am sure you would find it difficult to recall. You may live alone in your own house or flat, but very few of us work totally alone and even fewer never go shopping, have a drink in a pub or go somewhere where they come into contact with other humans. Even a lighthouse-keeper on the most isolated of lights is one of a team of three or four men. If you are forced into a survival situation you could well be on your own and that can be very frightening. Man is a gregarious animal and all his instincts are to be with others be it as part of a family, in a work group, in a sports team or whatever it may be. The recluse or hermit is considered a very odd sort of person and is himself sometimes feared because he is not quite normal. The character Robinson Crusoe was based on the actual experiences of Alexander Selkirk who did survive alone on a desert island. Trappers on the north-east coast of Greenland used to spend the entire winter alone apart from a dog team as they visited their traplines. Overcoming fear is a matter of gaining self-confidence in your ability to cope with any situation and you can, of course, experience being totally alone by going off for a few days' camping in some remote area like the Highlands of north-west Scotland. With experience and with plenty to occupy youself, being on your own ceases to be a problem. Alexander Selkirk and the Greenland trappers coped and so can you.

In the paragraphs above I have drawn your attention to some of the most common fears that are likely to assail you when forced into a survival situation. The knowledge that you will almost certainly, to a greater or lesser extent, suffer these fears is the best antidote to their effect. I have briefly suggested ways of alleviating the fears still further. The greak risk is that you will let fear so take control of you that you will no longer be in command of the situation. Then you will panic and start taking wrong decisions and initiat-

ing the wrong actions. If you begin to be frightened, stop, sit down and think for a while. Think about something totally different, and avoid taking any decisions until you have calmed down and are thinking rationally once more. Now I want to describe some of the material stresses that could face you.

PHYSICAL PROBLEMS OF SURVIVAL

Cold and heat are two ends of the same problem. Man is basically a tropical animal. In other words, for him to exist without some form of protective clothing he needs to be within a few degrees north or south of the Equator. Try spending 24 hours in Great Britain clad in nothing but a swimming-costume and you will soon decide that clothing, especially the warm sort, is a very good idea. If you go out for a winter day in the Scottish hills properly clad in the recommended clothing and are then forced to spend a night out with no additional clothing, sleeping-bag, etc., you will survive but I doubt if you will describe the night as comfortable. In temperate regions extreme heat will seldom be a problem unless you have a delicate skin or complexion. In the tropics it can kill you; and in a few hours unless you take very careful precautions. For survival you will never be able to select the ideal degree of heat or cold; you will be in it whatever it may be. The human body can survive a very wide range of temperatures, depending obviously on the availability of clothing, shelter, etc. Two friends of mine spent a night out at 28,000 feet on Everest, in a hole scraped in the snow and without sleeping-bags. The temperature was probably between $-30°$ and $-40°C$. They suffered from frostbite but they survived. At the other extreme people have survived temperatures of over 60°C. Extremes of temperature will cause stress but you can survive them.

Precipitation, be it rain, snow, hail or sleet, will in itself be little problem, unless it is associated with wind as in a blizzard. It is the secondary effect of rain-soaked clothing or cold which will cause the discomfort and, therefore, stress. Other than as a source of water, precipitation does you no good so should be avoided as far as possible by the use of protective clothing or other shelter.

Solar radiation is mainly a problem at high altitude, in places like the European Alps, especially when associated with snow-covered ground which reflects the sun's rays. However it can affect some people at sea level on a very hot sunny day, and sunburn causes discomfort and stress. The golden rule for survival is that you never sunbathe and you keep most of your skin, other than the weathered parts, covered at all times. Even the face may need some protection at sea level and it certainly will at high altitude.

Most people think that **hunger** is the thing to be most feared and that without eating you will die in a few days. Nothing could be further from the truth. Your stomach tells you, usually three times a day, that it wants food and you appease it by having a meal. While a feeling of hunger is mildly unpleasant it does, in fact, disappear after about four days with nothing to eat. Perhaps the stomach gives the whole thing up as a bad job and stops being difficult! In recent times we have had Irishmen on hunger-strikes and they survived for more than sixty days before dying. It might be argued that they had a death-wish rather than a determined will to survive, which is what I hope you have. A girl named Helen Klaben was a passenger in a light aircraft flying down the west coast of North America. It crashed in a wild, remote area and she and the pilot were not found for forty-nine days. Both were in quite good shape, having had little more than a packet of sandwiches and some berries to sustain them for all that time in weather which was below freezing.

You will die of **thirst** long before you die of hunger. In temperate climates you can last about fifteen days without any water at all. For every litre of water you have you should survive an extra day, so plan your water rationing accordingly. In hot climates the water needs of the human body rise dramatically. This will be dealt with more fully in a later chapter.

Shock will occur to some member of a survival party in almost every instance. It may be shock in the first-aid sense, which always occurs with any injury, or the shock to anyone finding himself in a dramatically different situation. Warmth, reassurance and confidence building are the proven treatment for shock and it is important to remember that all are likely to suffer from it to some extent in the immediate aftermath of any incident.

Motion sickness can produce considerable stress especially in those who suffer badly, and a small liferaft or lifeboat provides a lot of movement. Most of these craft have first-aid kits fitted and these include suitable tablets to lessen the effect of the motion. There is no virtue in being 'tough' or 'brave' and not taking such tablets. Sea-sickness produces dehydration and, almost certainly, you will have very little water to replace fluids lost by vomiting so anything you can do to minimize the loss of fluids will prolong your life.

Gas poisoning can occur with any sort of stove or combustion engine. All can produce carbon monoxide which is fatal to humans. Because it is colourless and odourless the risk is enhanced compared to butane gas supplied for camping stoves which incorporates a stenching agent to make an escape of gas from the cylinder very obvious. Adequate ventilation even in the worst weather is the only solution.

Wild animals, even quite small ones, are a major worry in the mind of the city-bred layman. Although Richard Attenborough and others have brought wildlife into our sitting-rooms by way of the television screen, the average person is not familiar with them in real life. The wild places of the world are not teeming with animals just waiting for a meal of juicy human. Most animals keep well away from all humans and since they will be aware of you long before you are aware of them your chances of having more than a fleeting glimpse are remote. Despite several years spent in wild and remote country I have virtually no good photographs of animals; the pictures you see in magazines and books are usually the result of waiting for days or weeks in a hide near a watering-place or where bait has been put out. Even then, telephoto lenses have to be used to get those close-up shots we all like. You must avoid putting temptation in the way of animal marauders by leaving food out. One of the big problems in the American national parks is where to put your food so that it does not attract bears. Usually it is hung high in a tree suspended in a bag from a rope, but I have read that the bears are learning how to get at the food even then. All food remnants such as fish and animal bones should be deposited a long way from your shelter area. Food preparation should be done by a stream which will wash remnants away. The rule is to do nothing to encourage animals and never to interfere with them. A female will defend her young very fiercely and this accounts for the majority of animal attacks on humans.

A few insects such as mosquitoes, lice, etc., can be dangerous for the diseases they carry, and the best protection is full body cover of clothing with the cuffs of sleeves and the bottoms of trousers drawn tight to stop them penetrating. Some, such as midges and blackfly, can drive people almost mad with their attentions as anyone who has camped in Scotland in July or August can testify. They cause no harm except irritation. If you have some form of anti-midge repellant use it. Failing that, total coverage of the body by clothing or some form of tentage is the only answer. A pipeful of some especially noxious shag tobacco is also useful to keep the bugs at bay.

One or more members of a party sustaining **severe injuries** will add stress to the situation. Obviously the casualties themselves will suffer stress and shock as a concomitant to their injuries, but the fit members will also feel some degree of stress. Will they survive? What happens if we have to move? How can we take them with us? Will this mean we cannot escape? What happens if they die? This last, is without being too callous, the easiest problem. If a casualty does die all you can do is place the body reverently in some quiet spot until such time as rescue arrives. If this is likely to be more than a few hours, a shallow grave or in a rock mound if ground is frozen is the answer. However, you must do all in your power to treat injuries or illness with whatever facilities you have. As far as possible your treatment should comply with what you have learned in first aid training (you have done some, haven't you?) about clean dressings, hygiene, etc. But those teachings must never overrule life-saving treatment. If the only available absorbent material is your grubby handkerchief, use it to stop major bleeding. If a few bugs get into the wound, that is far better than bleeding to death. Do remember also that most wounds look far worse than they are. Blood is only a red, slightly sticky liquid, and will do no harm to you so get on with the treatment and have no thoughts of fainting or being sick. Practise by watching a few medical programmes – in full colour – on the television, then perhaps the sight of a bit of blood will not worry you too much.

We live in a sanitized world of flush lavatories, sweet-smelling soap, frequent showers and clean clothes. In the wild there is a total **lack of sanitation.** If the calls of nature have to be satisfied behind a tiny clump of heather or in the middle of a totally bare glacier this will cause embarrassment to many who are not used to such coarse living. The lack of clean clothes or the chance of a good wash will affect the morale of many people especially after the first fortnight. I am not advocating that no attempt be made to maintain the highest possible standards of personal hygiene. The concern for such standards is a vital part of the whole survival process, but it is important to realize that even the best attempt to maintain standards will, in some circumstances be low compared to what most people are used to in civilized society. Oddly enough, despite our concern for cleanliness, little harm will come to you if you do not wash. The Tibetans have been proving this for centuries! In time you are likely to acquire fleas, lice, etc., depending on where you are, but they affect our sense of dignity rather than our bodily well-being. By all means try to keep yourself clean, but do not worry or fuss if you cannot. Ultimately those soft towels and hot water will seem all the more attractive.

If you are forced into a survival situation suddenly at any altitude over about 6,000 feet you could suffer from **lack of oxygen.** Most people will not suffer until they are above 12,000 feet and then only if they try to move quickly or energetically. It is important, if you are at altitude, to move very slowly and carefully at least for the first few days until you acclimatize. Himalayan mountaineers rightly lay much stress on slow and steady acclimatization before they attempt any high peak. After an aircraft crash, for example, you may

FIG. 2. SURVIVAL IS A STRESSFUL AFFAIR!

find yourself suddenly on very high mountains and have to cope with the splitting headaches, nausea, vomiting that can be caused. If at all possible descend to a lower altitude. Apart from reducing the risk of oedema – excess fluid in the lungs, brain or peripheral parts of the body – caused by being high up, you will also be warmer, nearer fuel, food and civilization in general.

SURVIVAL LEADERSHIP

In this chapter so far I have tried to outline and explain most of the fears and stresses which are likely to assail anyone suddenly projected into a survival problem. Coping fully with these is the most important thing of all. For you, a person who is interested in these things, the solution is fairly simple. Read this chapter again and make sure you realize what the fears and stresses are likely to be. Knowledge of them will go a long way to overcoming them. Next, consider how you would deal with them. You may have better ideas than those I have suggested. Follow this with training yourself in all the practical details of survival described in later chapters of this book. With this training you will gain a tremendous amount of confidence to deal with *any* survival situation you may find yourself in.

But what if you find yourself in a situation with a lot of other people; hysterical children, grown men in a total funk? You may not think you are the person to take control; you may have great inner doubts that you can do it, but it may well be that you will be the most suitable and experienced person because no one else will have thought about survival except you. You will have read about it and practised it. Every time you go into a building you notice, almost subconsciously, possible escape routes in case of fire. Flying to a holiday overseas you do not just think what a good figure the stewardess has got, but listen carefully to her when she describes the emergency exits during the pre-flight briefing. On a mountain walk you put as much effort into planning possible escape routes, for use if the weather turns bad, as into the main route for the day. Because you live survival you are almost certainly the one to take charge so make no excuses – get on with it.

If you are in a uniform; any uniform be it police, military, Scout or any other, that is a bonus. Frightened people will respond to instructions from such a person and they will not bother whether the person has any badges of rank. At first you may well have to raise your voice to get some quiet and order. Later you should be able to use a quiet but firm approach. A loud 'Stop that row at once!' to someone crying noisily should reduce the decibels. I leave the possible selection of adjectives to you. For a serious hysterical case you may have to say it several times or, as a last resort, slap the hysteric's face. Having gained some measure of control the next priority is to get everyone involved in a task so that they have less time to think about themselves and their predicament. The fit can comfort and treat the injured, others can start gathering, for example, wood for a fire, sections of aircraft to use for shelter, suitcases, etc.

Do not chase or harry people but keep them occupied. Only get involved yourself if there is a clear need for personal leadership – usually for a particularly unpleasant task. For the most part you should be thinking and planning what to do next. Activity reduces stress in people, but once the situation is under control have regular breaks for a rest, or a hot drink if it is possible. Let people have a laugh and a joke; a sense of humour is a very valuable thing in a difficult situation. After the initial few hours you should establish a routine. While hoping for early rescue you, at least, should plan on having to survive for day, maybe weeks. It is you that will have to keep a routine going and encourage those who get depressed. Change duties round so that the same people are not always doing the same chores. Encourage people to conserve their resources, both personal and material, and waste nothing. Not only should every scrap of food be consumed, but extra care should be taken of clothing, keeping it dry and as clean as possible. No one can have too much sleep and they should conserve their body heat as far as possible by not standing around getting cold. A sleeping-bag or other protection is not something to be in only from eleven at night to seven in the morning. If in doubt – rest!

Some people have the ability to switch off from their surroundings and bury themselves in a book. Others may prefer to talk, but try to keep them off morbid discussion of the survival chances and similar topics. Right from the start you or someone deputed by you should keep a diary of events. It is an ideal role for someone who is injured and cannot play a full part in other survival activities. A strong religious faith has proved immensely helpful to many who have been in the most appalling situations, and a person with such faith can prove a great strength and support. You may not have that faith and it cannot be learned, but an American polar survival expert has written 'Many men who have never met the Almighty in church, meet Him occasionally at the operating or delivery table, but really get to know Him at the ends of the earth.' Your survival situation will be an 'end of the earth' and people will appreciate time being made for a simple service or a few prayers on a daily basis. It will be a wonderful help to most of those with you. I would strongly advocate that part of your study of and training for survival should be to find out more about your religious faith so that it becomes more real. For the past thirty years I have found my own Christian faith a wonderful support in all aspects of life, but even more so at times of great difficulty. Let me relate one personal experience.

In the summer of 1972 I led an expedition to Axel Heiberg Island in Arctic Canada. For seven weeks we climbed, sledged and explored in mainly good weather, but at the end as the various parties were coming down to base camp to fly out the weather turned very nasty. Of the last party of four only two struggled back to camp. There had been an accident with one person killed and another injured who had had to be left up on a glacier in a tent. Clearly the rest of us had to mount a rescue and I, as the expedition leader, had to organize it but my mind was in a turmoil. What should we take? How would we find the casualty? What equipment did we need? Suddenly I knew I should commit the whole problem to God in prayer and I bowed my head and prayed for a few seconds. My mind cleared and without any shadow of doubt I knew what we needed to do, to take and so on. After a good meal we set off. Navigation was difficult in the thick mist and we were too near the Magnetic North Pole for the compass to be much use. Several times we went wrong but always found our bearings again. After about ten hours we were all very tired, our clothing was frozen and we were lost once more. I knew that a second problem was looming. How long before the rescue party themselves might need help? How long before they might succumb to hypothermia? Again I prayed and had a strong feeling that we should go on for another half-hour before turning back to wait for good weather. About twenty minutes later we came to an oddly-shaped bollard of ice which we had passed many times before and we knew precisely where we were. An hour or two later we were with the casualty. We prepared him for evacuation and after nearly 24 hours out we were all safely back at base camp. If you are a cynic you will say that my service background had trained me to deal with a crisis and come to the right decisions, but only I know the total change which came over me after committing the problems to prayer on those two occasions.

Let me remind you of the priorities of immediate action in an emergency:

1. Remove people from immediate danger.
2. Render first aid.
3. Stop, think and plan.
4. Provide shelter – from wind, wet and cold.
5. Allocate jobs.
6. Put out markers, signalling devices, etc.
7. Find water and fuel.
8. Fix your position as accurately as possible.
9. Decide if, and when, you will send for help.
10. Continue all the above until found. You as the leader need to keep going over these priorities again and again.

Survival is 110, not 100 per cent concentration and attention to detail. Always ask 'How can I improve the situation?' Have I done everything possible? You never say 'I can't be bothered,' or 'What's the point?' Survival is a mental discipline and it needs determination and confidence. You can survive if you want to. You must never, ever give up.

3. MAN IS A TROPICAL ANIMAL: Warmth and shelter

CLOTHING

Had he not been blessed with sufficient intelligence to provide clothing and shelter for himself, *homo sapiens* would have been one of the animals only found in tropical areas. He (and she) has virtually no hair, fur or feathers to keep the body warm. Even the fattest person is poorly provided with insulating fat compared to, for example, the blubber layer of a seal. The polar bear happily swims in the Arctic Ocean at all times of the year with no ill effect, yet man would succumb in a matter of minutes in such waters. The secret is the insulation of the main part of the body from the cold outside. In cold weather birds, when they are not flying look fatter than usual. This is because they have the ability to fluff up their feathers, especially the small down feathers close to the skin, to increase the insulating layer thickness. At the onset of winter, animals grow a thicker layer of fur to protect them through the coming cold months. Making the best use of the clothing you have available provides you with a micro-climate all of your own in the inch or two around your body. In the ideal situation this micro-climate will keep you comfortable – not too hot and not too cold. However survival is seldom ideal.

If you take part in outdoor activities such as climbing or sailing your choice of suitable clothing for such pastimes will be governed by the fact that you will often have to protect yourself from the cold or the wet. If you wait for a perfect fine day before you go on the hills you will do very little mountaineering indeed. It is accepted good practice for all outdoor activities that you wear or carry clothing and equipment to cope with the worst conditions you are

likely to encounter. Should you then become involved in a survival situation you have appropriate clothing with you, but what about the non-outdoor type or the outdoor person driving from A to B who runs into trouble? His clothing is likely to owe more to fashion or accepted standards of status or work. The same principles apply even if the end result is less satisfactory than would be obtained from garments designed specifically for rugged conditions. The American forces have an appropriate mnemonic 'COLD' as an aid to remembering how to use clothing to the best. Although it is designed to help you keep warm in cold weather most of the advice applies to keeping cool in hot weather.

Keep clothing	**C**lean
Avoid	**O**verheating
Wear clothing	**L**oose and in **L**ayers
Keep clothing	**D**ry

In survival conditions you will have no washing-machine, probably no soap and possibly limited water. Despite this you should keep clothing as clean as conditions and facilities allow. Dirty clothing becomes matted and the tiny spaces between the fibres cannot trap as much air as before and it is this trapped air which is the secret of insulation. Oil from the body also fills these tiny spaces. On the outside layer of clothing a film of dirt gradually builds up as we go about the chores in our survival location. Getting firewood, or digging turf to roof a shelter will soon make outer garments dirty. As far as your survival activities allow, keep clean. Do not be hidebound by convention. You may only have one pair of underpants but nothing will happen if you take them off, wash them and then have to do without them for a few hours while they dry. What mother may have told you is not always right when life gets rugged.

For various reasons it is important to avoid overheating. You should make a deliberate effort to carry out your survival chores slowly and steadily. This will conserve every bit of your available energy and it should stop you sweating. Moisture is a poor insulator and so sweat-soaked garments do not insulate you as well as dry ones. Sweating is part of the body mechanism to keep the body cool. Evaporation of sweat cools the body because body heat is used to change the sweat from a liquid state to a gaseous state. So again you are not helping yourself to keep warm. In cold conditions you should aim to feel slightly cold rather than too warm. Sweating produces various chemicals which are absorbed by the clothing thus making them dirty which again reduces their insulation value. When any active work is done clothing should be loosened or removed to prevent any overheating. Whether you are wearing specialized outdoor clothing or garments more suited to city streets the same principles apply. Avoid overheating and you will be cleaner and warmer.

For warmth all clothing should be loose fitting and in several thin layers rather than a few thick layers. An early part of your Survival – Immediate Actions should be to check and loosen any tight clothing. In extreme cases it could be better to remove it. Tight shoelaces or anorak cuffs will certainly give you cold hands and feet and could, in severe conditions, cause frostbite. Ties, belts and underwear should all be loosened. No matter how ample her bustline a lady will come to no harm if she slackens off her bra fastenings. There should be nothing to restrict the flow of blood around the body. An unrestricted flow keeps you warm and stops frostbite. Loose clothing traps pockets of air between the layers. Tight clothing, such as a pair of jeans, only provides insulation of the thickness of the garment material, usually no more than a frac-

tion of an inch. Loose clothing allows perhaps half an inch of trapped air over at least part of the body. Several thin layers rather than one thick layer increases the possibility of these pockets of air and allows much greater flexibility in the amount of clothing worn. Because the blood flows near the surface of much of the head there is proportionally a great loss of heat (about 20 per cent) from there compared to other parts of the body. Some form of head covering, even improvised, should always be worn to reduce this. Additional clothing might be improvised from old sacking, large polythene bags, etc., with grass or leaves used as insulation.

Clothing made damp by sweating has been covered above, but clothing can also become wet from rain or snow. Unless the rain is prolonged it is usually better to find shelter and wait for dry conditions before continuing your survival actions. Snow should be frequently brushed off outer garments before it has a chance to melt and penetrate clothing. It is especially important to remove all snow before entering any sort of shelter that you may have improvised. If clothing does get wet you should get it dry as soon as possible. If it is soaking wet, e.g., from falling in a river, it must be hung up and you must hope for what a housewife would call 'a good drying day'. Alternatively you may be able to dry it by a fire, but beware of sparks and flames damaging your very limited stock of clothing. A few years ago I got ashore from a swamped rubber boat onto Ruth Island in the Inner Fjord area of East Greenland. We soon had a fire going with driftwood and draped our clothing and equipment round it. Later we discoverd that while perforations are a good thing in teabags they are not good in a down-filled sleeping-bag. Garments which are only damp, e.g., a sweaty vest, should be removed, a dry layer such as a jersey put on next to the skin and the damp garment put on over that. A combination of body heat and air drying should solve the problem in an hour or two.

Whether you are a city type or an outdoor type I suggest that at least some of your clothing should be bought with survival in mind. Let me suggest the sort of garments you might buy. Stout boots or shoes will always serve you better than some fancy fashion shoe with pointed toes. The ideal socks would be fairly thick wool or loop stitched synthetic fibre. For the trunk and limbs you need clothing that will trap as much air in the fibres as possible. Wool sweaters, fibrepile garments, wool/cotton mixture shirts are all very satisfactory. Underclothes made from 100 per cent polypropylene have the property of 'wicking' away sweat from the skin and thus avoiding that clammy feeling you get from a sweat-soaked vest or shirt. Any of these materials are also suitable for gloves, mitts and head covering. Nevertheless, no matter how good any of these insulating garments are, their value will be largely lost if they are not covered by a windproof layer. Quite a mild wind of ten or fifteen knots will soon be felt through any of these insulating garments if they are not covered with a jacket or anorak of closely woven cotton or polycotton.

Various trade names such as 'Ventile' and 'Grenfell Cloth' are advertised, but

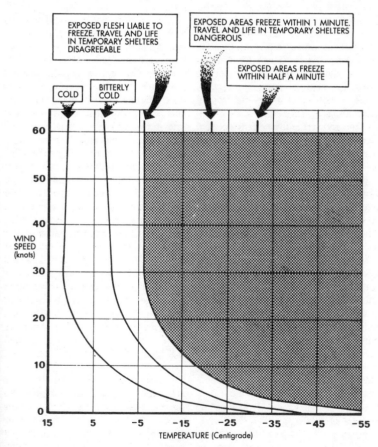

EXPOSED FLESH LIABLE TO FREEZE. TRAVEL AND LIFE IN TEMPORARY SHELTERS DISAGREEABLE

EXPOSED AREAS FREEZE WITHIN 1 MINUTE. TRAVEL AND LIFE IN TEMPORARY SHELTERS DANGEROUS

EXPOSED AREAS FREEZE WITHIN HALF A MINUTE

COLD

BITTERLY COLD

FIG. 3. A SIMPLIFIED WINDCHILL GRAPH

the basic material is a very good quality and tightly woven cotton. An alternative is to have an outer layer of waterproof clothing. Any waterproof garment is also windproof, but until recently this sort of clothing had the disadvantage of causing condensation to form on the inside of the garment as soon as any appreciable activity took place. This condensation transferred itself to the jersey or shirt and the process of losing insulation began. From a survival point of view the advantage of this moisture is that it is warm wet rather than the killing cold wet of penetrating rain. Recent developments in fabrics have produced what are known as 'breathables' which to a varied extent keep out raindrops but allow the passage of water vapour from the body through microscopic pores in the waterproof layer. Goretex is currently the best fabric for this, but any purchase should be preceded by discussion with a reputable retailer. Oiled cotton, and neoprene-proofed garments are satisfactory, but I cannot recommend polyurathene-proofed clothing for use in heavy or prolonged rain. For survival purposes the design of such garments is not critical, but a hood is vital and a full-length zip very useful since it allows flexibility in avoiding overheating. Beyond that it is a matter of personal choice. Your overall aim with clothing should be to keep wind, precipitation and cold out and your body heat in to maintain a comfortable micro-climate in which to exist. The simplified windchill graph at Figure 3 shows that a person in a 50-knot wind at 11°C is as much at risk as a person at minus 14°C but with only a 2-knot wind. Do not underestimate the danger of wind when in the great outdoors.

SHELTERS

Even if a person in a survival situation is fortunate enough to have plenty of clothing and/or a survival bag suitable for the climate he is in, there are good reasons to provide some form of additional shelter. First, it will provide yet more shelter from the elements than the clothing. In difficult circumstances you can never have too much protection and it is a lucky man, indeed, who can discard insulation because he is too warm when at rest. A shelter will bring members of a group together and there is much strength to be gained from one another in difficult circumstances. In strictly practical terms real warmth can be gained from a group of people who huddle together. The human body constantly radiates the heat of a 100-watt light bulb. While you should do all you can – see the discussion on clothing above – to reduce the heat radiated, some will inevitably escape. It is much better that this heat be passed to those with you rather than being lost to the atmosphere, so the closer you can get to your survival companions the better. The less surface area the body exposes the better since there is less heat loss, so never stand around in the open unless you have some task to carry out. Get into shelter and fold yourself up into a ball. To encourage you to do this keep any shelter small. Even if you have the materials do not build a palace. Any shelter should be just big enough for the party to sit and lie in comfort, but only just. The air in the shelter then heats up more quickly and keeps its heat more easily. The shelters illustrated in this book are the ideal, but you will seldom achieve this. The ground will be different or the best materials will not be available. The important thing is to grasp the principles and then modify the design to the location in which you find yourself.

NATURAL MATERIALS SHELTERS

The simplest shelter is a cave. It is often ready for use apart from removing the odd stone from the floor. Caves are not always dry, but usually some part of them will be better than trying to cope outside. A large rock or boulder, especially if it is overhanging, will offer some immediate shelter and you can soon improve it by building a stone wall or sangar round it – see Figure 4. A fold or a dip in the ground can also be the start of a shelter and you can improve it as time and available materials allow – see Figure 5. The gaps between the stones can be filled in with lumps of turf or heather to make an airtight windbreak. With a dry stone wall construction the problem of providing a roof remains. If any timber can be found it can be used as rafters and large flat stones laid across to form a flat or sloping roof. If you are trying to survive in wooded country the problem of a shelter is much easier. Figure 6 shows a simple one- or two-man shelter made from a framework of timbers with foliage as the roof. Many materials such as bracken, the foliage branches of pine trees or even large leaves like those from wild rhubarb can be used; if you have some sheeting, use it. The important thing is to start the thatching process at ground level and then fix on the overlapping layers progressively towards the top of the shelter. Notice how tiles are positioned on a house in order to shed the rain. Remember also that there must be plenty of overlap to reduce the risk of leaks. Figure 7 shows another sort of shelter commonly called a lean-to. Because of the large open side this is only suitable if you have such a plentiful supply of wood that you can keep a good fire going night and day. With such a fire the back of the shelter acts as a reflector to the heat and so warms your back as well. In Figure 7 I have shown another smaller reflector on the other side of the fire to make it even cosier. I have purposely left out dimensions because the size of a shelter will vary according to the number of people to be accommodated. A cave might well take twenty whereas a brushwood-type shelter can only take about four. Above this number you are better dividing into two or more parties and building additional shelters. If you can, keep the size of a shelter to the minimum possible for very modest

FIG. 4. AN IMPROVED BOULDER

FIG. 5. AN IMPROVED FOLD IN THE GROUND

FIG. 6. A ONE- OR TWO-MAN SHELTER (TWO VARIATIONS)

FIG. 7. A LEAN-TO

FIG. 8. TREE TRUNK SHELTER (BEFORE THATCHING OVER THE FRAME)

comfort; it will give you a chance to get to know people better than ever before! The trunk of a large fallen tree could provide a shelter for a very modest amount of additional work. Figure 8 gives an idea of how to do this.

If you are forced to survive in snow-covered terrain you are probably better off, apart from the lower temperature, than in a more temperate climate. Snow can be cut and shaped, within certain limits, to whatever you want it to do. The simplest and quickest shelter is what I call a snow grave, but since survival is a positive thinking affair most people call it a snow trench. Figure 9 shows that it is a simple trench cut in the snow. If the snow is in the right condition you can cut the roofing blocks from the trench as shown. However snow is not always, especially in the United Kingdom, suitable to cut easily into blocks; it frequently just crumbles. Try digging down through the surface layer and you may find more consolidated snow, but be prepared to find none that will remain in block form. Even without a roof a snow trench achieves a lot since you are below the surface and so out of the wind. In the absence of snow blocks any sort of sheet will make a good flat roof provided it is well weighted with snow or rocks. One big advantage of the snow trench is that it can be dug in very flat areas. Normally it need only be about eighteen inches deep and 20 to 25 minutes should see the finished article. Some years ago two of us dug one in this time just off the summit of Cairngorm in Scotland during a course run by Glenmore Lodge. Despite a lack of sleeping-bags it was with some reluctance that we emerged at midnight when the instructor relented and allowed the course to return to the comforts of the Lodge. We were quite snug and could not only have survived until morning, but we would have been in a fit state to carry out a normal day's mountain walking. What sort of shelter is possible depends to a certain extent on the tools you have or can improvise. Both the snow trench and the snow cave can be dug with just an ice axe and nothing more, although any sort of improvised shovel would make it easier.

Figure 10 shows the general design of a snow cave. I have managed to dig a one-man version in about 90 minutes with just an ice axe and a plate as a scoop and I doubt that one, irrespective of its size, could be dug in much less. Depending on the snow conditions and the size of the snow drift it is possible to dig very large caves holding as many as twenty people, but these tend to be dug as planned living accommodation rather than for survival use. The basic requirement is a snowdrift of well-con-

(A)

(B)

FIG. 9. SNOW TRENCH – (A) USING SNOW BLOCKS, (B) USING A SHEET FOR A ROOF

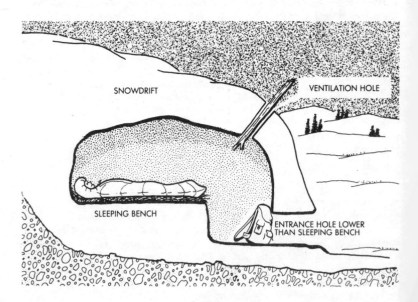

SNOWDRIFT

VENTILATION HOLE

SLEEPING BENCH

ENTRANCE HOLE LOWER
THAN SLEEPING BENCH

FIG. 10. SNOW CAVE

solidated snow at least eight feet deep both horizontally and vertically. Greater depth is even better. Before starting to dig you should put on waterproofs if you have them since it is a damp procedure. Tunnel horizontally into the drift and only begin to hollow out the cave when you are sure you have at least eighteen inches of good consolidated snow above you. Whether you hollow out to the left, to the right or straight ahead is a matter of choice *and* the shape of the ground under the snow. You may well hit a boulder. You just have to work round such an obstacle, but it does mean that few snow caves actually end up like the nice neat drawings used to show their design. How you improve your home from home is up to you. For basic survival, especially if you or your party are at the end of your tether, a simple cave is probably all you can manage, but as time goes on you may hollow out sleeping-bays, a cooking shelf or even a latrine. Figure 11 shows a design for a really de luxe cave for a large party of survivors. While such a design will require many manhours of work it is worth remembering, especially if you are the leader of a surviving party, that time may hang heavy after the initial

activity of establishing your camp, and it will be a good therapeutic activity to get the party improving their living conditions. It will be good for their morale and self-esteen but do not tell them this!

Whatever the design there are certain basic features which are critical. First, the entrance must be at the lowest point of the whole construction thus ensuring that warm air is retained as far as possible. The sleeping-shelf should be as high as possible for the same reason. You need only enough room to lie on it in modest comfort. Secondly, ventilation is vital. Make sure you have a ventilation hole which is kept clear especially if snow is drifting heavily outside. The entrance can be filled with a snow block or a filled rucksack. You will find that even if there is a howling blizzard outside, all is quiet in the cave. Combined with lack of oxygen, this will make you less aware of any lack of ventilation. This particularly applies if you are cooking with a possible buildup of carbon monoxide. For this reason you should always cook near the entrance. Thirdly, the internal roof of the cave should be domed and smooth. This will ensure that any water formed will run down the dome to the sides rather than drip in the middle of the

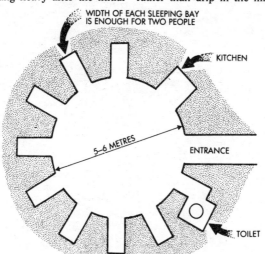

WIDTH OF EACH SLEEPING BAY IS ENOUGH FOR TWO PEOPLE

KITCHEN

5–6 METRES

ENTRANCE

TOILET

FIG. 11. DESIGN FOR A LARGE SNOW CAVE

cave. Smooth off all small projections on the dome. Additionally you may need small drainage channels round your sleeping or cooking areas. Fourthly, make sure you site your cave in a safe place where there is no risk of avalanche, stone fall, etc. Externally the entrance should be marked with a stick of some sort which needs to be as long as possible; quite an amazing amount of drifting can take place overnight and a cave entrance can easily be buried to a depth of some feet. Finally, remember to take all your equipment, food, etc., into the cave at night. Drifting snow can mean the loss of vital items. You should always have close at hand some sort of digging implement to get out in a hurry if need be. Remove all loose snow from your clothing before entering and keep any wet clothing or equipment well away from such dry things as you have.

A tree pit (Figure 12) is a variation on a snow cave which is possible provided you have snow at least three feet deep and suitable conifer trees. The pit can be dug in flat country and the aim should be to dig in under the lowest branches of the tree. The pit should be no bigger than the spread of the low branches since these form the roof of the shelter. Additional branches may have to be cut to improve the thickness of the roof branches. Any form of canvas or other sheeting could also be used to improve the roof. This is a more basic shelter than the snow cave, but it is quicker to make; an hour should be taken as an average time.

There can be few people who have not heard of igloos and for most people the word brings to mind a picture of fur-clad Eskimos standing in a sunlit Arctic snowscape and carrying harpoons. A romantic idea which is virtually a his-

FIG. 12. A TREE PIT

FIG. 13. IGLOO CONSTRUCTION

torical relic only since most of the northern people now live in modern sectional houses in the various settlements in the Arctic. However they retain the skill to build an igloo and will do it in about half an hour. This quick performance is achieved for two reasons; first, polar snow is usually very suitable in its texture and composition for cutting into large blocks with a good snow saw and secondly, the Eskimo has centuries of knowledge of all the nuances of igloo construction. Those of us from more temperate areas do not have this knowledge and only sometimes will the snow be really suitable for cutting into blocks for igloo construction. In a survival situation, unless you have a very good knowledge of snow structure and are very certain, as a result of much practical experience, that you can construct an igloo, my

strong advice is to ignore it and build something else. The fastest igloo I have seen built took three hours and that is just a nice sort of time in which to die in rugged blizzard conditions. However it is sometimes useful to cut some snow blocks to improve the entrance of a snow cave or for some other purpose – at 22,000 feet on Everest we had a rather elegant latrine built of snow blocks – so I add a few words on igloo-building.

An igloo can be built on flat ground or built into a gentle slope. Figure 13 gives the idea of construction which is a gently ascending succession of snow-blocks each of which is canted in. The construction is fragile until you insert the final 'king' block. The outside diameter of the igloo should be about nine or ten feet. This will give you room inside for about four people. The size of each snow block will depend rather on the density and texture of the snow than on predetermined dimensions. Try cutting them about two foot by one foot by nine inches and adjust accordingly. This size may not stay in one piece so cut them smaller. Above this size they will be awkward to handle. The ideal tool is a snow saw but it is possible to cut blocks with other implements although it is far less efficient. Rather than trying to build a long entrance tunnel as in Hollywood cartoons, make a short tunnel and excavate downwards to ensure that your entrance is the lowest point of the construction. This ensures that you retain the maximum warm air. An air vent is required just as it is in the snow cave. Once the igloo has been built loose snow should be used to fill the cracks between the blocks and to make good any defects in your handiwork. The inside should be smoothed to ensure that any melted snow runs to the sides of the igloo rather than dripping on to the occupants. Initially you can obtain some snow blocks from the circular area of the igloo itself, but once you have cut down about a foot you should take the rest of the blocks from a bank of well-consolidated snow.

Any shelter of natural materials will rest upon the ground be this earth or snow. Anything you can do to insulate yourself from the ground should be done. A thick layer of heather or other foliage will increase your chances of survival enormously – and will be a lot more comfortable. You may have something with you like a rucksack, a coil of rope or an aircraft seat that will provide some insulation. If the insulation available is limited, position it under the points where the body exerts pressure – the hips and shoulders. The cold earth extracts heat from your body if there is no insulation and your small body will never heat up the great big earth. Even a pile of newspapers or sitting on this book will provide some sort of insulation.

MAN-MADE SHELTERS

Many parts of the world are not as devoid of human habitation as you might expect. The 1,500 kilometres of the north-east coast of Greenland might seem a pretty inhospitable area, but until recently trappers made a living along that coast catching fox, polar bear, etc., for their pelts. To do this they established a chain of tiny wooden huts complete with built-in bunk, cast iron stove and a few basic utensils. The trapping has ceased but the huts remain albeit in an increasingly poor state of repair. The world is becoming increasingly leisure conscious and as a result holiday cabins can be found in some very remote areas, sometimes only accessible by boat or even helicopter. In Swedish Lapland small sectional wooden huts – *stugas* – have been positioned for the use of walkers as simple overnight stops, thus eliminating the need to carry a tent. Some judicious exploration from your survival site might reveal a very comfortable temporary home. In the United Kingdom the seemingly bleak and barren Scottish Highlands have many now uninhabited farms, shooting-lodges, keepers' cottages, etc., all of which provide a varying degree of comfort but are almost certainly better than lying out in the open for night after night. A ruined farm, thick with sheep droppings will seem a palace after your third night out in pouring rain. 'Bothy' is the general term applied in Scotland to such places.

If a habitation does not offer itself what can you do? You must improvise a tent. Its final form may not resemble the sort of tent you see in a camping shop but it will protect you from wind, precipitation and cold. A tent is basically a sheet, usually of cotton or nylon. Your 'tent' can be a sheet of anything; cotton, nylon, plastic, steel, wood, etc. Two rigid sheets such as corrugated iron can be placed against each other (Figure 14) to form the basic tent. Block in one end with turf and add some more

FIG. 14. A CORRUGATED IRON 'TENT'

FIG. 15. SIMPLE SHEETING TENT

along the ridge to make a rainproof seal and you have a very snug shelter. Those who indulge in outdoor activities normally carry a man-sized bag made of polythene, nylon, Goretex or similar material to use as a survival bag in an emergency. If your sheeting is flexible it will need support. In its simplest form this can be two trees with the sides of the sheet pulled out into the traditional A-shaped tent (Figure 15). Again, it helps to close one end or you will have a wind tunnel rather than a comfortable home. A large log or a small wall can provide a very simple lean-to with the aid of some kind of sheeting (Figure 16) and this can be improvised very quickly. In well-wooded country where branches are readily available near by, a more sophisticated shelter (Figure 17) can be built quite rapidly. This is similar to Figure 7 except that you are saved the chore of thatching your shelter with natural materials. Flexible sheeting can be made of many things. Cotton and nylon are obvious but also think of rubber sheeting or carpet taken from your wrecked aircraft. Industrial polythene sheeting is used for things like fertilizer bags and carefully cut open these make reasonable cover if several are roughly sewn together (even with

FIG. 16. A WALL SHELTER

FIG. 17. A SHEETING LEAN-TO (WITH REFLECTOR FIRE)

string) or pinned with twig 'staples'. Trees and bushes provide obvious supports, but look for the unusual. On Axel Heiberg Island in the Canadian Arctic I came upon about 40 large oil drums, presumably left by a bush pilot engaged on mineral survey. These would have made excellent supports with any sort of sheeting over them. The only extra would have been a strict 'No Smoking' rule. Your sheeting can be suspended by string or rope or held down by boulders or improvised tent-pegs. Some pipelines use tubes of very large diameter – 24 inches or more – and a comfortable shelter could be made in a spare section of such piping. In the 1950s an expedition to the Antarctic lost part of its base camp hut, but they were able to improvise very well using the large packing case in which their light aircraft arrived. Your comfort will largely depend on your ability to improvise shelter and thus provide warmth.

It is a salutary lesson to watch a well-trained and experienced soldier arrive in a new location, size it up, and set about making himself comfortable. He carries no tent, but has a poncho which he will rig within a few minutes while his cooker is producing hot water for a first brew of tea or coffee. Unless he has other duties to perform he will then get out his sleeping-bag, shake it and pummel it to get the maximum loft from the filling, get into it to minimise body heat loss and then set about cooking a meal or having another brew. At this stage the raw recruit will still be wondering what to do and, if it is raining, getting steadily wetter in the process.

In a survival situation you need to keep your body in the best possible condition. With adequate warmth and shelter you will be able to sleep. A well-rested person can think properly and take the right decisions. There are no rules about when to sleep when in the wild. A few hours in warm sun in a sheltered position are much better as a means of restoring the body than trying to sleep during the cold night. Shivering, believe it or not, is one of the body's mechanisms for generating heat, so never try to stop shivering, it is doing you good.

4. HEY, I'M HERE!: Signalling methods

You may be six feet six tall and weigh sixteen stones, but compared to the size of the earth you are microscopic, roughly equivalent to a germ floating around in your body system. This gives you some idea of the problem facing would-be rescuers when they start to look for someone who is lost. It is vital that you, the survivor, do everything you can to make your position known to searchers and you must start doing this in the very early stages of your survival planning after you have dealt with casualties and got some form of shelter rigged. Signalling aids range from the most sophisticated radio which can transmit round the world via satellites to you standing in an open space waving your shirt.

AERIAL SEARCH AIDS

If it is likely that a search for you will be made by aircraft, either helicopter or fixed wing, you must devise appropriate signals. If you yourself have escaped from a crashed aircraft, a radio or distress beacon may be available. Approach any wrecked aircraft with care and only when you are reasonably certain that there is no longer a risk of fire. Remember that jet engines work at very high temperatures and will take an hour or two to cool down. If a member of the aircraft crew has survived, obviously he should take the initiative. All aircrew, including cabin staff, have been fully trained in safety procedures and the use of beacons. They will also know the safest way to approach an aircraft. If no aircrew have survived you must use your common sense. A careful inspection of the exterior should reveal wording to indicate where to make an entry. Do not let everyone get in and poke about. If you have someone with

technical knowledge of radios, etc., so much the better. In the survival packs there is usually a beacon which starts to work by pressing a button or turning a switch. Remember that such a beacon will normally work best on high ground, unobstructed by trees, rocks, etc. The aircraft's main radio will be a more complicated affair and may well not have survived the crash, but it is worth your 'technician' having a go. Do remember that military aircraft have additional hazards lurking. They may be armed with bombs or rockets which may have been rendered unsafe by the crash. Also, the crew in combat aircraft sit in ejector seats. If these are not made safe first a rescuer can be badly injured if the seat is activated when he is near it. Usually a locking pin has to be inserted in a hole on top of the seat. This pin is normally fixed to a red label and kept in a pocket near the top of the seat.

Even if you think the beacon is working or you have made the radio work it must be backed up with visual signals. At least one and preferably three fires (see Figure 20) in a triangle should be prepared. Ideally the triangle should have a side of at least 20 metres. The prepared fires must be kept covered to keep the wood as dry as possible. They must be capable of being ignited quickly; if possible, use some petrol to achieve a rapid blaze. Many a survivor has wept with rage and frustration at being unable to get a fire going when an aircraft has been heard. It is vital that someone keep constant watch with ears and eyes for an approaching aircraft. It will pass by in no more than about a minute so speed is vital. Attracting the attention of a search aircraft should not be left to chance. At night the aim must be to produce a fiery blaze. By day your requirement is for smoke; black, if the

FIG. 18. PURPOSE-MADE HELIOGRAPH MIRROR

background is snow or other light-coloured ground, white if it is to be seen against conifers or other dark vegetation or rock. Black smoke can be made by adding oil or rubber to the fire; white by adding green grass or vegetation or small quantities of water. Remember that one of the fires can be your camp/cooking fire which will be going much of the time anyway and it should be easy to take glowing embers to the other two fires when necessary. Keep feeding the fire in case the aircraft has to make a wide turn to come back to check that he has found you.

If you have survived an aircraft crash it is more than likely that you will find in the wreckage, unless it is totally burnt out, some pyrotechnics. These will be either handheld flares, sometimes with smoke at the other end, or cartridges to be fired from a pistol. If you use the cartridges fire them well ahead of the flight path of the aircraft; the pilot will not be amused to have them fired *at* the aircraft and due to the time lag it is unlikely that he would see them.

I was once told by a very experienced pilot that the finest aid to attract the attention of a searching aircraft is flashes of sunlight reflected on a shiny surface. This can be a specially made

heliograph mirror, but the mirror from a compact or a shaving mirror will do. This pilot told me that he had picked up flashes like this long before his aircraft radio had detected the signals put out by a SARBE beacon. If you have no mirror, any shiny surface will do, so find one and clean and polish it ready for sudden use. The method of using the specialized item is shown in Figure 18, but if all you have is something improvised, you must try to ensure that the angle between the sun and the mirror and the mirror and the aircraft is the same. Figure 19 shows this. Remember that these angular equivalents must be the same in the vertical and horizontal planes. Once the pilot has seen you he should waggle his wings from side to side in acknowledgement. If he does this do not go on blinding him with your mirror reflections; he is now concentrating on trying to see you on the ground and he needs unimpaired vision for this. The one limitation to this method is that it needs sunlight, and temperate zones have their share of cloudy days so you must use other signals as well.

Ground signals can be laid out and these require little maintenance. The most obvious is 'S O S' (see Figure 20).

FIG. 19. IMPROVISED HELIOGRAPH MIRROR

FIG. 20. SOS IN SNOW AND SIGNAL FIRES IN A TRIANGLE

This should be in letters as large as possible depending on the available materials. Large boulders, preferably of a contrasting colour, can be used as can strips of brightly-coloured material. The letters can be stamped out in snow, ideally in a north–south line to make the most of shadows. Better still is to fill the trenches you have stamped out with dark contrasting material like tree branches, heather, etc. If you want to convey more than the basic 'S O S' signal, there is an internationally recognized series of signals you can lay out in the same way. Some of the more useful of these are shown in Figure 21. Ideally each symbol should be about 6 metres long, but lack of materials may reduce this. You may have other large or brightly-coloured items such as parachutes, cabin carpets or seats which can be laid out in regular patterns. You must try to make the patterns as unlike nature as possible. Nature is never regular, square, or rectangular.

You may have a torch. If so conserve the batteries and do not use it for reading in bed at night or for illuminating a shelter. Keep it for the possibility of an air search. If an aircraft approaches, keep giving long flashes pointed straight at the sound. Make each flash about five seconds with a two-second interval. If it is not possible to switch the torch on and off easily, keep it on but move it in as wide an arc as possible still keeping it all the time pointing towards the aircraft. If you are with a stranded vehicle remove both the headlamps but leave them electrically connected. When the aircraft is heard turn on the headlamp switch and point both headlamps in its direction. You can produce flashes if someone holds something in front of the headlamps every five seconds. Remember that you must endeavour to make yourself and your position as big and obvious as possible.

GROUND SEARCH AIDS

Aircraft searches can cover a lot of ground in a short time, but they are limited by their availability, the weather and the terrain, so you should always make alternative plans to help a ground rescue party. Remember they may be trying to find you at night or in bad weather and you must do all you can to help. There is an internationally agreed mountain distress signal which is six long blasts on a whistle/flashes on a torch/waves of a garment in one minute, followed by a minute's interval before the signal is repeated. Acknowledgement that the distress signal has been recognized is three long blasts/flashes/waves. Although the signal is designed for mountain use it is equally suitable for any other terrain. If you were to keep making these signals for 24 hours a day you would eventually run out of lung power or your torch batteries would go flat. It is important therefore to decide the best possible time to use the signals.

If you have had an accident, on a rock climb for instance, it is likely that there may be other climbers in the area and the sooner you attract their attention

1. REQUIRE DOCTOR; SERIOUS INJURIES	4. REQUIRE FOOD AND WATER	7. ALL WELL
2. REQUIRE MEDICAL SUPPLIES	5. REQUIRE MAP AND COMPASS	8. NO
3. UNABLE TO PROCEED	6. AM PROCEEDING IN THIS DIRECTION	9. YES

FIG. 21. A SELECTION OF RECOGNIZED GROUND TO AIR SIGNALS

the better so immediate use of the signal should be made. If, however, you are in a remote area with little likelihood of anyone else being near no one is going to start worrying about you until you are overdue at your planned destination. It will then take time to initiate a search and for the rescuers to move into your area. Allow the shortest reasonable time for this to happen and then start making signals. Unless you are a large party you are more likely to see the search group before they see you especially if you have sought out a sheltered spot in which to wait. It is vital therefore that one or more of your group be posted as lookouts. You are much less likely to be found if you are carefully tucked away in a collection of boulders well out of the elements, but since you *should* be here for warmth and shelter you *must* have your watchers out.

At night it will be even harder for searchers to find you even if they have a good idea where you are so if you have a climbing rope stretch it out full length across the likely line of approach, thus instead of being a small group only a few feet across you have become a hundred or more feet long – a much easier target to find. Leave the rope out by day; it can still help as can brightly-coloured clothing prominently displayed. You may need your orange anorak for warmth, but someone in your party will be wearing bright underwear and that will be equally eye-catching especially if it is trimmed with lace! The whole secret of signalling to rescuers is to make yourself as big, colourful, noisy and obvious as possible. If you think of the most brash advertisement you have seen on a hoarding or television and try to copy it you are probably on the right track.

5. HELP! I'M LOST!
Survival navigation and movement

In this chapter I have assumed that you have a basic knowledge of map-reading and also of how to use a compass to orientate yourself to the terrain. I have also assumed that this knowledge is with 'proper' maps such as those produced in the United Kingdom by the Ordnance Survey at a scale of 1:50000 for travel over rough country. If the term '1:50000' has already got you puzzled, do read a basic manual on map-reading before you venture much further. 'Being lost' can range from not being quite sure where you are in one of the woods in the New Forest in Hampshire, to being tens, if not hundreds, of miles from civilization in the wilds of Canada. In the first case provided you walk on a constant bearing for no more than half an hour you will come to a road, track or other sign of civilization. You were not really lost – just slightly misplaced. In the second case you have the much bigger problem of deciding whether to stay put and let others find you or whether to try to find your own way out and it is this major problem that I wish to deal with first.

TO STAY OR TO MOVE?

If you are surviving as a result of an aircraft crash in a wild and remote area you stay with the wreckage. It is a large, easily seen object and it should provide some degree of shelter and other useful equipment. The pilot should have filed a flight plan before he took off and may have crashed on or near his planned route. This is the first thing that search aircraft will try. Once you have dealt with the more important of your 'Survival – Immediate Actions' you should send out the fittest pairs in your party on short exploratory trips to see if they can find any sign of civilization. It could

be that there is a forestry logging trail only a mile from where you are. In this case you would be foolish to stay put when by walking even 30 or 40 miles down an easy track you will reach habitations. If you find nothing, you stay put if in the desert or the Arctic. The problems of travel in both these areas cannot be over-estimated. The jungle offers much in the way of aids to comfortable living and local people inhabit many jungle areas. Jungle streams will lead, ultimately, to the coast, but will almost certainly pass centres of habitation on the way.

In temperate zones the decision is more difficult. You should ask yourself if you know your position, even roughly. If you have no idea, staying put is indicated. If you do have some idea of your location, ask yourself if you could navigate to some linear feature such as a coastline, major river, road, etc. The advantage of a linear feature is that your navigation does not have to be too accurate for you to hit it somewhere. Then consider if it is realistic to believe your party, or at least some members of it, could cross the terrain involved and make the distance. Other points to be considered are the prevailing weather, the availability of food and water. A person at rest can last 60 or more days without food, but someone travelling across rough country will last only a fraction of this time without food. Your survival party may contain injured, the very old or the very young. This will influence your decision although there is no real reason why the party should not split with some going for help while others remain. Consider the basic fitness, both mental and physical, of your party. It might be the right decision for a bunch of fit, lean soldiers to try to walk out, but it probably would not be the right decision for elderly, overweight businessmen.

All the above questions are variable factors and must be considered carefully and fully after you have recovered from the initial trauma of being thrown into your survival situation. Twenty-four hours would not be too long to allow for this recovery. If you do decide to travel there are certain things to plan carefully. Those remaining (if any) must be sufficient in number and capability to care for any casualties. Those going must select carefully any equipment they plan to carry with them. They should aim to take the minimum consistent with their own survival. Nothing should be taken 'in case its needed'. They will need to improvise some form of rucksack (see Figure 22) to carry this equipment. Canvas, nylon sheet and straps or rope will provide the basis for such a rucksack. A compass is probably the most vital item and other items are given in the list of survival kit contents at Appendix 2.

The party should pick the easiest route going round difficult terrain rather than fighting their way through it. They should go at a slow steady pace which is comfortable for the slowest member. Never travel at night, and make camp in time to cook your evening meal in daylight. Always blaze a trail both for those who might follow your route and for yourselves if you have to backtrack. A route always looks very different coming the other way and you should never trust to memory especially if you are getting towards the end of your tether. All the above is in the rather more dramatic type of situation, but what about being lost in the British hills?

ACTION WHEN LOST

Everyone gets lost at some time. I well remember a few years ago being out on the Moelwyns in Snowdonia in thick mist. I was with a friend and we had both recently obtained our Mountain Leadership Certificate as it was then called. He was also a full-time instructor at an outdoor centre. We set off up a path and talked hard about all manner of things until we came to a junction of paths where we both stopped, each obviously expecting the other to take

FIG. 22. IMPROVISED RUCKSACK

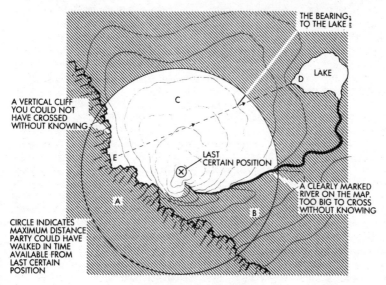

THE BEARING
TO THE LAKE

LAKE
D

A VERTICAL CLIFF
YOU COULD NOT
HAVE CROSSED
WITHOUT KNOWING

C

LAST
CERTAIN POSITION

E

A

B

A CLEARLY MARKED
RIVER ON THE MAP.
TOO BIG TO CROSS
WITHOUT KNOWING

CIRCLE INDICATES
MAXIMUM DISTANCE
PARTY COULD HAVE
WALKED IN TIME
AVAILABLE FROM
LAST CERTAIN
POSITION

FIG. 23. RELOCATION EXAMPLE

the lead. It then dawned on us that we had both assumed that the other knew where we were. In fact neither of us knew where we were and so, rather shamefacedly, we had to carry out the procedure described below.

The first rule is: Never Get Lost. This may seem to beg the question, but it is a reminder that everyone should frequently check the map against the ground, even in fine weather, and confirm exactly where they are. To do this you must be able to get at your map in five seconds and your compass in ten. That means having them in your pocket not deep in a rucksack. In good weather you have no need of a compass; you orientate the map by natural features, but at the first sign of approaching mist or bad weather you bring your compass into full use and set it to the bearing you want to follow. You are then prepared when the mist suddenly reduces visibility to a few metres only.

If, despite everything, you are lost or even just 'slightly displaced', as an optimist might describe it, *stop* and perhaps sit down. This will discourage

any feeling of panic and the urge to rush on. It will also reassure others who are with you. Think back to the last place where you were quite certain you knew your whereabouts; perhaps a mountain top or a lake clearly marked on the map. (See Figure 23). Then decide, possibly with the help of others in your party, how long ago that was. It is to be hoped that it was only a few minutes; if it is more than 30 minutes I doubt your ability to be in the hills at all. Decide the maximum distance you could have walked in the time that has elapsed. That gives you a circle of distance round your last known location. Beyond that you cannot have gone, so you have narrowed down your present position quite a lot. Now try to reduce it further. Look carefully at your map and see if there are any natural features you could not have crossed without noticing – a vertical cliff is an obvious example! If there is such an obvious feature on your map, you can probably eliminate quite a large slice (Area A, Figure 23) of your circle. Think again about any feature which you might have crossed quite easily, such as boulder-hopping over a stream and which should be marked on the map. This may take another large slice (Area B, Figure 23) out of your circle. Now look at the contours. Have you been going gently or steeply up or down hill? Find the area on the map which corresponds to the ground you have traversed. A break in the mist may give you the chance to get a quick compass bearing on a lake (D, Figure 23) or some other feature in the valley. Are you slick enough with a compass to do this in a few seconds?

A combination of all or some of these actions should be enough to enable you to decide where you are to within a hundred metres or so and Figure 23 demonstrates this process (i.e., you are in area C on line D–E). Having found your position you can then plot a new course either to regain your original planned route or a new route avoiding any hazards shown on the map. If, despite all your efforts, you are still very unsure as to where you are, search your map for a linear feature such as a road or river which can be reached safely from anywhere within your possible area and set a compass course to reach it. This compass course can be fairly rough, e.g., SE or SW, since you are heading for a large feature several kilo-metres long. It might be useful or necessary to climb *up* a little way if this will give you a better view of the lie of the land. For 99 per cent of the time this procedure will bring you back to civil-ization, but you could be caught out by the other 1 per cent and much of the rest of this book then applies.

In the mountains it has long been a routine practice to leave details of your planned route with some responsible person, e.g., police, a hostel warden, etc., so that in the event of your being benighted, someone will have some idea where you are. A suggested layout of such a Route Card is shown at Figure 24 and on the basis that prevention is better than cure it is commended to all who venture into the wilder areas.

SENDING FOR HELP

The 'Survival – Immediate Actions' at Appendix 1 and listed at the front of this book have been produced as a suit-able set of actions applicable to any survival situation anywhere in the world. To that extent they have to be somewhat general in content. Since this book is likely to be used mostly in Great Britain I want to deal specifically with the actions you should take if you have some sort of accident or incident in the

FROM	TO	MAG. BEAR	DIST	HEIGHT GAIN-ED	DESCRIPTION OF GROUND	EST. TIME
OGWEN COTT. 650604	PEN YR OLE WEN 656619	028	1·5 K	676 m	VERY STEEP AND ROCKY	86 MINS.
PEN YR OLE WEN 656619	CARNEDD DAFYDD 663630	038	1·2 K	124 m	BEAR 330 FOR FIRST 200M THEN FOLLOW RIDGE.	27 MINS
CARNEDD DAFYDD 663630						
TOTAL						

FIG. 24. A ROUTE CARD

wilder parts of this country. It is strongly recommended that you take the actions strictly in the order as given.

1. Remove the people from immediate danger. This means getting away from a risk of rockfall, getting the casualty out of the river, etc.
2. Render first aid to any casualties. This is first aid for major injuries not sticking plaster on a slightly cut finger. For the priority of treatment remember C-H-A-S-T-E (Appendix 1).
3. Improvise some shelter. Get casualties into survival bags, build a rock wall to keep off the wind, put on spare clothing, etc.
4. Fix your position accurately. This means a six figure grid reference, and determining any other nearby features.
5. Decide the easiest and quickest route to go for help. This may well not be the shortest. Eight miles down an easy glen is easier and quicker than four miles over a 3,000-foot mountain ridge.
6. Produce a *written* message (possibly on the back of a map) giving the following information:
a. Exact location of accident. Include grid reference and near-by well-known features such as a named lake or footpath.
b. Time of accident.
c. Casualty(ies) name and suspected injuries.
d. Number of fit persons with the casualty(ies), and whether they have food, sleeping-bags and stoves.
7. Send two people for help. These should be the best navigators provided they are fit. Remind them that the vital thing is to arrive safely at some habitation not that they break all records – and possibly a leg – trying to get there.
8. Dial 999. The two should go to the nearest habitation and find the telephone. They must not go all the way to the nearest mountain rescue post marked on the map. Having contacted the police they then take their orders from them.
9. Those remaining at the site of the accident carry on doing all the things listed in Appendix 1.

DIRECTION FINDING

If you have a compass and good maps of an area you should have little problem knowing where you are and finding your way across country. If you are short of one of these vital items you must improvise. Here are some useful wrinkles. Let me deal with finding north first. If you have a watch which keeps reasonably good time and the sun is out, Figure 25 shows you how to find south and therefore other points of the compass. With a digital watch just draw a watch face with the hands at the time indicated and proceed as if it were a real watch. If you can spare several hours in the middle part of the day, set up a stick as shown in Figure 26 and mark on the ground every fifteen minutes or so the position of the end of the stick's shadow. The shadow will gradually shorten and then begin to lengthen again. The shortest shadow was cast at noon local time and thus the shadow is pointing north. This must be done on level ground. Remember to allow for variations such as British Summer time if it is in force. This is only applicable, because of the tilt of the earth, north of 23.4°N latitude (a line through the middle of the Sahara, the Red Sea, the middle of India, Hong Kong and Miami). From 23.4°N to 23.4°S the shadow can be north or south depending on your position and the date. South from 23.4°S the shadow always points south. This method is good if you are setting up a survival camp but not if you are travelling. You cannot stop for a day every time you want to check your compass direction, but you can make a stop at noon and make a check then to see which direction the shadow is pointing.

At night your best method of finding north is by the stars. In the northern hemisphere the Plough or Great Bear (Figure 27) is the most obvious of the

FIG. 25. FINDING NORTH BY SUN AND WATCH

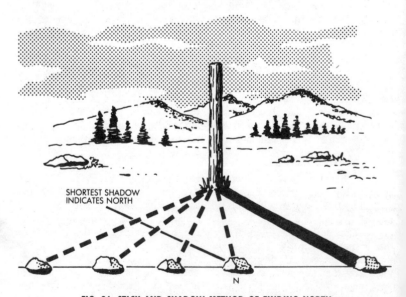

FIG. 26. STICK AND SHADOW METHOD OF FINDING NORTH

FIG. 27. THE PLOUGH AND NORTH STAR

FIG. 29. THE SOUTHERN CROSS

FIG. 28. ORION

In the southern hemisphere the Southern Cross (Figure 29) is the major constellation to look for but beware of the so-called False Cross. Those trained in celestial navigation will be able to apply many more methods of finding north, but the above must suffice for the average layman concerned with survival. It is important to remember that all these constellations revolve so may well appear upside down or sideways when compared to the diagrams given.

There is no scientific proof that humans have an in-built sense of direction. Certain people such as shepherds, trappers, poachers may appear to have this sense, but it is more likely that because of their calling they have become very familiar with every square inch of their territory and thus they give the impression of knowing precisely the right direction to go. Take them out of their own area and they would be as uncertain as the rest of us and this is the reason why a compass or an improvisation of one must always be believed. Some people do have an uncanny

constellations and the North Star, which can be found by projecting a line from the two end stars of the Plough, is always due North for all practical purposes. Another constellation, Orion (Figure 28), is also useful if the Plough is obscured by cloud. Normally Orion is lower down on the horizon and cannot be seen at all in the middle of summer.

FIG. 30. TREE RINGS INDICATING NORTH

ability to select a good route over rough ground or on a rocky crag but this is not a sense of direction.

There are a number of other alleged methods of finding north. Each has a germ of truth or sense, but it must be stressed that a single example should never be taken as positive proof of direction. If a number of such indications all support one another, the weight of evidence can become very strong and is worth accepting if you are totally without compass or map. In all travel or movement across country remember that everyone is lop-sided to a certain degree and will veer to left or right. In the same way we all have a dominant eye which may or may not coincide with our tendency to veer. To determine your dominant eye keep them both open and hold a finger upright at arms length. Then close each eye in turn. With one eye open your finger will remain lined up on an object, with the other eye your finger will appear to jump to left or right. The open eye which does not jump is your dominant eye. An unbalanced rucksack or carrying a load in one hand will make you veer as will a strong wind or driving rain and snow.

Trees and shrubs often develop in a windswept shape. If you know the prevailing wind for the area you have quite a good indication of direction. Trees normally, provided they are not influenced by rock outcrops, other

trees, etc., grow the maximum foliage on the sunny side, i.e., the south side (in the northern hemisphere). If you find a tree which has been felled with a saw the annual rings (Figure 30) will be wider apart on the north side. Moss tends to grow more abundantly on the north side of a tree trunk and the bark on some trees, notably the poplar and alder, is lighter on the south side. In contrast to moss on trees, lichens on rock will be most prolific on south faces. Anthills are usually on the south side of rocks, trees or other objects.

Most seabirds, it is alleged, fly out to sea in the morning to feed and return to the land at night. I doubt that the cormorants which nest four miles inland from where I live know this. They seem to keep up a steady pattern of flying to and fro from the sea to their nests throughout the day so be careful not to place too much emphasis on this type of indication.

It is possible to improvise a rough compass which can be used in conjunction with the sun (if it is shining). First, cut out from card or paper two triangles; one with dimensions 1:2 (see Figure 31) and one cut diagonally from a square. By using one or both triangles in combination you can determine angles as small as 15°, which in survival terms is not too bad. Link this to the fact that the sun revolves around the earth at 15° every hour and you can get bearings accurate to within 15°. Figures 32 and 33 show this in simple form. Figure 32 shows examples of angles which can be achieved by use of the triangles. In Figure 33 an example is given at 1000 hrs, i.e., when the sun is on a bearing of 150° (180° less 2 hrs at 15°). The example shows that the desired bearing for travel is 210° and this is measured with the help of the 60° angle. By 1100 hrs you would have to use the 45° angle and at noon the 30° angle, and so on. A modest knowledge of geometry helps for this method. When cutting out the triangles the dimensions can be anything – inches,

FIG. 31. TRIANGLES FOR IMPROVISED BEARINGS

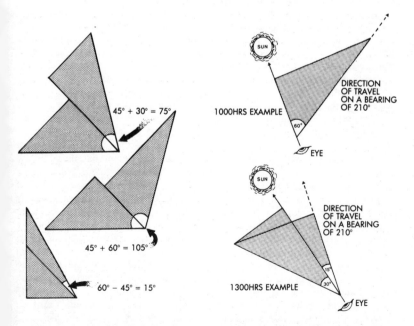

FIG. 32. EXAMPLES OF THE USE OF TRIANGLES FOR IMPROVISED BEARINGS

FIG. 33. EXAMPLES OF THE USE OF THE TRIANGLES TO FIND A DIRECTION OF TRAVEL

centimetres, thumbnail widths, etc., provided that they are the same on each triangle.

CROSS-COUNTRY TRAVEL

The distances people can travel on foot in a day can vary enormously. On a good road or track with little or no gradient a fit man might make 50 or 60 kilometres in a day. The same man might only cover one or two kilometres in bamboo thicket or mangrove swamp. Before deciding to try to walk out to civilization it is important to assess the type of terrain you will have to cross. Before setting out you should leave details of your intended route at your point of departure and then clearly mark your route with small cairns of stones, a blaze mark on a tree, a sapling broken off in the direction of travel or any other clear indication that someone has passed that way recently. Do not rely on footprints, a rain storm will soon wash them away. Keep a sketch map of your route with the major features, bearings and changes of direction marked in. It is important to be able to measure distance and pacing is the most likely method you will have available. You should know from prior survival training how many normal paces you take per 100 metres. It is easier to count every second pace, i.e., every left or right step rather than every pace.

You will almost certainly encounter streams and rivers. Many books on mountaineering advise against following streams since they have a habit of going over a cliff edge. This is so in some, but by no means all, cases and it is reasonable to assume that you would follow any route carefully and prudently. I see no risk in sensibly following streams and rivers. They lead to low ground and eventually the sea. Civilization tends to be in the lower areas of the world and along the coast. You may be able to build a raft on which to float down a river. This is slow but conserves energy. Do listen and watch for any signs (roaring or a haze of spray) of a waterfall and get in to the side if in any doubt. A raft can be made from logs (Figure 34) or from a sheet of canvas or similar material wrapped round a circular bundle (Figure 35) of twigs and saplings to form a coracle which has been a traditional form of boat on Welsh rivers for centuries. Poles, oars, sails, etc., can be improvised according to your skill and inclination.

FORCE CLOSED WITH TIGHT LASHINGS

FIG. 34. A LOG RAFT

River crossing is a vital part of any mountain training course, and it is not a subject to be treated lightly. The nearest I have ever come to death was when I was swept away in an Arctic river and battered over boulders in ice-cold water. Remember always to so fix your load that you can easily shed it if you fall over; but having shed it remember also that any rucksack or similar load will act as a float with the aid of which you can half swim half float to the shore. If you can avoid a river crossing do so even if it means quite a detour. If you decide to attempt it look carefully for a good crossing place. You want good entry and exit points. Where a river widens and flattens out it is likely to be shallower. Ideally choose a point where the river is flat and even, and without boulders; shingle and small pebbles are good. It is always worth removing your socks, but put your boots back on to protect your feet. For a short crossing it is probably worth taking your trousers off to keep them

FIG. 35. A WELSH CORACLE

dry, but for a long crossing they do provide some insulation against the numbing cold of most river water. If you are on your own look for a stick to provide a 'third leg' (Figure 36), face upstream and progress by a series of sideways shuffles rather than normal steps. If there are two of you, the weakest of the pair stands close behind the other, grips his waist and they move in unison. For greater numbers a similar method applies. A variation for a group

FIG. 36. RIVER CROSSING WITH A 'THIRD LEG'

of three is to stand (Figure 37) in a triangle looking in and with arms around the shoulders of the other two. Again careful control of movement is required. The strongest one should face upstream while the other two face down stream.

If you have an actual or improvised rope the continuous loop system (Figure 39) can be used. The diagram gives one example of how to use it, but additional members of the party can assist by bracing the rope out to give greater support against the force of the river or by providing a downstream recovery loop. If someone falls it is better that he swim/or is pulled to the side rather than try to regain his foothold. In some instances it may be easier to rig a tight rope between two trees, boulders, etc., and each person, except the first and last, ties some sort of loop to the tight rope. Ideally (Figure 38) they should have a safety rope around

DIRECTION OF FLOW

STRONGEST PERSON

FIG. 37. RIVER CROSSING – 3-MAN TRIANGLE METHOD

the waist so that should they fall they can be hauled in to one side or the

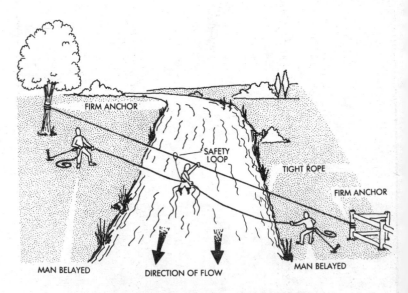

FIRM ANCHOR

SAFETY LOOP

TIGHT ROPE

FIRM ANCHOR

MAN BELAYED

DIRECTION OF FLOW

MAN BELAYED

FIG. 38. RIVER CROSSING – TIGHT ROPE SYSTEM

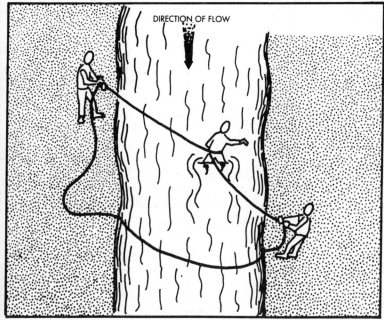

FIG. 39. RIVER CROSSING – CONTINUOUS LOOP SYSTEM

other. In all river crossing you should allow yourself to move partially downstream with the current as you progress across the river. Frozen rivers provide an easy means of travel, but you must be sure that the ice will safely bear your weight. Remember that the ice will be thicker on the inside of bends in the river. It is seldom that a sufficient thickness of ice builds up on rivers in Great Britain and all but the smallest lakes are equally suspect.

Ridges and other high land normally provide dryer and easier conditions under foot and also allow you a better view of your route ahead. Against that they are usually colder and more windswept. Remember that contouring can save a lot of energy. Contouring is the art of never losing or gaining height unnecessarily. Climbing up takes much more energy than walking on the level and it is often worth walking further on the level than taking the shortest but steepest route. If you are not sure how two routes compare apply Naismith's Rule and take the quickest route unless you are really exhausted when it will always be better to take the contouring route. Naismith's Rule is three miles per hour of horizontal travel *plus* an extra half hour for every thousand feet climbed. You treat downhill stretches as if flat. Figure 40 gives an example of how the rule works. In metric terms you should calculate this as five kilometres per hour plus one minute for every ten metres climbed.

Scree and boulder fields should be avoided as far as possible, as should any very steep slopes since all these are very tiring to traverse. Snow will add to your

A–B 500m (50 min) + 2km (24 min) = 74 min
B–C NIL   + 1km (12 min) = 12 min
C–D 750m (75 min) + 2km (24 min) = 99 min
D–E NIL   + 1km (12 min) = 12 min
               TOTAL   = 197 min
               or 3 hours 17 min

FIG. 40. EXAMPLE OF NAISMITH'S RULE

FIG. 41. CORNICE DANGERS

difficulties on any terrain. Soft powder snow without the aid of skis or snowshoes will sap your energy almost as much as swamp. Hard frozen snow or ice is hazardous without crampons and iceaxe. On a snow-covered ridge keep well back from the edge of a cornice (Figure 41) and note that the fracture line is often much further back than one might think. Avalanche risk is a science in itself, and several complete books have been written on the subject. In simple terms you should keep well away from steep slopes covered in new powder snow, and warm days increase the risk on any slope. Avalanches are not limited to high mountain areas and do frequently occur in Great Britain. Dry glaciers are those with no overlying snow; they are just ice. Because the crevasses are easily seen, travel on a dry glacier is reasonably safe, but even so a rope is a useful aid and only the most

level of such glaciers allow comfortable walking without the help of crampons. Wet glaciers are covered with snow which can bridge quite large crevasses. These snow bridges frequently give way under the weight of a body. It is vital that a party be roped in groups of not less than three. Linear depressions should be treated with suspicion especially if they appear to continue the line of obviously open crevasses. It cannot be stressed too strongly that snow-covered glaciers should only be traversed if all alternative terrain is exceedingly difficult.

Technical mountaineering books explain a number of different methods of crevasse rescue, but the non-mountaineering survivor wants a method (Figure 42) that is simple and easily remembered. The diagram shows how a party should tie on the rope. The principle is that if anyone falls into a crevasse there

FIG. 42. ROPING UP

(A) 2-MAN SYSTEM

(B) 3-MAN SYSTEM

is sufficient rope not under tension to the person in the crevasse for a looped end to be dropped to him. When the loop reaches him he puts a foot into the loop thus relieving the rope pull on the body. It is important that the loop rope runs over something such as a pack, clothing, stick, etc., on the lip of the crevasse otherwise the rope will cut into the snow causing additional friction and difficulty to those trying to pull him up. Unless he is injured the fallen person should do all he can, by pulling on his rope, bracing his feet against the crevasse wall, etc., to assist with the haul. It is possible to reduce the effort required by rigging two-to-one pulley systems, etc., but such systems are seldom retained in the mind unless frequently practised, and this volume is not aimed at the experienced mountaineer who should be well-practised in such arts. Survivors should take heart from the fact that when putting a foot through most snow bridges it is soon sensed and the person is able to throw himself forward or back, or if he does go in he often lodges no more than waist deep, and can be easily pulled out. If you see one of your party fall you should immediately brace yourself and if you have an iceaxe or similar equipment thrust it into the snow or ice. I was once able to hold not only a man but also the weight of a loaded *pulka* (one-man sledge) which hung from his waist when he went into a crevasse. Some instinct had told me he was going through the snow bridge and I turned my skis to take the pull. On my own all I could do was to hold him, but others in the party were able quickly to rig an anchor and we soon had him out. It is better not to carry coils of rope in the hand but to keep the rope tight at all times. On glaciers and where there is an avalanche risk, travel in the early part of the day when it is colder. If you deem it safe, travel at night and sleep during the warmth of the day.

A mountaineering technique which could be useful in a very limited number of situations is abseiling (Figure 43). If you have a rope, double it round some suitable anchor such as a tree, rock, bollard, etc. Do make sure it is free-running because once you have abseiled down you pull one end of the rope to retrieve it for future use. Only abseil if you cannot climb or scramble down easily. You can abseil down a totally sheer face, but before doing so you must be quite certain that you are on the right route and that you will never have a need to climb back up. When abseiling remember it is the downhill hand (the right hand in the diagram) which is the controlling hand. To reduce your speed of descent bring your right arm round towards the front so that the rope is wrapped more around your body thus increasing the friction. To increase speed do the reverse. Keep your legs straight, feet flat on the rock surface and spaced well apart.

FIG. 43. USE OF A ROPE FOR ABSEILING

If, in a survival situation, you have a map and a compass you are indeed lucky, but the map may not be suitable for cross-country travel. It could be an air navigation chart at a scale of 1:1M (16 miles to the inch) – hardly the thing for a party on foot; they might take three days to cover an inch! It might be a panoramic picture map as sold in tourist shops. Very pretty and worthy of a place on your wall but not ideal for accurate navigation. If you decide to move from your survival camp do make sure you understand your map first. Study it. What does it show? Do you really understand how the shape of the ground is indicated? What do all the various symbols on it mean? What is the vertical distance between contour lines? If, for example, contour lines are 500 feet apart a great number of small hills will not be shown on the map. If the contour interval is 1,000 feet things will be a lot worse. Do check the date the map was surveyed. A map is out of date on the day it is printed. Twenty years later it will be even more inaccur-

ate with even such apparently long-lasting things as forests swept away. The only features you can rely on are the shape of the ground and water symbols, and even here remember that a valley could have been flooded for a hydro-electric scheme. Remember to check the magnetic variation. In some parts of the world this is massive compared with the five or six degrees current in Great Britain.

No compass is totally accurate and everyone, when they walk, has a tendency to drift to right or to left. Because of this you should never try to navigate directly to a point object such as a single building. In the example (Figure 44) there is a lone hut on the bank of a river, and it is well hidden by forest and so cannot be seen from a distance. If you set a bearing to travel to it, it would be luck or chance if you hit it spot on, especially if you had been on that bearing for several kilometres. You would be to the north or to the south of it. In Figure 44 the traveller has veered off to his left (north of the hut). He

FIG. 44. RISK WHEN NAVIGATING TO AN ISOLATED POINT

thought he was to the south, so he turned north to find his objective. After travelling some distance he realized he was wrong and so had to backtrack finally to find the hut after yet more time and effort had been wasted. The river, being a linear feature, stopped him going too far beyond the hut: it is a linear feature that you must always look for when trying to find a point object. The safe thing to do is deliberately to aim off to left or right by only two or three degrees; then when you reach the linear feature you will know which way to turn to reach the point object.

Navigation may well be a crucial part of your survival in a difficult situation, but it is a subject which needs a lot of experience before you can be said to be proficient. Half a dozen lessons on 'map reading' in a barrack room or a Scout HQ will only give you the very basics and far less than you need to confidently navigate anywhere in any conditions. Even for the simplest of walks on the local common with the dog take a map. See what it shows. Trace out the footpaths. Get a simple Silva-type compass and follow a bearing. See how accurate you are over 1,000 metres. Try orienteering as a sport; you may not win any medals but you will become a very good navigator. For the enthusiast half an hour with a good map will be as enjoyable as half an hour with a good book. If you have not yet reached that level of enjoyment you need more practice.

6. WATER, WATER EVERYWHERE...
Finding water

The shipwrecked sailor's lament continues '. . . Nor any drop to drink'. Fortunately for the survivor in the temperate parts of the world this is seldom the case. However the water that is available will not be coming out of a tap so 'water' must be considered in a survival manual.

At total rest the human body will lose about two pints per day by way of loss through breathing, perspiration and urine. Even if the body is dehydrated there is no appreciable reduction in this quantity. In normal civilized circumstances medical advice recommends that one drink plenty of fluids and the same applies in a survival situation. In the latter case, however, water may not be easily obtained and it is vital to conserve it as much as possible. In Chapter Three I have already mentioned the need to avoid sweating, and the need to conserve the body's store of liquid is another good reason for it. Ideally you need six to eight pints of water per day. As a minimum you need the two pints quoted above, to which must be added a varying quantity according to the amount of work you do during the day. If water is limited there is no value in rationing it to some microscopic quantity per day. There is a real risk you could breathe your last while some water yet remained! Medical advice is that the maximum fluid that can be lost is 20 per cent of body weight.

As an example, with a ten stone person that is 28 pounds or about 23 pints. Assume that the daily water loss is three pints (two pints normal daily loss plus one pint for the additional work of modest survival activity). Without any additional water this will give the survivor seven and two-thirds days. If this person had only a fixed amount of water available, say ten pints, he would survive for an additional three and one-third days (at the three pints per day rate). His total survival time is thus eleven days. To make maximum use of the fluid available in his body at the start of his survival situation he should drink nothing for 24 hours, but thereafter should drink an equal amount on each of his expected day's survival. In this example he has ten remaining days and ten pints of water so the ration will be one pint per day. If he drinks less than this he will die before all his water has been drunk. If he drinks more he will not be eking out his available fluid to the best advantage. Should he find water he can drink unlimited quantities if the supply is unlimited. If it is not, he must recalculate his daily ration figure.

Hot weather or a hot climate will alter dramatically the minimum amount of water required for the body's basic existence. The following table gives the quantity required assuming that the body remains at rest and in the shade.

Mean Temperature °C	Pints per 24-hour day
24	2
27	2½
30	4½
33	6½
35	9

From this table it is quite clear why desert survival without adequate supplies of water is such a shortlived matter. At nine pints per day a person will have lost his 20 per cent of body weight in about two and a half days. The best one can do is to rest in shade during the hottest part of the day and undertake the bare minimum of activity during the cool of the night. A person approaching the 20 per cent fluid loss point may well not be capable of taking rational decisions. For this reason it is probably worthwhile increasing, during the last few days, any daily ration slightly – perhaps by ten or fifteen per cent – to get the fluid into the body before the brain becomes incapable of ordering the action to drink the daily ration.

There is no substitute for fresh water. Urine, blood, petroleum fuels, alcohol all require water if the body is to assimilate them and certain fluids such as petroleum fuels are positively harmful in their own right. Much has been written about drinking sea water especially in relation to survival at sea. However, it now seems clear that since the average proportion of salt in sea water is considerably more than the body can cope with and remain healthy, sea water can only be drunk if there are adequate supplies of fresh water to take up the surplus salt and thus maintain the correct salt balance in the body. Thus it would be much simpler to just drink the available fresh water.

Parts of the Arctic are sometimes described as 'deserts', but this is not unreasonable since the total precipitation per year is often only a few centimetres and is thus comparable to deserts as we usually understand the term. And the term 'desert' can also be applied in relation to the problems that man will have in obtaining water in such areas. Although he may be surrounded by millions of tons of water it will be in a frozen state as snow or ice and every drop for drinking will have to be melted, often by the use of precious fuel in a stove. It is important to remember that the amount of fuel required to change ice into water at freezing point is roughly the same as that required to raise the same amount of water to boiling point for a hot drink. Exactly the same applies in mountaineering at altitude and for this reason climbers and explorers delight to find any source of running water and will

often go to some lengths to use the heat of the sun to melt ice in cooking-pots or spread out on groundsheets, etc. Dehydration is a well-known risk when one is active in cold conditions, and polar and high-altitude rations include a more than average quantity of drinks. The amount of body fluid lost by respiration in cold climates is also greater than in hot and this further compounds the risk of dehydration in such climates. Despite our ability to eat a modest quantity of ice in the form of icecream or ice lollies, eating ice or mouthfuls of snow should never be resorted to in cold climates. The 'fuel' to melt it has got to come from your body heat and in a survival situation you can spare none of that. Eating snow also frequently causes a sore mouth and lips which is painful and unpleasant. Always melt ice in preference to snow. Even a full cooking-pot of snow produces a pitiful amount of water. To avoid burning the pot melt a little snow in the pan first and then gradually add ice to the liquid.

In temperate climates finding water is not normally a great problem, but collecting it and storing it in a survival situation may be. When selecting a possible site for a survival camp one of the factors you must consider is: How far to the nearest water? There may be something of a conflict between proximity of water, of fuel and the need for shelter. You will probably have to improvise water containers from tins, plastic bags, etc. Many good sources of water will only be a trickle. Some Alpine climbers carry a short length of rubber or plastic tubing which acts as a flexible straw and can be used to suck water from the tiniest runnel of water flowing over a rock. You may have to think of something similar and certainly you may have to scoop water, almost literally by the thimbleful, from some trickle source. Some years ago I was climbing in Turkey in an area where the whole climbing programme was governed by the location of two or three waterholes. We first had to find them and from a distance the only indication was the few blades of vegetation – just a tiny splash of green – to show that there was water there. The actual water-hole was only about three feet in diameter and covered with a fair crop of flies and other assorted insects, so the first action was to skim the animal life from the surface and then gently bail out the water with a small mug to avoid disturbing the mud on the bottom. Finding water will often need care and effort.

On another expedition three of us were using a rubber boat with an outboard to travel north in the Inner Fjord area of East Greenland. A sudden squall blew up and we hurriedly made for the nearest land – Ruth Island. We landed and sorted out our wet kit and I went looking for water on an island only about half a mile in diameter. I searched for a long time and was on the point of giving up and accepting that we would have no water that night when I tried one more dried-up water gully and heard the faint sound of trickling water. A bit of digging and removal of boulders and I got down to the water level and used a cup to scoop out the water bit by bit.

Apart from the obvious sources such as rivers, lakes and pools, and by digging in gullies or other water courses, you should always, unless water is plentiful, collect water from groundsheets, plastic sheeting, etc., whenever rain falls. In many streams water only flows in winter or when there has been a lot of recent rain. At other times the watercourse may be dry on the surface but water can often be found by digging down a foot or two. When you find it fashion out a pool to collect the water as it flows in and for sediment to settle out. Green vegetation is often a good indication of the presence of water especially if the vegetation is lush and plentiful. Unlike the jungle where there are plants such as bamboo which actually hold water in liquid form, there are no plants of this type in temperate climates.

Having found your source of water and begun to collect it you have two further problems: to clarify it and to treat it for possible pollution. In the first case, the water may have tiny particles of rock and vegetable matter floating in it. These may be easily visible or they may be tiny. The particles will not give you any dread disease, but they may irritate the walls of the stomach and lead to diarrhoea or vomiting which, apart from being unpleasant, lessen your chances of survival since they remove from the body the very thing – water – which you are trying to get into it. The answer is to allow the water to stand for an hour or two thus allowing the heavier particles to settle in the bottom of the container. Then gently decant the water from the top of the container into another container and discard the possibly murky remnant. Do not be discouraged if, despite this treatment, the water is still peat-coloured especially in an area like the Scottish hills. Just think of it as looking like whisky!

Having removed the large lumps construct a simple filter (see Figure 45) using closely woven fabric. Good quality handkerchiefs are an obvious example or a piece cut from an anorak. If it is a very good-quality anorak made

FIG. 45. SIMPLE WATER FILTER

from Ventile or a similar cloth you may find the water only soaks through very slowly, drop by drop, unless you can provide quite a few inches' head of water to increase the pressure. This is the one time when having a high-quality garment is not an advantage. Nylon stockings or tights make another good filter. I must admit that I have drunk water from all sorts of doubtful streams, glacier melt pools, etc., for the past 30 years and have not come to any harm, but I believe that I have a very rugged stomach capable of accepting almost any punishment without a murmur. I have friends for whom the slightest change of food or water seems to mean an automatic dose of Delhi Belly, Montezuma's Revenge, Kathmandu Quickstep or some similar malady according to their geographical location!

Having partially, but at your own peril, dismissed the need to clarify water, the second problem is purification. Doctors will assure you that almost anything except housemaid's knee can be caught from drinking unpurified water and this is certainly true. In the Western world it is possible, with a very high degree of safety, to drink from high mountain streams and I have done this for many years in Wales and Scotland. The proviso is that drinking straight from a stream should only be done above the highest habitation. Water below a farm or house should always be treated as suspect and if you have any doubts use purifying tablets. East of Suez and anywhere else you should always take precautions with the local water even if it comes from a tap. Unlike the British hills where an accurate map will tell you if there is any habitation above you, you can never be sure even quite high in the Himalayas. What appears to be a crystal-clear stream coming down a steep jungle slope from high mountains may be anything but pure. If you follow it up for a few thousand feet you will find some one with his simple house and patch of ground and his pride and

joy – a constant flush loo! The only trouble is that his constant flush loo is flushing straight down the hillside into your water bottle. Be warned.

In a survival situation there are three things you can do. First, water-purifying tablets are often found in aircraft survival kits and should form part of your own personal survival kit. They are very light in weight; enough to purify several hundred litres of water weigh less than an ounce, so they should be high on your list of priorities. Without such tablets the next possibility is two or three drops of iodine or a few grains of permanganate of potash in a litre of water left to stand for 30 minutes. Finally, you can boil the water. The pessimists will say that you must boil for at least 20 minutes to ensure you have killed every last bug, but three minutes is usually accepted as a very adequate time especially if fuel is short. Do remember that in most cases water will be boiled automatically to cook food or make drinks. There is no need to boil it, leave it to cool and then boil it again as part of cooking. This will only waste fuel. Running water is usually sweeter to the taste, but is no guarantee of its purity. Conversely, even stagnant water may be pure although it may have a decided taste to it which for the first few days will be deemed unacceptable but will eventually seem like the proverbial nectar. In a survival situation never get so paranoiac about the water supply that you end up dead from thirst but in the best of health in all other respects. It is better to survive alive even if you have suffered a nasty dose of an upset stomach.

If you have any choice in the food you can eat when water is in short supply, limit yourself to carbohydrates – the sweet and sugary things. Both protein and fat need additional water for them to be assimilated into the body. In a survival situation you will succumb for other reasons than a lack of either protein or fats. To sum up, if you have unlimited water drink as much as you like and eat what you like. If you have only a limited amount of water available work out your daily ration and limit yourself, if you have choice, to carbohydrates. Do not worry too much if you cannot clarify water, but beware of drinking it unpurified. Always, for a variety of reasons, avoid sweating and adjust your work rate and clothing to ensure this.

7. FUEL FOR THE FURNACE: Finding food

Your body is a machine and your digestive system is the boiler or powerhouse. In general if you keep the furnace well stoked with fuel the machine can keep going. In a survival situation your furnace may well have to accept a variety of fuel and fortunately it does compare very well with a multifuel engine. When the going suddenly gets hard, it is not the time to have petty likes and dislikes about food. You may not like rice pudding but if all you have with you is a case of tinned rice pudding you have got to eat it. Tom Bourdillon, who was a member of the successful 1953 Everest expedition, when talking about food once said 'The main thing is that there shall be some' and that just about sums up the hope of anyone who is trying to survive. Vilhjalmur Stefansson, who spent much of the early part of this century exploring the Arctic and often lived off the land entirely, once said '. . . any traveller who complains about going three or four days without food will get scant sympathy from me'. A forthright statement maybe, but it does demonstrate the right approach to the question of food. As I have quoted earlier in this book, food is almost the least of your worries if you are forced to survive in the wild. You will live for weeks without any and you will succumb much more quickly to a lack of water, shelter, etc. However 'any fool can be uncomfortable' and a full stomach will add to your general well-being and help you through some of the other rigours of being a survivor.

If you are thrown into a survival situation you will carry out all your Survival – Immediate Actions and then turn your attention to food. The first thing to do is to determine what food resources you have with you. This may be anything from specially provisioned survival rations in a crashed aircraft, through bars of chocolate, packets of nuts, etc., being carried by individuals, to the remains of a sandwich lunch. Put someone in charge of the food, under your direction, and he can decide what will be eaten, and when. There is much to be said for eating nothing for 24 hours other than perishable items like sandwiches. Even the leanest of us has fat on the body and the sooner the body starts to draw on this the better. Some people appear to have several weeks' reserves scattered around their midriff and similar areas! One idea is that you estimate the probable number of days until rescue and split the available food into thirds. Two-thirds are eaten during the first half of your survival time and the remaining one-third during the second half. Unlike determining a water ration there is no simple way of deciding the amount to be eaten daily other than to say that if the body is kept in a state of food shortage this will ensure that such food as is eaten is digested to the full and every bit of nourishment extracted by the digestive system.

If you decide to send some of your party for help it is only right, since they are likely to be much more active, that they take more than their share of the food. Twice as much should go to the walkers as to those staying behind, provided that the quantity is not so much that they are burdened down by it. As explained in the chapter on *Water* you should, if you have any choice, avoid foods which are mainly protein or fat when water is limited. Most foods are made more palatable and digestible if they are cooked and it also makes them much safer since the cooking process will kill any unwanted bugs. However, cooking does not add food value and in some cases, such as over cooking cabbage, the food value can be much reduced, so do not be afraid of eating food raw if you cannot cook it. To the Eskimo raw liver straight from the still warm body of a seal is gourmet eating beyond measure.

Almost inevitably, unless you are a wildfood enthusiast, you will know very little about the food possibilities in the immediate area so it is important to establish some guidelines on how to decide if a certain berry, fish, etc., is edible. First, avoid all fungi unless you are very experienced in their recognition. In any case 'there's not a calorie in a barrelful', as one American expert has so aptly put it. You will expend more energy bending down to pick the thing than you will get from it. Try unknown foods one at a time. If you try several at once and one (or more?) clearly proves that it is not good for man, how do you know which it is? Prepare an unknown food in the way you plan to eat it. Take no more than a teaspoonful in the mouth and hold it there for a few minutes. If there is no burning, nauseating or bitter taste, swallow it. If within the next eight hours you have no ill effects (nausea, diarrhoea, stomach cramps) eat a handful. If there are still no ill effects the food is safe to eat although for the first few meals it would be wise not to over-indulge. Remember that some foods are inedible when raw, so do not assume that something which passes the test when cooked can be eaten raw. Watch what animals eat. Food eaten by mice, rats, rabbits and similar animals are all safe for you to try.

PLANT FOOD

There are many thousands of plants which will provide you with food; far too many to give you lists of suitable ones. As a general rule avoid those with a milky sap and avoid heads of grain which have a black spur in them. Beyond these two points you must apply the tests given above. While actual species names are too numerous it is worthwhile reminding you of the different types of plant food. Nuts are probably familiar to everyone if only as one of the traditional items at Christmas. Almonds, hazelnuts and walnuts are well-known and easily recognized and they are widespread in the temperate zones, but other nuts should also be tried. Most of the tiny nuts inside fir cones can be eaten. Beech nuts are also suitable to eat raw. Acorns vary in their suitability. Sweet ones can be eaten raw but bitter ones should be boiled in changes of water, or they can be ground up after being roasted. A type of coffee can be improvised from them in this form. Nuts are a very good source of food as any vegetarian will tell you.

Ferns and bracken, besides providing good insulation or roofing on an improvised shelter, can also provide food. The young, curled-up fronds can be eaten raw or can be cooked if you prefer. Just use the tips since the main leaves will be bitter. We are used to eating wheat as flour in bread, cakes, etc., but all seed-bearing grasses can be eaten. Discard any seed heads with black spurs instead of grain and also any which look as if they have fungus on them. The remainder you should remove from the stalk and then either boil or grind into a coarse flour. The stalk does not make good eating for humans even if it is good for cows. The flour can be used to make any form of bread or bannock. Depending on the sophistication of your survival camp you can make loaves in an improvised oven, or you might wrap a 'sausage' of dough round a peeled green stick to bake a twist over a camp-fire, or cook thin round cakes of dough on a hot surface, such as a sheet of metal. Figure 46 shows a twist being cooked, and Figure 66 an improvised oven design.

Berries and fruits pose problems. Some, such as blackberries and bilberries, are very edible and often form part of a normal civilized diet. At the other extreme are the berries of deadly

FIG. 46. COOKING A TWIST

nightshade and yew which are highly poisonous even in small quantities. However, many more berries and fruits are edible than are dangerous so do not be frightened to try them, but under controlled conditions over successive eight-hour periods. Remember, you can eat the more unusual ones such as rose hips, wild strawberries, elderberries, sloes, rowan berries and many others.

Flowers and their leaves and stalks are another very wide field with many which are edible and a few which are not. The humble dandelion provides tasty young leaves for a salad, a form of coffee if you dry and grind up the roots and the actual flowers can be made into wine. Chickweed, which makes its way into many a garden, can be eaten raw as a salad item or boiled to make a soup. The leaves of the lime, hawthorn and beech are also suitable for salads, as is wood sorrel. The following is a fairly random list of edible plants. Fat Hen, Greater Burdock, Silverweed, all the Vetches, Red Clover, the Plantain group, Yarrow, Goatsbeard, Chicory, Wild Rose, Common Wintercress, Sheep Sorrel; Bulrush (pith of stalk only). Now for the ones to avoid at all costs. Hemlock and Cowbane are both of the carrot family and have leaves somewhat similar to the domestic carrot. Because of this they might be

thought suitable to eat but they are not, being poisonous in quite small quantities. Baneberry, Foxglove and all the Hellebores should also be avoided, as should the humble buttercup. Some of these plants have been used in the past for medicinal purposes in strictly controlled doses, but this does not make them suitable for general consumption as food.

At first sight the idea of eating tree bark may seem odd, but the inner bark of poplars, birches and willows is suitable. Scots and Lodgepole Pine bark can also be used provided that you strip away all the outer brown parts and use only the inner white pithy parts. It can be eaten raw but is probably better cooked, either roasted or boiled.

The roots of plants should not be ignored. We regularly eat carrots and parsnips so why not try dandelion, the common reed, and others. Although not strictly roots, the bulbs of onions, tulips and similar plants are all worth trying. Water-lilies and other aquatic plants should not be despised. The world is full of plants and vegetation (including lichens) even in the tundra regions and most of it is good to eat. A book with suitable colour illustrations is the best aid to finding known edible plants and for avoiding the known poisonous ones.

MEAT AS FOOD

Weight for weight meat is the best food you can get, but unlike plants which stay still and allow themselves to be picked, most animals are very wary of other animals and especially of humans. The effort required to find and catch an animal must be measured against the likely food value. Since meat is largely protein, which requires water to digest it, you should avoid meat if water is short. Everyone is familiar with beef, pork, chicken, turkey and other similar meats which form part of our everyday diet, but for the person trying to survive, anything on earth that is animal, bird or insect should be considered. Almost certainly you have eaten a caterpillar in salad or cabbage without realizing it and you may well have eaten all sorts of other things in food. It is the idea of eating such things that we find difficult to accept, and yet in some parts of the world grasshoppers, for instance, are a delicacy.

Since the beginning of time the art of hunting has been slowly perfected by many different communities across the world. Because it is a difficult art, the idea of domesticating certain animals and birds began to be developed a few thousand years ago and now we have reached the point where virtually all meat comes from this source. Only a very few remote and primitive tribes still rely totally on hunting for much of their food although hunting as a sport has become increasingly widespread in the Western world. The survivor has to go back to thinking like his ancestors and thinking 'animal' when it comes to setting snares or deciding where to look for food. Ask yourself where animals (who normally are creatures of habit) would go for water or food. Where are his regular paths? Where would he make his burrow, warren or den? Animals are not unthinking brutes, they like their comfort.

Some years ago I was with an expedition in East Greenland and we were at first puzzled by narrow tracks which looked very like the sheep tracks on the Welsh or Scottish hills. East Greenland, however, has no sheep: but it does have musk ox and these were their regular routes. We then began to realize that they had an unerring instinct in picking the easiest route across country and it soon became the cry of the expedition to 'Follow the musk ox trail!' since that would be the easiest route for us as well. Tracks, droppings, trampled vegetation all indicate the passing of animals. Hole-dwelling animals can be poked out of their burrows but you need to stop up the other exits or have someone there ready to catch them. Hunting at night is possible with the aid of a torch since that will partially blind an animal. Normally animals will be out foraging for food early or late in the day especially if it is hot in the middle of the day.

Before going on to deal with the catching of animals, note that you should avoid some animals or parts of them. You should not eat toads, but you can eat frogs. The internal organs of all animals are best kept for bait, although you can usually eat the heart and liver without ill-effect. The exception is that you should not eat the liver of polar bears or seals, nor should you eat the heads of rats and snakes. Finally, the skin of the snake and hairy caterpillars should not form part of your diet. Beyond these few prohibitions, all creatures which run, fly or slither are good food, but you should try to make sure that the meat is always well-cooked. Some of the meat, while quite suitable as food, may have a flavour which, to put it mildly, is an acquired taste. An example is that the flesh from fish-eating birds such as gulls may have a very 'fishy' taste. However, as the great Arctic explorer, Stefansson, has said '. . . hunger, the best of all sauces, sweetens every sort of food'.

It is convenient to divide the methods of obtaining meat into active and passive. Let me deal with active methods first, although in any survival situation you are likely to try every idea in this book and possibly some ideas of your own; a survival situation wonderfully stimulates the imagination and inventive capability. The active methods are those where you actively seek out and catch your prey, most obviously with a rifle or shotgun. You will be very fortunate, unless you are a soldier, to have such a weapon available, but let us assume that you are lucky. The first thing is to realize the limitations and advantages of the actual weapon. A shotgun, which fires a cloud of tiny pellets over a limited range, is ideal for rabbits, birds and similar-sized animals, but you would be running a grave risk if you fired such a weapon at a bear. Unless you were extremely lucky with your shot you would only antagonize and enrage such a large animal which would then seek out its adversary, and you might well become breakfast for the bear. If you have only a small rifle such as a .22 or a shotgun you would be well advised to stick to small game. If you have the sort of rifle that a soldier might carry in war you can try for larger animals, although you should take care to shoot only if you are sure of a killing. The most vulnerable spot varies between animals, but for a non-hunting enthusiast the most you can expect to remember is that you should aim for the head, neck or just behind the shoulder for the best chance of a kill.

For the novice hunter the best chance of success is to find an obvious location, such as a drinking place or regular track, and to position yourself, hidden as far as possible but with a clear view of your target area. You must note the likely path of the sun since a few hours later you could be trying to shoot into the sun. You must also note the direction of the wind. No animal will approach if your human smell is wafting gently across the water-hole or game trail. Remember that, like the sun, the wind can change direction and you may have to select a new position because of this. Make sure you are com-fortable, you may be there for many hours. Avoid having any non-animal smells about you. The smell of solid-fuel cookers, paraffin, etc., in your hide, and strongly scented soap, deodorant, tobacco and similar odours will make an animal even more uneasy than your natural unwashed, unadulterated smell. Only clear the minimum of vegetation to allow you a good sight and shot at your quarry. Avoid making any unnatural noise; make sure you have no coins clinking in your pocket, make sure the sling buckle on your weapon does not rattle. Remove all twigs from around your feet to avoid them snapping. Make sure your clothing does not rustle and that the pull on a zip does not flap against the metal of the zip. Only such constant attention to detail will give you any chance of a successful shot.

If you are very familiar with the weapon you will know its characteristics, but if you are not you must spend some time before attempting to hunt anything in finding out how to load it, make it safe by unloading or other means and how accurate it is. You may not be able to adjust the sights, or to 'zero it' in military terms, but you should be able to determine, by firing two or three carefully aimed shots, if it is firing high or low, left or right. Then when you take your shot at an animal you can aim off to allow for any of these variations. Do not waste ammunition, especially if you have only a few rounds, but you must spare two or three cartridges for this or you may well waste all your ammunition anyway. A few years ago I was with an exploring party in north-east Greenland and we had with us three rifles because of the polar bear risk. Only two of us were soldiers so having landed we had a short instructional session and let everyone have a shoot, aiming at a piece of wood with a symbol on it. This was set at the height of a bear approaching and assumed that you waited until it was only about 25 metres away before firing.

Even those who had never fired a rifle before were pleasantly surprised with the accuracy of their shots, although they did express some doubt about whether they would wait until the last 25 metres before firing. Even an absolute novice can be quite an adequate shot if required. A good position, a careful aim and a gentle squeeze of the trigger is all that is required.

If you choose or are forced to stalk your animal your chances of success are much reduced. I have known skilled Eskimo hunters spend fifteen or eighteen hours trying for a caribou without success. However, if you do attempt this form of food gathering keep in mind the following points. Look for any signs of the animals' passing and try to estimate how long ago that was. Move slowly and avoid looking over a ridge or other skyline; look round a boulder, or a clump of vegetation instead. Always stalk into wind and use any available cover. Remain stockstill if the animal lifts its head. Make sure your clothing is dull in colour. Apart from obvious water sources, feeding places and tracks, look along the edge of forests, in sheltered re-entrants, near ponds or lakes. Thick woodland, high mountains and dry areas with poor vegetation are not very fruitful sources of game. Some animals are curious and stand and watch an unusual object such as a man pretending to be an animal on all fours. Closer in a noisy kissing of the back of the hand or imitation of the noise an injured bird or animal might make can also attract their attention and curiosity. If you have already caught your first sheep, goat, deer, etc., use the skin to cover yourself as you stalk.

If you do not have a rifle or similar weapon, try a catapult (Figure 47). It will need to be a powerful one, but rubber ropes (like those used in conjunction with car roof racks) will provide some strong elastic. Small round pebbles will make the best ammunition and you must be ready with a stick or other implement to kill the animal

ELASTIC ROPE OR SIMILAR

LEATHER, CANVAS, OR SIMILAR MATERIAL

FIG. 47. A CATAPULT

which may only have been stunned by your catapult shot. Even without a catapult a stick or rock may be sufficient to kill one of the slower moving animals such as a sheep especially if, by a combined effort with one or two other people, you can corner it against a rockface or force it over a small cliff. I have never heard of anyone using throwing knives to kill an animal or use a bow and arrow, but I see no reason why such methods should not work.

All birds and their eggs are good to eat, but they have the additional advantage over animals that they can escape in three dimensions (by taking wing) rather than two. Much that applies to hunting animals also applies to birds. If you find their nests the eggs are readily available and many birds especially in remote areas are very tame. At the settlement of Mestersvig in East Greenland I have gently stroked a red-throated diver on its nest without its making any attempt to escape. In the breeding season the young of many species can be easily caught by hand and in the moulting or eclipse season (July–August) many duck are flightless as they grow their new feathers. Birds often nest in colonies and if you are trying to survive near one of these your food problems are at an end even if the diet is a little monotonous! Ptarmigan are usually very tame and can be taken by hand. Some form of net if you have one or can improvise one could help.

Let me now go on to deal with the passive methods of catching your meat. In broad terms these are traps and snares. Indiscriminate setting of these devices will catch little or nothing. You have got to decide the best place for catching your animal or bird; these are generally the same as those for active methods discussed above, but with more emphasis on tracks and regular runs. A simple snare is shown in Figure 48 and consists of a loop of thin wire formed with a slip knot which tightens when the animal runs into it. If wire is not available cord, etc., can be used but the vital feature is that the loop must be held open to allow the animal to get into the snare. For small game such as rabbits the diameter of the loop should be about four to five inches with the bottom only an inch or two off the ground. This type of snare will hold rather than kill the animal or bird.

A refinement of this type of snare is the trigger snare which has the same loop, but the end cord is attached to a branch or twig held in a simple trigger device which is activated by the struggles of the animal, thus lifting it into the air. The device is shown in Figure 49. The trigger can be a stick thrust into the ground, but loose enough to come out when the animal is caught, or it can be a notched stick which is displaced by the movement. A deadfall can be used to kill both animals and birds. This can be either self-actuating or operated by a hidden man operating a cord. Figure 50 shows the first type and Figure 51 the second. In both cases some form of bait will attract your quarry. Remember that bait is not always of animal origin (internal organs, etc.); for many animals and birds it must be seeds, grain, etc.

I have seen a spring snare (Figure 52) work very effectively to catch small birds in the foothills of the Himalayas. There the materials used are split bamboo canes, but other springy twigs or branches can be used. It is important to conceal the device with grass or other vegetation, and to position it on a likely animal or bird track. Haphazard positioning of traps and snares will achieve little; you must study the animals you

FIG. 48. A SIMPLE SNARE

FIG. 49. A TRIGGER SNARE

STICK TO
AID BALANCE

STONE OR SMOOTH SURFACE
SUNK TO GROUND LEVEL

BAIT

FIG. 50. SIMPLE DEADFALL

BAIT

CORD

FIG. 51. DEADFALL – CORD OPERATED

FIG. 52. SPRING SNARE

are likely to catch and plan accordingly. As an example, squirrels are tree-living animals and spend very little time on the ground, but if they are plentiful in the area it is worth setting snares on tree branches to catch them. In addition to man-made substances such as rubber elastic, many natural saplings and twigs have a natural elasticity which makes them ideal for spring-type snares. A rather sophisticated one is shown in Figure 53. Unless you have practised making this type before, you will probably need a set of working drawings to use it! Either practise beforehand or carry this book if you ever are likely to need the diagram. Remember that simple ideas are usually the best, but if a party are forced to survive over a long period of time the design and construction of more sophisticated snares, shelters, cooking methods and the like all have a very therapeutic value in maintaining morale.

A deadfall trap is a hole dug on an animal trail or similar place, lightly covered with vegetation to camouflage it. An example is shown in Figure 54. Dimensions will vary according to the animal you expect to catch – and the effort you put into digging the deadfall trap. This is the sort of trap normally used for larger animals and if they are wanted alive. In the past, lions and similar animals have been caught in this way for zoos. The principle can work for smaller animals provided that you remember that most of them are quite good climbers so the sides of the hole must be at least vertical if not overhanging. Remember also that vegetation soon dies off and will require renewal at least once a day.

Gulls can be caught with a gorge hook (Figure 55) which is laid on the beach or wherever gulls congregate, or it can be floated on a piece of wood on the sea. The needle can be made of wood, bone or similar material and must be well disguised with bait; a nice juicy morsel of fish would probably be best. The size of the needle should not

FIG. 53. ANOTHER SPRING SNARE

FIG. 54. DEADFALL TRAP

NEEDLE

BAIT

FIG. 55. GORGE HOOK

exceed one inch and the line should be as inconspicuous as possible. Nylon fishing line would be ideal.

FOOD FROM WATER

The sea, rivers, lakes and almost any other area of water will provide food. In the temperate zones of the world the flesh part of fish is good to eat. You should avoid fish with an unpleasant smell, those with flabby skin, slimy gills and sunken eyes. With all fish apply the thumb test by pressing the flesh with your thumb. If the impression remains do not eat that fish (but remember that it could be used for bait). Avoid all jellyfish, those fish with a bony skin instead of scales and those with spikes. Many of the molluscs are good to eat and these include limpets, mussels, cockles, clams, sea-urchins, starfish and many others. Do not eat dead ones; a simple test is that any that are rock huggers will move slightly when touched and cling more tightly to the rock. Crabs, lobsters and crayfish are a delicacy at all times and would be very welcome to any survivor.

Fishing for survival is very different from fishing for sport. There are no conventions about only fishing for trout with a fly or only taking fish over a certain size. You should have a number of fish-catching devices in use all the time, preferably while you are away doing something else. Fishing with hook and line is traditional and you may have someone in your party who is a fisherman anyway. Just as with trying to catch animals it is vital to chose the right place to fish. Indiscriminate fishing will produce little. Normally early morning and late evening are considered the best times, but if you can leave your lines out for 24 hours at a time do so. Pools and the calmer reaches of a river should produce fish especially if there is shade from over-hanging vegetation and there are eddies caused by submerged rocks or logs. Like humans, fish seek cool waters in

hot weather and shallower easily warmed water in cold conditions.

It is unlikely that you will have proper hooks and line, but these can be improvised (Figure 56) from pieces of hard-wood such as hawthorn or blackthorn. Lengths of wire, a sliver from a food tin, unravelling a few yards of wool from a jersey or separating out threads from a piece of nylon cord or rope. A hook and line are almost the easiest of things to improvise. Almost always you will have something suitable for the job. For bait you want as far as possible, to simulate what the fish might eat naturally in the waters you are working in. Remember the trout fisherman ties flies to approxi-mate to the flies that are found on or just above the surface of the water. However it is much more likely that you will have to make do with a fragment of meat from a sandwich or a scrap of sardine from a tin you happened to have in your rucksack. Fish will also be attracted to shiny or brightly-coloured objects, and a tiny piece of silver paper from a cigarette packet or a coloured thread from a garment may do the trick. Do also remember that a worm, grub or beetle may also appear very attractive to the fish you are after. You will need to improvise a float from a piece of wood or cork because you cannot allow your-self the luxury of casting your 'fly' in the best traditions of a good salmon river. You want to set up several lines and leave them to work for you.

Having got your initial fishing set-up going you might move on to more 'com-mercial' methods. One of these is to build a fish trap (Figure 57). Although the one shown in the diagram has a wide mouth, I have seen traps on the fast flowing rivers in the Himalayas with much narrower mouths and these caught fish just as well. Alternatively you can narrow a stream with boulders, etc., so that the fish are forced into a narrow channel. You can then either stretch an improvised net across the gap or attempt to spear the fish or stun them with boulders as they swim past. A

HOOK MADE FROM SAFETY PIN

SIMPLE WOODEN HOOK

HOOK MADE FROM SARDINE CAN KEY

FEATHERS AS AN ATTRACTIVE LURE

BASIC LEDGER RIG

WOODEN 'STOP'

SIMPLE SPINNER

RIVER FLOW

PEBBLE SINKER

FIG. 56. IMPROVISED FISH-HOOKS

CURRENT

FIG. 57. A FISH TRAP

FIG. 58. ANOTHER FORM OF FISH TRAP

FIG. 59. BAITED LINES SUSPENDED IN A RIVER

possible design of net is shown in Figure 58, but you may have to improvise. The mesh should be about one inch unless you know you are dealing with much bigger fish. If you have access to both sides of a river, suspend a rope or cord across the river and attach a number of baited lines (Figure 59) at intervals along the rope.

Do not forget to search tidal pools on the shore or the backwaters of streams.

These often contain small fish which half bury themselves in the sand and can be gathered by hand or some easily improvised hand net.

FOOD PREPARATION

Having acquired your food by fair means or foul, you then have to prepare it and cook it. If you have any fuel available it should be used to cook your food. Cooked food is always safer in a survival situation since any unpleasant parasites should be rendered harmless in the process. The preparation of fruit, plants and vegetables will normally follow the same process as dealing with them in a civilized kitchen. Anything will cook more easily and quickly if it is chopped small rather than being left in large pieces. A modern cook will discard the less attractive outer leaves of a cabbage or the core of an apple. You cannot be so fastidious and you should cook virtually every part of the food, only discarding the really inedible parts which remain after cooking.

The preparation of meat for the pot requires more effort. If the animal is still alive you must kill it. Small animals and birds should be grasped firmly by the head and body. A strong pull with a sharp twist should break the neck quickly and cleanly causing no pain to the animal. Snakes, frogs and similar animals should be hit on the head with a stone or stick. You may be squeamish but by one means or another you must kill your food if you want to eat. An alternative method, and the only one for large animals, is to hold the animal down, pull the head back to expose the throat and cut the jugular vein which lies on each side of the neck. Cutting on the front of the neck merely cuts into the windpipe and will prolong the agony for both the animal and you. Animals should be skinned and gutted as soon as possible. Hang the larger ones up in order that the blood can drain out of the jugular vein. Birds should also be hung up in the same manner. Catch the blood and use it later to add to stews, etc.

To skin the animal place it on its back and cut through the skin on the belly from the anus to the bottom of the breastbone. There is no particular objection if you chose to insert the knife at the base of the breastbone and cut towards the rear of the animal; the

FIG. 60. SKINNING A SMALL ANIMAL

important thing is that you do not stab at the animal. If you do the blade will go deep and rupture the bowel, bladder or various glands which may spoil the meat. You should concentrate on gently using the blade of the knife as if you were a surgeon operating. Having made the full incision, open it as wide as possible, reach in and sever the intestines as high up towards the head as possible. For small animals such as rabbits this can be done with the fingers; for a deer a knife will be required. Remove all the entrails carefully, keeping the kidneys, heart and liver to eat, but remembering that the remainder still have a use as bait. Wipe out the stomach cavity with a damp cloth. Now sever the legs at the first joint if you have a knife or can break them. With larger animals you may not have a heavy enough implement for the job so the answer is to cut through the skin at the joint right round the leg and then cut through the skin along the thigh to join your original cut.

Assuming you have removed the legs at the joint, ease the upper limbs out of the skin and then pull it back inside out towards the head repeating the process with the front legs. If you chose not to use the head for food, keep it for bait. With a large animal you will not be able to pull the whole hide inside out so you must carefully pare the skin away from the flesh. As far as possible you should keep the hide in one large piece rather than hack off small segments. A full skin can be additional insulation between you and the ground. It is often easier to sever the tail at its base before removing the skin. Figure 60 shows the sequence for skinning a small animal.

Having skinned your animal, the next thing is to joint it. The bone joints give you the best guide as to where this should be done, but you may have to resort to some odd shapes in order to fit your cooking-pot.

Snakes, frogs, lizards, birds and all other animals should be skinned and the internal organs discarded or used for bait. If there is any suspicion that the snake is a poisonous type, remove the head and a small margin of the body to avoid the poison sacs. Birds should be plucked preferably while they are still warm as this eases the task, but skinning is usually best in a survival situation. Remove the head and the legs at the first joint. When taking the head off take the neck as well by making the cut close to the body. Follow this with an incision down the back. Ease off the skin as if it were a small mammal. Having done this you should be able carefully to remove all the intestines. As when skinning animals, you must avoid rupturing the gall bladder, bowel, etc.

Fish are easy to gut. Remove the tail and the head at the gills. Lay the fish on its side on a flat surface and with as sharp a knife as possible cut on the underside of the fish from the tail end to the head. Remove the internal organs and wash the whole fish, preferably in running water. A professional fishmonger with his array of knives will fillet a fish with ease, but in a survival situation it is probably best not to attempt this, but to cook the fish whole or at least in large cutlets, then removing the meat from the bone when cooked.

COOKING METHODS

You may be fortunate in your survival situation and have some form of cooking-stove. This may run on paraffin, petrol, meths, camping gas or solid fuel. This is the ideal, but there are two limitations. First, you must know how to use the stove safely. Correctly operated, all stoves are safe but they all depend on using a very flammable fuel which will cause bad burns if misused. Any survival situation produces problems; do not compound them by having a badly burned person in your party as well. Secondly, you will almost certainly have a finite amount of fuel. In an extreme case you might be with an aircraft which has crash-landed successfully with a tankful of aviation turbine fuel intact. This could be thousands of litres and would keep the average primus type paraffin stove going for months even if you burned it 24 hours a day. Whatever fuel you have, conserve it to the utmost.

Recently on an expedition to Greenland I cooked for ten days with one litre of meths. I had reasonable meals and did not stint myself on brews of coffee, but I never let the stove burn for an instant without something on it even if it was just a tiny drop of water for washing up. You must never 'waste' fuel for space heating. Your bodily warmth must come from clothing, sleeping-bag or other insulation. Eventually your fuel will run out and you are then back to natural materials.

Before dealing with types of fires and improvised cooking methods a word or two on means of ignition might help. All the fuel in the world is just so much useless rubbish if you cannot set light to it. Matches and cigarette lighters are the most obvious forms of ignition but should be used in conjunction with a candle if you have one. They could well be the means of saving your life, and you cannot take too much care of them. Always carry matches in an inner pocket, wrapped and sealed in a polythene bag and where the warmth of your body can help to keep them dry. Never be content to carry just one box or book of matches; their weight is negligible so always have one or more spares in your clothing or kit. It is well worth carrying some in a waterproof container and you might consider having an emergency reserve either of ordinary matches which you have previously waterproofed by covering in candle wax, or of what are known as lifeboat matches. These will burn fiercely in almost any conditions of rain, wind, etc. A cigarette lighter is another way of causing fire and this should be carefully nurtured in some warm dry place about your person rather than left to get at least damp if

not wringing wet in an unprotected outside pocket.

Non-smokers should remember to carry matches or a lighter in case they are ever in a survival situation. It is perhaps the only advantage in being a smoker that you will automatically have a means of fire with you. Treat every match and every flick on the lighter as if it were your last one. You may have to ration matches just as you ration food and it should be a firm rule that you never, no matter how bad the situation, light a match until the fuel and everything else is ready and you have taken every precaution against wind, rain and any other natural hazards. Only then do you light your stub of candle and use that to light your fire or stove. Once that is alight, extinguish your candle and keep it for next time.

If you have not got matches or a lighter what can you do? Provided the sun is shining, a lens removed from a pair of binoculars or a camera will do the trick. Focus the rays of the sun through the lens to a pinpoint on the tinder and it should soon start to smoulder and eventually burst into flames. On the commercial market are a number of gadgets which will produce a spark. Most of them depend on the phenomenon that striking steel against flint or similar substance will produce a spark. If you are devising your own survival kit you might choose to include one of these things instead of or in addition to matches. They have the advantage that they will usually produce more sparks than a single box of matches, but your tinder (which is

FIG. 61. FLINT, STEEL AND MAGNESIUM FIREMAKING

sometimes also provided by means of a magnesium block) must be even better at igniting than tinder used with matches (see Figure 61). If you have a powerful battery from a car or aeroplane, this will produce excellent sparks by shorting across the terminals. Flints sometimes occur naturally especially in parts of the country where the basic rock is chalk. They will be single, hard and usually misshapen rocks embedded in the chalk. Dig one out, split it open and you will have a readymade flint.

Some native tribes can make fire by rubbing two sticks or other pieces of wood together. These tribes are almost exclusively found in places where tinder-dry wood is readily available. In temperate zones this is very unlikely and even the aforementioned tribes, having kindled their fire, will often carry it with them when they move on rather than go to the trouble of relighting it. You are more likely to have success with a firebow (see Figure 62). The stick should be a hardwood (from a deciduous tree) with a sharpened point at one end. The board is softwood (from

a coniferous tree) with a depression cut out of it to take the pointed end of the stick. Make the bow from a flexible branch and use string, shoelace, or something similar for the string of the bow. Nylon cord is not very good for this because it does not grip the stick well enough to turn it. Press down on the top of the stick with a flat rock or similar pad and move the bow backwards and forwards to rotate the stick rapidly. Some of your tinder should be in the depression. This is the theory and I know people who have succeeded, but I must confess that I have not done so myself. It certainly needs a lot of effort!

Having got your means of ignition you need tinder. The vital requirement is that it be bone dry. We use the term 'tinder-dry' in everyday speech to indicate something which is extremely dry. Leaves, the bark from birches and hawthorns, wool from sheep or your jersey, virtually any bits of fluff, feather or down, scraps of lint, cotton wool, materials, tiny wood shavings taken from the inner wood of a tree branch of a pine, grass and other similar-sized

USING THE BOW

BEARING BLOCK

DRILL

CORD OR THONG

BOW

BASE BOARD

GROOVE CUT

FIG. 62. A FIREBOW

pieces of vegetation are all possible sources for tinder. If you are fortunate enough to have some petrol, meths or similar fuel, a few drops – and no more – will make lighting the tinder much easier. Quite apart from the danger of a sudden flareup if you use too much petrol, remember you conserve everything and anything when you are a survivor and even something as insignificant as a little bit of fuel could be the difference between life and death.

Before lighting your tinder, however, make sure you have twice as much heavier fuel ready as you think you will need. There is nothing worse than getting a fire going nicely and then seeing it die because you have not gathered sufficient fuel to keep it going. If you can, choose the type of wood for the fire you need. For getting a fire going use birch or almost any coniferous tree. Once the fire is going and if you want a good cooking-fire (or warming-fire) to last a long time, change to oak, ash or beech. Poor woods for any sort of fire are elm, chestnut, willow and poplar. If you can pick and choose you will be very lucky indeed. It is much more likely that you will be burning heather roots, ground willow and other not very satisfactory fuels. Remember that dried dung, peat and animal fat can also be used as fuel.

Having gathered your fuel you are at last ready to start your fire. Choose a

CUT
HERE

FIG. 63. A FUZZ-STICK

sheltered spot on dry ground. An overhanging rock could shelter you and your fire from rain and snow. If there is snow on the ground build a platform of green logs and build your fire on that. It can be useful to have a fuzz-stick (see Figure 63) as the centre post of your fire to help start it. Put your other tinder round it and then some slightly thicker twigs (no thicker than a quarter of an inch) in a pyramid shape. Leave a small opening for your match to be applied. Figure 64 shows what it should look like. Shelter the fire from the wind with your body and cup the matchbox in your hands. Light the match carefully and get it well alight before applying it

TINDER!

KINDLING

FIG. 64. HOW TO START A FIRE

LAZY MAN'S FIRE

RADIATOR FIRE

FIRE FOR WINDY CONDITIONS

WIND

ALTAR FIRE (SAVES BENDING)

PIT FIRE (NEEDS NO ATTENTION WHEN ALIGHT)

STONE FIRE

STONES OR BRICKS

AIR SPACES

WIND

TRENCH FIRE

LAYING A TRENCH FIRE

SEMI-OVEN FIRE

STAGE 1

STAGE 2

OPEN FIRE

GREEN TIMBER

AMERICAN TRAPPER'S FIRE

FIG. 65. A SELECTION OF DIFFERENT TYPES OF FIRE

to the fire. Add fuel gently so that you do not stifle the fire. In the early stages you want dry wood so you may have to split the timber open to get at the centre wood. Gradually build up the fire until it is the size you want. This will normally be the smallest possible for cooking your food. Large fires are no better for cooking and are difficult to get near, but more importantly you will waste energy gathering timber to keep such a fire going and a survivor must conserve everything – not least his own energy. If you want a fire to sit round or to dry clothing, still make it a small one but sit close to it. Camping books usually show a number of neatly drawn diagrams of different types of fires. Figure 65 gives some examples, but do not try to follow these slavishly, your facilities or surroundings may not be right. Remember that a good bed of ashes is best for cooking rather than a mass of flames which the cook cannot get near.

It may seem odd to talk about improvising an oven in a survival situation but it can be useful and the devising of it can interest several people for some time – a good fillip to morale in difficult circumstances. A five-gallon oildrum or similar container is the sort of thing you need. Figure 66 gives an idea of the possibilities. The 'fire' could be a cooking-stove or a wood fire. Ideally it should be dug into an earth bank but this is not vital. There must be a through draught to keep the fire going and you need some form of sheet as the door. Some years ago on an expedition to the Canadian Arctic one of the party found an old oildrum in the middle of the tundra and improvised an oven. We had some breadmix with us and he produced some very acceptable loaves.

We have dealt so far with what is basically a camp-fire even though it can be made in many different forms and with all sorts of variations; but what other methods of cooking are there? If you have an easily ignited fuel such as petrol you can make what was known during the Second World War as a

FIG. 66. IMPROVISED OVEN (SECTIONAL VIEW)

FIG. 67. A BENGHAZI BURNER

Benghazi Burner. Put an inch or two of sand or similar soil in the bottom of a tin. Punch, bore or cut holes just above the sand to provide a source of oxygen for the fire. At the top of the tin (see Figure 67) cut some slots to allow the smoke to escape. Depending on what is available and the amount of fuel this could be done with a very small food tin or a large Army biscuit tin. A variation of this uses a candle instead of petrol and sand. Obviously this can only be done with a very small food tin, but because the heat is contained within the tin very little is lost to the surrounding atmosphere and a flame as small as a candle will heat water for tea, soup or coffee. If you have the ingredients you

FIG. 68. IMPROVISED STOVE FOR OIL, FAT, ETC.

FIG. 69. ANOTHER TYPE OF IMPROVISED STOVE

can even make tiny drop scones on a small piece of metal placed across the top. A similar principle of heat conservation is used by the makers of the Trangia type of cookset.

For centuries the Eskimos have used seal blubber as a source of heat and light, but for this and when using any of the less combustible oils you need a wick, so if you have engine oil, animal fat or even some insect repellant make yourself a stove or 'koodlik' as it is called by the Eskimos. For a wick you can use string, a strip of rag, nylon cord or even dried moss. Figure 68 shows a stove using an upright tin and Figure 69 a shallow tobacco-type tin. Do be careful when lighting the more volatile fuels, and if you want to make a petrol stove last longer add a little oil or similar less explosive fuel.

These designs for improvised stoves are also useful if you are very restricted for fuel – perhaps nothing more than a few heather roots. Substitute these for the candle and keep the tiny fire going carefully and you will again be able to heat water for a hot drink even if you cannot cook a meal.

Cooking is an art. One person will, from a few odds and ends, produce a meal fit for a king. With the same odds and ends someone else will produce an almost inedible mess, except for the fact that for survival nothing is inedible – all must be eaten. As far as possible maintain your standards and try to produce meals as close as you can to those you might eat in civilized circumstances. Beware the man who wants to throw everything into one pot. You may only have one pot but try to do better than that. Such a meal will always be a tasteless mess. The best way of cooking food in a survival situation is by boiling. Almost all food can be boiled and it loses little of its food value in the process provided that you keep the cooking water and consume that as well in the form of soup or mixed with other foods. For the pedantically minded cook the term boiling should be taken to include stewing. It is the safest form of cooking to ensure that parasites in meat are killed, vegetables are softened and allows even the most unlikely food such as lichens to be added. You may be lucky enough to find some wild

FIG. 70. SPIT ROASTING

herbs to add to your stew and make it more appetising. Your boiling-container may have to be improvised so do not be too rigid in thinking solely of the saucepans you would find in a proper kitchen. You can boil water in a paper-bag with care. the air-sickness bags provided in aircraft are very good for this.

If you have no means of boiling you will have to resort to roasting. Almost any small animal or fish can be cooked (see Figure 70) on a spit over a good bed of embers. For a quicker meal cut the meat and vegetables up and skewer the

FIG. 71. GRIDDLES

FIG. 72. COOKING ON A STRING

pieces on a suitable piece of metal or a peeled green stick. The result is kebabs – a very popular barbecue dish. Avoid sticks from yew, laurel and pine which will taint the food. Griddles improvised from thin saplings or branches (see Figure 71) can also be used to roast meat. If you have the ingredients to make any form of bread, roll out the dough into a long 'sausage' and wrap it round a green stick (see Figure 46) to bake in the heat of the fire. This is known as a twist. Dough can be shaped into a round disc and baked on any flat surface over the fire. You could suspend a succulent bird's leg from a string (Figure 72). Before cooking any meat by roasting thrust it into a flame for a few seconds to seal the outside surface.

If you are going to bake your food in the embers of your fire, only gut your animal, bird or fish; leave the skin, scales or feathers on. Wrap the whole thing in clay, mud or large, wet leaves and scrape away the embers of a fire which has been going for some time so that the ground underneath is well heated. Place your food pack in the embers and rake them over it. A rabbit-sized animal will take at least an hour. This is a traditional gypsy method of cooking hedgehogs. When the meal is cooked break open the clay and you will find that most of the fur, feathers, etc. (or spines in the case of a hedge-hog!), will come away with the clay, leaving the meat or fish ready to eat. If you wish you can use the same method (with leaves only) for a piece of meat and include some vegetables with it. Aluminium foil, which is often used in aircraft for various technical parts, can be used instead of the leaves. The gourmet touches can be provided by including some herbs with the food. Instead of just scraping away the embers of your fire you can dig an oven hole (Figure 73). Heat some stones in your fire and then place them in the bottom of the hole. Some types of stones have a tendency to split when heated, and these should be discarded. Let the stones start to warm the hole and then put in some embers, followed by your food and some more embers. Add some new fuel to the top layer of embers and keep it going like any other fire. You can cook something else on this top fire. Cooking times will vary according to the size of your meat, fish, etc., but 40 minutes would be a good start. Trial and error will show how to adjust this time. If you want to cook something slowly, perhaps while you

FIG. 73. AN OVEN HOLE

are away from your survival camp, omit building the fire on top and just put some turf over the hole. Smaller items of food such as eggs, shellfish or snails can be cooked in this sort of pit. Wrap them in leaves, grass or cloth, cover with half an inch of sand or soil and build a fire on top.

Frying food should be your last resort, but if you have a plain sheet of tin which you cannot fashion into a better cooking-pot, then by all means fry your food. A hot flat stone can also be used for frying but you must maintain its heat. All food is best cooked as soon as possible after you have obtained it. If you have a ready source of food only gather what you need as you require it. However, this is very much an ideal and most of the time you will be only too glad to get any food that is available when it is available. Previously prepared rations are dealt with on page 120.

I started this chapter by saying that food was not your most pressing problem in a survival situation and that you could live for several weeks without it. While this is quite true, nevertheless, within a few days the lack of food will begin to take its toll of your physical and mental capabilities, and this in turn will reduce your chances of ultimate survival. For this reason you should make every effort to find, prepare and consume food of all sorts. The morale of a party will sink to a very low level if they do not eat. Determination will dwindle and apathy will ensue. This is the road to failure and death. Find food and eat it!

8. A HEALTHY MIND IN A HEALTHY BODY: Survival medicine

You stand a better chance of survival if you are mentally and physically fit. This is one good reason why in everyday life you should keep yourself in this desirable state, because a survival situation is hardly the time to start a regime to improve your fitness. However, even the fittest person can be injured or be taken ill. The very action of your being precipitated suddenly into a survival state may have caused injury to you or one of your companions, but even if this is not the case initially, something may happen before you are rescued and you will be faced with a medical problem of some sort. Just as with every other aspect of survival, training and practice before the event is of great value, so it is with the medical aspect, but here there is a much greater chance of your training and skills being used. Only a small proportion of the population will, within their lifetime, be likely to find themselves fighting for survival. For those who work or take their leisure in the outdoors the proportion will, of course, be higher. Few, if any, of us will go through life, however, without needing some knowledge of first aid or minor medicine. We will arrive on the scene of a road accident, our child will be badly cut by broken glass on the beach, a husband will electrocute himself doing a household repair or a wife will burn herself badly on the kitchen stove. One or more of these incidents will come our way during our 70 or so years on this earth.

In the Survival – Immediate Actions (see Appendix 1) I have given a mnemonic – C-H-A-S-T-E – as a help to you when suddenly presented with an accident. Even if you have done a course of training with one of the national first aid organizations, when you approach your first accident all that you have learned will seem to disappear from your brain just when you need it. Remember CHASTE and what it means and you will do things in the right order. Let me deal with each part in turn.

C – CHOKING, CARDIAC

With any casualty the vital thing is to get him breathing again if he has stopped. Clear his mouth and throat of any obstruction and then begin one of the methods given in first-aid manuals. The generally recommended method is popularly called the 'kiss of life'. Get the casualty into the position shown in Figure 74 as quickly as possible, give four quick full breaths with your mouth sealed over the casualty's and with his nose pinched shut between your fingers and thumb. When you have done this settle down to a breathing rate of about twelve to fifteen cycles per minute, i.e., you breathe into his mouth then take your mouth away to allow him to exhale. As well as not breathing the casualty's heart may have stopped. Check this by feeling his pulse at the wrist with your fingers. If you cannot detect it you should endeavour to get his heart going again. Figure 75 gives you the method of doing this. Remember that the heartbeat is much faster than the lung rate so your pressure applied at the base of the breastbone should be about 70 per minute. Do not muddle this with the twelve to fifteen breaths per minute to get the breathing going! This is just a brief summary of the methods in common use (and there are other methods you can use if, for instance, your casualty has a badly damaged face or mouth), but you cannot learn to do these procedures correctly from a book. Take a proper

HEAD HELD
TILTED WELL BACK
TO ENSURE
CLEAR AIRWAY

FIG. 74. KISS OF LIFE POSITION

FIG. 75. CARDIAC RESUSCITATION

course or at least get someone who is already trained to show you what to do. Remember that if the pulse has stopped and the lungs are not functioning irreversible damage will soon occur to the brain and other parts of the body so you must have a go. Even if you are not sure of every detail, you will seldom have time to wait for more skilled help to arrive. You may get it wrong, but you are much more likely to get it right and save a life.

H – HAEMORRHAGE

The next most likely cause of early death is heavy bleeding. Having got your casualty breathing and his heart going you must do a rapid body check to see if he is bleeding badly; not a badly grazed hand or even a deeply cut finger, but major bleeding, probably from an artery or vein where the blood is literally pouring out, and already soaking into the clothing. The first treatment is to apply pressure to the wound with a pad of some sort. Check quickly that there is no piece of jagged glass in the wound, but do not worry about getting out all the tiny bits of dirt that may be there, nor should you worry about having a clean, sterile dressing to apply. This is nice if you have it, but it is better for the casualty to be alive even with a few extra bugs floating round his system (which modern antibiotics will deal with) than dead while waiting for a clean dressing to arrive. If you have no cloth pad of any sort your fingers will provide a very good means of closing a wound, and blood, even lots of it, is just a red, slightly sticky liquid which can do you no harm whatsoever. If the blood begins to soak through the first pad apply another, tying it firmly over the first. If possible, and other injuries allow, elevate the wound above the level of the heart. With bad bleeding you may also apply pressure at one of the pressure-points situated in various parts of the body. Tourniquets should only be applied by trained medical staff

except in the case of total severence of a part of a leg or an arm.

A – ASSISTANCE

Having dealt with the real killers of Choking, Cardiac Arrest and Haemorrhage, you can now take a very short breather and consider getting some Assistance. At a normal road accident this would mean sending someone to find the nearest telephone and to call an ambulance. In a mountain accident a mile or two from a road, you would send off two of your party to contact the police. The assistance would, in due course, arrive and this sort of thing is now a routine affair in most civilized countries. However, if you are miles from anywhere, or in an area with no sophisticated facilities, you have got to do a lot more for yourself. Your Assistance must come from those with you and you must appoint someone to look after the casualties while you get on with the bigger problem of the survival of the whole party rather than just those who are injured.

S – SHOCK

Shock will occur with every injury no matter how small, even if there has been no physical injury but only an emotional one such as being involved in a car crash. The shock from a cut finger is so slight that we normally take no notice of it and carry on with whatever we are doing, but the shock from a major injury, if left untreated, can be a contributory cause of death. The treatment is simple. Warmth, comfort and reassurance are required, and a hot drink provided that the casualty has no internal injuries. After something as traumatic as an air crash everyone including yourself will have some degree of shock and you should remember this. The will to carry out lifesaving procedures must be summoned up, but thereafter a time of rest and recovery should be allowed for everyone. A quickly organized camp and then time set aside for sleep will deal with shock.

T – TREATMENT

Having made your casualties warm and comfortable you can now deal with their other injuries. Speed is no longer the priority so you can attend to them with more care and consideration. If the casualty is conscious start at his head and work gently down the body asking him where, if at all, he has any pain. Some injuries such as a bad burn will probably be obvious, but others, such as a simple fracture may not be obvious especially if concealed under clothing. A conscious patient will naturally adopt the least painful position. It is normally best to leave him in this position but to provide support, e.g., with splints for a broken arm, or a sling to support the arm if the collarbone is broken.

If the casualty is unconscious carry out the body check and take any precautions you think fit to avoid an injury being made worse. An open fracture where the broken end of the bone has pierced the skin should obviously have a dressing placed over the wound. Any burn should be covered with a dressing to exclude the air and thus reduce the pain. No attempt should be made to give food or drink to an unconscious patient nor do they need pain-killers of any sort; their natural body mechanism has done the job for you. Most casualties respond best when the minimum of treatment is given, and warmth and comfort are still the best medicines for most conditions.

E – EMERGENCY

The last letter of the mnemonic – CHASTE – is also the easiest. All that you have done so far is the action you must take in an accident crisis. It has been an Emergency and you should have treated it as such. There should have been no question of decision by committee; the natural leader should have taken charge and given orders, albeit in a firm but friendly manner. Your actions should have been brisk but calm, you should have been a defusing influence on the situation. Everyone else should have been able to breathe a silent sigh of relief and be glad that X had taken clear charge of the situation. In an Emergency those who make most noise are usually least hurt. The hysterical should be firmly taken out of earshot for the benefit of all. Think of the calm and efficient way that a trained nurse goes about his or her duties and you should emulate this.

Remember 'CHASTE' and you will not go far wrong when faced with a medical emergency be it in a survival situation or otherwise.

OTHER MEDICAL PROBLEMS

So far I have covered the emergency situation but it is likely that, during your survival state and before you return to civilization, you or one of your party will become ill in some way. Shortage of food, lack of proper sleep, cold, damp, etc., will all, because they debilitate the body as a whole, contribute towards possible sickness. For this reason it is important that you take more than the usual care of yourself. A general lassitude will affect most people after a few days and this can lead to inattention when using a knife or other sharp object with obvious results. If your feet are constantly wet and you make no attempt to dry them out you may well succumb to a disease known as 'trench foot'. This odd name originated during the First World War when this was a very common complaint among soldiers who spent long periods standing in trenches, very often deep in mud and water. Some men were crippled for life as a result. Survival is not a time to promote your macho image, but un-

FIG. 76. THE RECOVERY POSITION

ashamedly to give yourself and those with you a lot of tender, loving care of the human frame.

What you can do will vary a lot. At best you will have in your party a doctor or trained medic. Diagnosis of any medical problem should then be fairly easy. What that doctor or medic can do will depend on the resources available and this could range from a very full expedition medical pack complete with a wide range of drugs to nothing more than a dirty handkerchief. As in all survival matters you must do the maximum with the minimum and improvise to the utmost. To give adequate coverage to the treatment of the medical problems likely to be encountered in survival would require most of this volume, but in case you have failed to learn a reasonable amount of first aid and allied medical information the following very brief notes may assist you. The ailments are in no order of priority.

Open Wounds. Remove any obvious foreign bodies and cover with as clean a dressing as possible. If the bleeding is profuse apply the dressing with some pressure. Elevate the limb if applicable.

Cessation of Breathing or Heartbeat. (See page 93).

Unconscious Patient. Provided that the patient is breathing normally and there is a satisfactory pulse, place him in the recovery position (Figure 76) but keep him under close observation by frequent checks. Heart or lungs can cease to function even some time after the initial accident. Treat for shock (see page 95).

Pain. This will occur with varying degrees with most injuries. Time will reduce or eliminate it, but if it is severe the patient should be given suitable pain-killers. Remember that morphine should not be administered if the patient has head injuries or difficulty in breathing.

Eye Injury. Wash with plenty of water. Gently try to remove any foreign bodies but do not persist after the first few attempts.

Fractures and Dislocations. Treat any open wound. Move the patient as little as possible and gently position the limb (if broken) in the most comfortable position for the patient. With broken ribs, collarbone, etc., patient comfort should be the guide as to where and how to apply supporting slings or bandages. Splints can be improvised from branches, rolled up papers, part of a rucksack frame, but if the patient is not comfortable do not persist with a method just because you have read it in a first-aid book.

Sprains. These could actually be dislocations or fractures masked by swelling so be careful. Normally all that a sprain requires is a bandage (preferably of a crepe-type) and rest.

Burns. Do not try to pull charred clothing away from the burn. Cover it with a clean dressing with plenty of padding. Do not try to renew the dressing at a later stage by pulling it away from the burn. Reduce the pain if it persists and remember that burns can reduce body fluid, so give plenty to drink.

Infection. This can manifest itself in anything from a septic finger to massive infection producing high temperature, delirium and other nasty symptoms. Administer antibiotics if you have any and remember that most of the modern type depend on being used as a five-day course. Do not stop the course just because the infection seems to be clearing up. With an open infection frequent changes of dressing should help by removing pus. Don't tell a dentist this, but I have on a couple of occasions got rid of an abcess under a tooth by wiggling the tooth and biting hard. This seems to break open the abcess and allows it to drain away. This may not be the recommended treatment but it seems to work without any ill effects afterwards.

Cold Injury. This can be anything from slight frostnip to deep frostbite. It is avoidable. Watch yourself and those around you to notice the first whitish spots on the face or hands. Keep thinking about your toes. Can you feel them? If not unlace your boots and warm them in your hands or clothing. Remember to lace boots loosely and have no tight restrictions at the wrist. Under sophisticated conditions it is possible to treat deep frostbite with warm water, but in a survival situation this will probably not be possible. Body heat is the best, either from the casualty himself or his friends. Greater love hath no woman than that she allow her husband to warm his cold feet on her warm stomach!

Heat Injury. Lay the patient down in the shade. If conscious give plenty of liquids with salt (half a teaspoon to a litre) added. If unconscious cool the patient by fanning and saturating his clothing with water. On recovery keep at rest. Sunburn is avoidable. Keep the body covered if there is any risk.

Constipation. This will normally sort itself out in a few days but beware of enforced constipation when it is too cold or too wet or too uncomfortable to go outside. It can also result from people being embarrassed by primitive or no sanitary arrangements.

Diarrhoea. This is normally a symptom of something else, but some people seem to be affected by a change of diet or even water. No food should be given, only liquids to prevent the body becoming dehydrated. Take suitable medication if available.

Blisters. Although minor in themselves they can be critical if your survival depends on walking. At the first sign of a blister or sore place on the foot apply some sort of padding to the area. Adjust the tightness of lacing since this may also cause blisters. Remember your feet can be your passport to safety so look after them.

Carbon Monoxide Poisoning. This can occur in a confined space when using a stove or lamp. Usually there are no symptoms but sometimes, a headache or nausea may give you some warning. If someone collapses get him into fresh air and apply artificial respiration if necessary. Keep a system of ventilation going in any confined space when you are using a stove.

Bugs, various. In the temperate zones of the world none of the ticks, fleas or lice that you may pick up will do you much harm. We just feel it is not nice to have fleas! Check yourself and your clothing. Do not scratch a bite as this brings a risk of infection.

Hypothermia. Caused by a combination of cold and wet conditions. Symptoms are lethargy, slurred speech, stumbling, shivering, pale skin, brief outburst of anger or sudden energy, varying respiration and pulse. Get the casualty into warm and dry conditions and apply body warmth from someone else. Do not assume that apparent recovery is actual recovery. A period of rest is required, normally of some hours.

FIRST-AID KITS

I have deliberately not suggested a list of contents for a first-aid kit. There is no such thing as a standard kit and you should tailor yours to the occasion. The first-aid kit I keep in my car is geared towards road accidents so it has several large dressings suitable for dealing with wounds which are bleeding profusely. It also contains travel sickness tablets suitable for a car journey. The kit I keep in my climbing rucksack still has the dressings but there is no need for travel sickness tablets. When planning the kit for any activity think carefully about the likely risks involved. This will decide some of the contents. Next consider the size of the party. A party of four going off into the hills for a week do not need the sort of kit required by an expedition going to the Himalayas for three months.

Are there any special factors involved? If you are going to a malarial area you must take Paludrine or an equivalent. Have you got to provide medical facilities for local porters, inhabitants, etc.? Is anyone in the party allergic to any of the drugs you have, e.g., penicillin, and should an alternative be provided? How far will you be from sophisticated medical support? If you will never be more than a couple of days from a hospital you will not require a large stock of prescription-type drugs. These are some of the points to bear in mind when planning your first-aid kit. If you are unable to decide what to take your first-aid training is inadequate, and you should not be going on the expedition.

PREVENTIVE ACTION

The human body is both frail and robust. A relatively minor complaint like influenza will make a person feel very unwell and very much reduce his physical ability. His reaction will be to curl up into a tight ball until he has recovered. That same person, when fit, may cover prodigious distances, perform great feats of strength and endure extremes of heat or cold. In a survival situation you are very dependent on the well-being of that human frame be it

yours or someone else's. In all walks of life prevention is better than cure so what can you do to minimize the risk of your body breaking down when it most needs to be in perfect working order?

You may be thrown into a survival situation at any time, so you must keep yourself physically and mentally fit as a general mode of life. The real enthusiast will consider every aspect of what he eats, drinks, does, etc., and how it might affect his survival. For the average person, however, let it suffice that he (or she) keep himself reasonably fit and attend to any minor injury or sickness as soon as it occurs. There is no virtue in being a martyr to some ailment which, for the sake of a little time and effort, could be cured. Those who work or take their leisure where there is an enhanced risk of survival action need to think further. It is not wise for the hillwalker to go off to the hills in winter within a few days of apparently recovering from a bad cold. A fisherman on a trawler should not be nursing a torn muscle or ligament. The human machine should always be kept running smoothly and sweetly.

For certain activities you would be wise to take special precautions. For a canoeing holiday on the River Wye you probably need do no more than check that your bouyancy aid is in good order and that you have some plasters for blisters. For a major overseas expedition a medical check before you go would be useful; certain innoculations would be vital. Once in the field you and your party may need to ensure that you drink not one drop of water that has not been purified. A bad dose of Kathmandu Quickstep at 13,000 feet is no laughing matter. You may decide that eating local food uncooked is too much of a risk. In camp, the siting of a latrine area (downwind and downhill) is important. If someone does become ill treat him early. If there is a risk of infection, start the course of antibiotics early not late. In remote areas it is never wrong to use a sledgehammer to crack a nut. A casualty can hinder a party to the point of danger. If you are a leader you must be firm about the treatment of those with you, and you need to keep your eyes on everyone to make sure they are not quietly but irrevocably leading you all into a survival situation.

IMPROVISED REMEDIES

In an ideal situation a sophisticated first-aid kit sufficient to treat any ailment will be available to you. In reality this will seldom be the case and you will have to improvise. Remember that modern medicine is just that – very modern. People have been improvising treatments and cures from natural resources for thousands of years. The following is a miscellany of cures (not all of which I claim to have tried!) culled from prisoner-of-war accounts, old woodcraft-type books and other sources. There are tales of the Old Wild West when men amputated limbs with nothing more than a knife and a saw-blade. Only you, in the situation you are in, can decide how far you go with the treatment of a casualty. All I know is that I would rather be alive after some rather unusual treatment than dead waiting for the perfect treatment.

For diarrhoea you can take powdered chalk or charcoal. If you have any bones, burn them and grind them into powder and take it. Strip the bark off a tree (oak is claimed to be best), boil it for at least twelve hours and drink the result. The tannic acid in the brew is the part that cures, so very strong tea can also help and as a by-product it gets fluid, always vital for any diarrhoea case, into the system. If you think you have got worms, two tablespoonfuls of paraffin should cure you.

If you have lice or other 'bugs' you must pick them off yourself, your clothing and other people at least daily.

If you want something sterile for washing wounds, burns, etc., human urine straight from the source is satisfactory. Unpleasant though it may

sound, maggots in a wound do no harm. In fact they do good because they only eat dead tissue and that is a useful thing in the treatment of wounds.

Dressings can be improvised from any sort of absorbant material. Sphagnum moss was collected and dried in large quantities for medical use during the First World War, and gipsy women used to use it as sanitary towels. Slings can be made from any sort of sheeting, cloth, plastic or paper. Splints can be made from anything that provides support, and I have used tree branches, rolled up newspapers, iceaxes and metal tubing.

If you have an abscess or a boil you should use a poultice. Try soft boiled rice wrapped in a cloth applied hot, or a cloth impregnated with soap and with sugar worked into it, also applied hot. If you have no rice try boiled potatoes or oatmeal in a cloth. Finally clay or cow's manure heated and spread over a cloth covering the abscess is claimed to have very good drawing properties.

Stings and bites can be rubbed or covered with a piece of onion or dock leaves. If you need to make someone vomit a good emetic is a lot of salt or dry mustard in lukewarm water.

DEATH

Only a doctor may certify death, but a time may come when, despite your unremitting efforts to apply the 'kiss of life' or other treatments, there is no response. No one sign of possible death should be taken as confirmation of the fact but the following, if mostly present, can be accepted as probably indicating death: no heartbeat or pulse, no misting of a mirror or similar object placed close to the mouth and nose, eyes glazed, pupils dilated and no movement under strong torchlight, body cold and skin remains indented when pressed with the thumb, lips may be blue and the muscles stiff.

If you finally decide that someone is dead you should place the body a little way from the camp. In a temperate climate a body can remain unburied for a few days and this is probably the best course if early rescue is anticipated since if possible the body should be taken back to civilization for proper burial. You may have to protect the body temporarily, by covering it with stones, etc., against interference by animals. In a hot climate burial should take place soon after death, but do remember first to remove the contents of pockets, watches, rings, etc., to return to the next of kin in due course.

If you decide to effect your own rescue by walking out, you must never reduce your own chances of survival by trying to carry a body with you. Bury it and mark the grave clearly so that it can be recovered later.

For the benefit of those remaining, some form of simple service or prayer should be conducted during the burial as a fitting mark of respect. Afterwards the routine of the camp should be quietly re-established as soon as possible to ensure everyone continues their own personal efforts to survive.

9. BOATS AND WATER

The previous chapters of this book have been devoted to survival on land, but since the greater part of the earth is covered by water it would be wrong if it did not deal with the problem of survival in water. Water poses some problems of survival similar to those on land, and some which are very different. The risk of hypothermia in water is as great, if not greater, as on a rain and windswept mountainside. On the other hand, the sources of food at sea are very much less, generally speaking, than those on land. Those readers whose work or leisure involves them only with water must not think that they can ignore the rest of this book. On the contrary, they should read all of it and consider how it applies to their particular environment even in an adapted form. In order to keep this chapter within reasonable limits only inland and coastal waters will be considered; those who venture on Round the World Yacht Races and the like will be presumed to have studied the problems of ocean survival in detail. In keeping with the treatment accorded to the rest of the book, this is not a training manual on 'how to swim' or the specialized life-saving techniques taught by the relevant societies.

Going on any sort of vessel or aircraft (except as a totally unthinking passenger) involves a deliberate act by choice, and it is probably for this reason that most boat owners, private pilots, etc., take care to provide at least the recommended items of survival equipment in the way of radios, marker flares, lifejackets, etc. Many amateur yachtsmen take a very professional pride in their safety gear and the overall standard of their craft. This is in contrast to those on land who go out for a walk, often in high places, without so much

as a map or compass. The mariner anticipates that the weather could change, his boat could founder, and he caters for such an event as best he can. The landsman sees no hazard in going for a walk; and within reason rightly so, but it is never clear when a walk on the local bit of rough ground with the dog begins to be a walk in more rugged terrain requiring additional knowledge and equipment.

Any safety equipment, from a canoe throwline to a highly sophisticated radio, is only valuable if you know how to use it. It is not like an insurance policy where the mere possession of it covers you against certain risks. The ownership of safety gear does not do likewise. You must know how to use it under all conditions; not just in the comfort of the shop where you buy it, but at night, when you have lost your torch, in appalling weather, when you are dog-tired and probably very frightened. You may not want to fire off a succession of expensive flares, but you can read the instructions until you know them by heart and you can sit, with your eyes closed, and feel the flare all over to determine what it would feel like in the dark and how you would activate it. You would not be popular if you practised with your radio on the emergency frequency, but you can have a dry run with the power off or use a frequency which will not affect anyone. The important thing is to know what buttons to press or knobs to turn.

The person who is only an occasional boat user is probably the person most at risk rather than the man who is a highly enthusiastic canoeist or yachtsman. I am thinking of the man on holiday who hires a boat 'for a bit o' sea fishing' or buys a rubber dinghy 'for the family to have some fun'. No matter how infrequently you use it, no boat can be considered complete without the accepted scale of safety gear.

INLAND WATERS

Most of these are very innocent and under the right conditions offer very little risk, but there is no shortage of rapids and weirs on our rivers and canals. The first thing that any reputable school of instruction or responsible friend will teach a novice is what to do if his boat turns over (capsizes). Only a canoe (of the kayak pattern) poses any real problem and even here the technique of forward rolling out of the upturned boat is soon learned. Do not try to right the canoe, but use it as additional buoyancy and, floating with the stream or current, swim towards the bank. It is easier to hold on to the end of a canoe rather than the centre. Recover your paddle if you can, but do not put yourself at any increased risk. Always stay with the canoe, it is a bigger, brighter object than you, and you will be more easily seen by others. You should know by previous reconnaissance whether there are any hazards ahead. If there are, a time will come when you must abandon your canoe and swim for the side. If you capsize a canoe in rapids, hang on to the upstream end endeavouring to steer it clear of rocks.

A sailing dinghy or similar boat can usually be righted by standing on the keel and pulling on the gunwale, but if this is difficult the correct procedure, as with a canoe, is to stay with the boat because it is a much bigger and more colourful marker than a human being, even one clad in a brightly-coloured lifejacket. If you have capsized a rubber dinghy climb on to one side, reach over for the lifeline on the other side and heave, at the same time pushing down with your feet or knees on the near side. If successful this deposits you back in the water so pull yourself round to one end of the rubber boat and climb in over that end. Figure 77 shows this manoeuvre.

If for some reason you become separated from your boat and cannot reach it – relax. Let your lifejacket or buoyancy aid hold you up and swim slowly towards help. If you find anything that will assist buoyancy use it. If you are not even wearing a lifejacket or buoyancy aid – still relax. Try to float on your back, using one arm to wave and attract attention and shout at the same time. Again swim gently, using any current or flow, towards safety. Discard only boots or shoes and an overcoat or similar garment. Keep the rest of your clothing on, it will help to keep you warm. When resting wrap your body up into a ball; again this helps to retain heat. The exception to this is if you decide to use your clothing to make an improvised buoyancy aid. Trousers are the most suitable for this so take them off, knot the ends of the legs, do up the fly and

FIG. 77. RIGHTING A LIFERAFT

FIG. 78. TROUSERS AS AN IMPROVISED FLOAT

holding the waist firmly and wide open reach up above your head and bring them down smartly (Figure 78) onto the surface of the water. Air will be trapped in the legs and if you now draw in the waist tightly you have a good improvised float. A similar but not so efficient float can be made from a shirt. If wearing a skirt do not take it off but float on your back, pull the skirt up to your waist and out of the water, then pull it down with the hem entering the water first to trap air over your thighs. Long full skirts are best for this technique!

COASTAL WATERS

What follows is applicable, in most cases, to aircraft ditching in the sea, as well as to ships of all sizes. A professional crew should have been fully trained and practised in evacuating passengers should the need arise, but a sensible survivalist is never going to rely totally on someone else. In any ship or aircraft make sure you know where the escape hatches are, where the life-jackets are kept and how they are put on. Remember you might not be able to use the nearest escape route so look for an alternative. Read the escape instructions on your cabin wall or in the pocket of the seat in front of you. Remember that other passengers will not have disciplined themselves, as you have, to reacting quietly and calmly in an emergency. Some may panic, others will think only of themselves. At times you may have to apply the principle of minimum force to restrain some people from impeding the crew in the execution of their duties.

When there is no professional crew you become, in effect, part of the crew even if a fairly amateur member. While the skipper is always in charge you should make sure you know where the emergency equipment is and how it is used. Even the captain of a boat is mortal and could be knocked out at the moment of crisis or washed overboard and you might have to take over. In

such vessels no one goes along 'just for the ride'. They must be able to take a reasonable part in manning the ship, and this includes an emergency.

A large craft is only abandoned if it becomes quite clear that everyone will be better off in the emergency facilities, but it is wise to take precautions in good time so as to avoid any last-minute panic. If you are well-prepared before you leave the aircraft or boat your chances of survival are that much better. Fresh water is vital, but food, compass, charts, spare clothing, emergency radio and distress signals all need a place. You or the manufacturer may have prepacked items such as tinned water (or a solar still), emergency rations and a compass, but it is unlikely that charts will be included. If you have a radio do not delay sending a distress signal until the last minute. Ideally, you need to send an accurate position, details of the size, type and name of your craft and the number of people on board. It may be helpful to say that you can use alternate radio frequencies. If time is short the vital information to transmit is 'Mayday' (three times) and your position.

Remember that inflatable liferafts, like lifejackets, should never be inflated until required for use and then only *outside* the aircraft door or the boat's hatchway. I was once on an American service aircraft when for no obvious reason one of the liferafts suddenly inflated itself in the cabin. There was no emergency; it just happened, but it did show what a totally unwieldy thing it was. It seemed to fill the fuselage and we only got it out through the door by deflating it; we would never have got it out otherwise. Ideally you launch on the lee side, but the aircraft doors or the list of the ship may prevent this. Remember that sharp objects such as ball-point pens or stiletto-heeled shoes are a real danger to inflatable craft. Leave them behind. Also remove heavy clothing such as an overcoat, but retain close-fitting items such as anoraks, trousers and light shoes (but not heavy wellingtons); you will need all you have got to keep warm. Try to get into the liferaft dry clad, but if you do go into the water get out of it as soon as possible. In cold water you will soon be chilled through.

Once everyone is in the lifeboat or liferaft, they all have the same survival problems, even if some were originally professional seamen and others amateur sailors. The sea is not man's natural environment even to the most experienced sailor let alone aircraft pilots who, almost to a man, never contemplate the possibility of a ditching, although I did once, and only once, meet a RAF helicopter pilot who deliberately wore boots, puttees, etc., in anticipation of having to walk back from a forced landing. Because the sea is unnatural the numbing shock is likely to be greater than being thrown into a survival situation on land. There is a risk of lapsing into total lethargy when there are urgent matters requiring attention.

Your boat, however big or small, is literally your life. Without it you are almost certainly doomed unless the rescue services find you very quickly. Your first, and continuing concern must be for the well-being of the boat. Is it correctly inflated? Is it leaking? Does it need any repair? Is all the equipment secured? Is there any hazard outside, such as jagged debris? Is the bailer to hand? Has a sea anchor been streamed? As in all survival situations you must apply 110 per cent concentration to the task. Although needing some modification for the sea situation the 'Survival – Immediate Actions' given in Appendix 1 are a good guide to your future efforts. You have got the party clear of danger and either you or someone else has taken charge because even the smallest of vessels needs a skipper. Now look outside your own circle for a moment. If there were others on the ship or aircraft where are they? Look for people in the sea or on other liferafts. Currents are fickle so move quickly to link up with other boats before they drift away. There is strength in numbers in this sort of situation. Looking for other survivors is not just a five-minute effort; it must go on, so appoint your first lookout or watchkeeper. Just as important is the watch for and signalling to rescue services. The largest liferaft is a tiny dot in the sea so a lookout is vital night and day. Everyone does a turn at the job except the sick.

After life-saving first aid has been given the additional need will be an issue of sea-sickness pills. Except on a mirror-calm sea the motion of a lifeboat or raft will make all but the strongest seasick. Vomiting leads to loss of liquid which is very dangerous if water is in short supply so an issue of pills all round should be made.

Warmth and shelter are your next priority. Modern liferafts are fully enclosed and give good shelter, but make everyone wring surplus water from all their clothing? It takes a lot of vital body heat to warm up soaked clothing so reduce the water content. In the temperate zones of the world you are very unlikely to become overheated. You cannot get a fire going so every scrap of heat must come from the survivors' body heat. A dry layer next to the skin is the aim, with damp layers over that being dried by the general warmth generated. Make sure the hatch is kept shut and that everyone is insulated as far as possible from the cold sea water. You will never heat up the ocean! In due course food will provide heat to the body, but if this is limited wait until any sea-sickness has been overcome.

Allocate jobs. Someone must control the available food, another should apply himself to water provision, a log or diary writer is important. Any responsibility does wonders for morale and keeps people occupied. You cannot move about much in a lifeboat, not even a few yards away for a 'bit of peace and quiet'. Tempers will fray, hates will develop. Activities and jobs will go some way to coping with these interpersonal problems.

Signalling is paramount. You must use every means possible to attract attention to your situation. Every signalling device you have or can improvise must be brought into play. If you have a radio, use it but remember that its batteries have a finite life. Emergency beacons also have a limited life and if you have both it is probably best to use only one at a time. For visual signals the flashing mirror is probably the best, as it is on land. Marker dyes and smoke-flares are best used when you have been spotted and an aircraft or ship needs to turn and come back to find you again. Remember neither can turn 'on a six-pence' and they virtually have to search for you again on their second approach. If you can rig a mast with some sort of radar reflector this can help. Despite your efforts you may not be seen and rescued by the first or even subsequent ships that pass. Not every lookout has perfect vision or dedicated attention to duty. Be mentally prepared for this sort of disappointment.

Water will be more of a problem than on land, but you are likely to have less need of it. You will not be out hunting for food, looking for fuel, etc. Much of your time will be spent sitting still. The liferaft equipment may contain desalting tablets or a solar still and these should be used in preference to any bottled or tinned water. Be ready to catch every drop of rainwater by rigging sheeting, sails, etc., to channel the water into containers. Look back at the chapter on 'Water' to see how to work out a sensible rationing scheme. Even when you appear to have plenty you should continue the scheme, albeit with a revised ration. Only when every possible container is full and you are still collecting rainwater can you feel free to drink your fill. Under no circumstances should you drink seawater (even mixed with fresh), urine, alcohol or bird's blood. Smoking increases thirst and protein foods such as meat need an increase of water intake to digest. Your watchkeeper should keep his eyes open for the approach of rain clouds and be ready to catch the rain when it falls. If it rains take the opportunity to have a shower or wash in fresh water to remove salt from your skin. Old sea ice, which is blue and wellrounded will be salt free and can be melted for fresh water. Much more than on land your efforts must be directed to reducing your body's need for water. You cannot help losing about 2 pints per day; your aim must be to lose not a single drop more. A bead of sweat is a drop of water wasted.

Your ability to fix your position will depend on your knowledge of navigation and the equipment you have with you. If you are an offshore sailor you should be able to continue navigating as if you were in your original boat since you should have taken charts and other aids with you when you abandoned ship. If you are a passive passenger from an aircraft ditching you may not be able to do very much and are unlikely to have navigational equipment. Between these two extremes there is infinite variety. What you should appreciate is that you will almost certainly move in some direction due to the ocean currents. Initially you should try to remain in the area of your ditching. This is the location you gave in your distress signal and that is where rescue services will search first. If you are aware of the currents that affect that area it is worth making efforts to keep yourself as static as possible. A traditional lifeboat can be rowed, but the average rubber liferaft is a singularly unmanageable beast if it is round and only marginally better if it is not.

Ultimately you must decide if you are going to stay put as best you can or try to move. The currents and the prevailing winds will probably make the decision for you to a large extent, but by careful trimming of a sail or a certain amount of paddling you may be able to modify drift. Obviously your aim is to reach land or get into the busy shipping lanes. Make a very conservative estimate as to the time it may take to reach help if only to give a guide to food rationing. Unless you can navigate accurately you should aim to hit a long coastline rather than an isolated landfall such as a small island. An increase in the number of birds seen is an indication of approaching land and you should note the general direction of their flight. Many will be coming to the sea to catch food and then returning to land. Drifting vegetation is another useful indicator as is fixed cloud which will indicate high ground on the land. Once land has been sighted, every effort, by sailing, rowing, paddling and anything else you can think of, must be made to reach it. Then your problems of land survival may begin!

Food sources at sea are likely to be more limited than on land, but this is not always so. On a recent expedition to Greenland, someone had only to sit out in the fjord in a boat for half an hour and hang a few lines over the side to catch almost any number of fish and large, succulent arctic char at that. A fish diet may not be everyone's choice, but it is a nourishing one. At sea, apart from any survival rations in your liferaft, you will be dependent on fish and perhaps birds. Because they are packed for long storage you should always eat your survival rations as a last resort.

Fresh food will not keep for very long. In temperate zones all fish are safe to eat. Just clean out the entrails. Do not rely on one method of fishing, try casting from the boat as well as dropping lines over the side. If you catch more fish than you can consume, clean them and cut the flesh into strips and dry it for consumption in leaner days to come. Try anything as bait. Fish may be attracted by even such things as a sliver of silver paper from a cigarette packet or a tiny piece of coloured cloth. Do remember, however, that fish are protein and need a reasonable availability of water. If water is very short it is better to go hungry. You can survive quite well for weeks without food, but you cannot afford to squander limited supplies of water by using it to digest protein foods.

The sea or any large stretch of water with no land in sight poses its own psychological problems. It will never seem as friendly as land because man is a land animal. The constant motion, the close proximity of a lot of people in a liferaft, the constant wetness will all tax survivors to the utmost, but you can survive. Poon Lim, a Chinese sailor who was on a ship torpedoed during the Second World War, survived for 133 days and was in quite good shape when rescued. Most of the contents of this book apply as much to sea as to land survival. The ideas and methods may need modification but the principles apply.

10. WHEN NATURE STRIKES: Natural hazards

Survival is usually considered against the natural elements as they exist. These elements may vary from extreme heat to extreme cold, from bare mountain rock to impenetrable jungle, but they are 'as found' in the world as it is. Sometimes Nature goes to the limit and produces flood, fire, earthquakes and the like; what insurers usually call 'Acts of God'. This chapter will consider briefly the special survival problems associated with these natural disasters. Each could justify a book of its own, but a few guiding hints may be useful since your basic survival situation could be compounded by one of these additional natural hazards.

AVALANCHE

These can happen even in the modest hills of Scotland and are not limited to major mountain ranges. Seldom a winter passes without at least one accident involving an avalanche. The causes are numerous; being an interaction between the weather, angle of slope, type of snow, its degree of metamorphosis and other factors, even to the disturbance caused by the tracks of a skier. No walker, skier or climber should be on the winter hills unless he has some knowledge of avalanches and the conditions under which they are likely to occur. The survivor who does not have this knowledge should note the following precautions. In warm weather avoid traversing below cornices (the overhanging curl of snow and ice often seen on a ridge or at the top of a steep slope) (Figure 41), steep slopes and gullies, especially if there has been a recent fall of new snow (within the last 24/48 hours). If an avalanche does occur avoid it if you can by rushing for the nearest bit of higher ground, shed-

ding your rucksack at the same time. If you are enveloped keep your mouth shut and make a swimming motion with your arms and legs. Ideally this should be towards the surface if your are not totally disorientated. As the movement slows bring your arms around your face to form an air pocket in which you can breathe comfortably. Just before all movement stops make as massive an effort as you can to keep your body loose in the snow. Once everything has stopped, keep calm and try to decide which way up you are. Once you have decided this try to move towards the surface, although this will often not be possible. Shout for help but not continuously or you will soon run out of voice and effort. If you are not caught in the avalanche yourself, but someone else is, try to note the last point at which he was visible and then follow his likely path at the rate at which the avalanche is moving. When it stops note where you think he might have got to and start your search there.

FLOOD

In temperate zones of the world you are unlikely to be suddenly caught in a flood. Rivers may rise rapidly but not instantaneously. The obvious thing to do is get higher, either to an upper floor in a building or to higher ground. This is what might be termed a controlled survival situation, where you can take some precautions before the situation actually happens. Before retreating to your upper floor think what you will need for a prolonged stay. You will want warmth with extra clothing, blankets, etc. You will want water, food and a means of cooking it. A couple of books or children's games would not go amiss if you have a young family. A bucket as an improvised lavatory would be useful plus any of the other items you might take on a camping holiday because that is, in effect, what you are going to do – camp in your bedroom.

FIRE

This can be from natural causes or as the result of a man-made error. Make one quick attempt to put the fire out. If this fails get out of the building, closing doors and windows as you go. Raise the alarm and keep well out of the way of the fire and the fire brigade. If caught out in a forest or similar fire, head either for open country or, if the fire is moving faster than you can run, find a river, pool or other patch of water and get in it. Even in open country you should keep close to water because a moorland fire, fanned by a strong wind, can move very rapidly. Bare rocky ground, which offers no potential fuel for the blaze, is another place to head for. Wet clothing is an aid to survival in a fire so do not be afraid to jump in a river. Note the direction of the wind and therefore the fire and move out of its path. If you have a fire from a stove in a tent, kick or throw the stove outside. Do not try to put the fire out. You will only lose your tent which may be vital to your survival.

BLIZZARDS

If caught in a blizzard your first priority is shelter. In winter you should be aware of your nearest refuge if your work or play takes you out into rugged conditions. The combination of wind, cold and driving snow can be very energy-sapping and you should beware of pressing on if your party is not as strong as you are. A time may well come when a hastily dug snow trench is better for your party than pressing on to a better refuge. It is very much a question of judgement. During the winter you might well keep a sleeping-bag, shovel, emergency food, towrope, etc., in your

car especially if your travels take you over exposed roads or through sparsely inhabited areas.

LIGHTNING

Thunder gives a good audible warning and lightning a good visual warning of the risk. If caught in the open do not do the obvious thing which is to seek shelter under trees, boulders, etc. Keep off exposed mountain tops and ridges. If you want to stop do so on a slope and make yourself as small as possible. Sit on your rucksack or on a dry rope to minimize your contact with the ground. But there is no special value in stopping. A building, car or flat ground offer the safest places. A person struck by lightning is not always killed, but will usually need first aid so treat him as a normal first aid casualty. Do not discard your iceaxe if you have one, you may need it later.

ANIMALS

Animals can be a hazard; people do get gored by bulls and bitten by snakes but so infrequently that virtually every occurrence is media news. Newcomers to the jungle are struck by the apparent lack of animals. Probably the major risk, worldwide, is where man has done something which attracts wild animals. An obvious example is campsites in America where campers have attractive food which brings bears and other animals to investigate. It is at times like this that animal/man accidents happen. If face to face with an animal do nothing to frighten or antagonize it. Back quietly away. If the animal follows, discard an object or a garment; it will usually stop to investigate. With some animals you can climb a tree as a refuge. Tree-climbing bulls have yet to be invented, but bears like to climb trees. Some animals do not like water so a nearby river could be a haven. Never hold out a hand to a doubtful animal even a dog which is not known. A long hard look such as a duchess might give a recalcitrant second footman may have the desired effect. If actually entangled with an animal fight as dirty as you like; shout and scream, and aim to hurt tender parts of the animal.

11. CIVILIZATION IS A DANGEROUS PLACE: Man-made hazards

Survival is usually thought of as something which happens in an emergency miles from anywhere in bad weather, but our allegedly civilized society of the late twentieth century is not without its hazards. This chapter offers a few hints on just some of the possible survival situations you may meet, probably in places where you least expect them. The situations are in no particular order of importance.

CAR CRASH

Whether it is your own crash or someone else's makes little difference except that if you have been involved you will soon begin to suffer some degree of shock. First, you should make a very quick assessment as to the hazard caused by the crash to other traffic. If the crash is on a bend or not obvious to approaching vehicles, send someone out to wave them down. An uninvolved vehicle with its hazard warning lights flashing positioned in front of the crash is very useful. The next quick decision required is should you remove any injured persons from the crash vehicles? If there is a smell of petrol it is probably wise to do so, but remember they may have serious injuries to back or neck which need very careful handling if you are to avoid increasing the damage. In any case it is worth turning the ignition off. C-H-A-S-T-E should now be your guide. When you get to 'A for Aid' make sure the person going for help realizes that he needs the nearest telephone which, except on a motorway, will usually be in a private house. He must not go for miles looking for a public call-box. At a private house he may have to be quite forceful about using the telephone and must not be put off by an unhelpful householder.

Emergency calls are free so there is no need for coins. Once the police and other services arrive let them take over.

CAR BREAKDOWN

Normally this is just an annoyance, but at times it can involve a survival decision. A few months before writing this book I was driving over the mountain road from Machynlleth to Llanidloes in Central Wales. It was March and the weather at sea level was mild. Near the top of the road at about 400 metres I found snow on the road and was thinking of turning back when the car stuck in a small snowdrift. I reversed out and decided to back down the hill only to find that I had just come over a rise which was now too thick with snow to back the car up. I was stuck in a dip between two quite minor slopes, but they were sufficient to prevent a two-wheel drive vehicle going either way. I had a sleeping-bag, shovel, food and a flask and was well clad. Should I stay or should I walk back the way I had come? It was snowing, but the depth was not enough for me to miss the road and wander off across the moors. About half a mile back was the last house up that road and thereafter there were cottages or houses no more than about half a mile apart. Weighing up all these factors I decided it was worth walking back and that it was safe for me, as a reasonably fit outdoor person, to do so. It would not have been the right decision for a young mother with two toddlers. If your car breaks down do, before you start getting involved with fault-finding, give a quick thought to the question of survival. It could be better to leave the car and get out while you can, or perhaps allow yourself ten minutes and if you have not started it by then, take the decision to go. This book is not the place for a course in car mechanics, but a modest knowledge of fault-finding is very useful, as is membership of one of the motoring organizations!

FIRE

See Chapter Ten.

AIRCRAFT CRASH

The procedures to be followed if you are in crashed or ditched aircraft have been covered earlier in this book, but what happens if you see an aircraft make a forced landing and you arrive on the scene shortly afterwards? The first rule is to keep well away from both ends of jet engines, and from propellers. Unless the fuselage breaks open on impact an aircraft is effectively a sealed metal cylinder and you have got to gain entry. Look around the aircraft and you will find signs indicating that by pulling, pushing, twisting or turning something you can get in. Also note that there may be additional warning signs telling you to keep clear in certain areas. If the aircraft is a military one, in addition to the hazard from engines, it may be armed with rockets, bombs or ammunition, which can also offer a risk and should be avoided. In fast jet military aircraft the crew will sit in ejector seats and these must be made safe before you do anything else. Usually this is done by inserting a split safety-pin, normally labelled with a large red label or tag, into a hole on the top of the seat. Having gained entry you carry out the first aid sequence and alert the emergency services, just as you would with a car crash. The difference is that you may have many more casualties than in a car accident. The sheer numbers will appear overwhelming at first, but if you deal only with the real killers of lungs and heart not functioning and severe bleeding you will not go far wrong. Because of the numbers you must con-

centrate in getting others to do things. Even someone who is slightly injured himself can apply pressure hard to a handkerchief held to a major wound on somebody else.

MAN OVERBOARD

This is not an infrequent event and it is a drill which should be practised before it is needed in real life. If someone falls overboard announce the fact as loudly as possible. Everyone should then keep their eyes on the person in the water because even in good weather the easiest thing to do is to lose sight of a person in a large expanse of water. Whether you are under sail or power it takes time to bring a vessel round onto the reverse course and it is during this turn of 180° that someone can be lost from view. Despite the urgency of the situation the man in the water must be approached slowly. Especially under sail, it is possible to overshoot and the turning process has to be repeated. As the approach is made, a lifebuoy on a line should be got ready and looped lines put over the side. If he is in the water for more than a very few minutes he will need a lot of help to get him on board again. A ladder over the side will also assist. Once on board, dry clothing and warm surroundings are the priority followed by a hot drink. Alcohol in any form, as in all hypothermia cases, should be avoided. It hinders rather than assists recovery despite its apparent warming effect.

ELECTROCUTION

The first requirement is to cut off the current by turning off the switch, pulling out the plug, turning off at the mains, etc. If this is impossible, push or pull the casualty away from the source of power with a *dry* object which does not conduct electricity. Assume that any metal object will conduct current so avoid these. Wood, rubber, paper, etc., provided that they are dry do not. Most likely first aid requirement will be to restart the casualty's breathing.

GAS HAZARD

Anyone who has collapsed in a room with a gas appliance in it should be removed from the room and resuscitated with the 'kiss of life'. If you suspect a gas escape, remove everyone from the scene, call the local gas authority and try to turn off the gas at the main supply. Carbon monoxide is produced by most processes of burning. It is colourless and odourless so is difficult to detect. It is very common from the exhaust funes of a car or burning a stove in a confined space. Get any collapsed casualty into fresh air and resuscitate him.

TRAIN CRASH

The safest position in a train is a seat with your back to the engine. If a crash occurs it will be similar to an aircraft crash with possibly many casualties. As with a road crash there may be a risk to a following train, or one on the other line if the crash has blocked it. Try to find out from train staff if this is likely, but do not delay too long before going up or down the line to give a warning. Remember that trains need a long distance to slow up – hundreds of metres – so go a long way. Telephones can be found on some lines at intervals beside the track.

HUMAN ATTACK

These can range from a belligerent but unsteady drunk to a determined, if mentally unbalanced, terrorist. Unless you are trained and *experienced* in one of the forms of unarmed combat, discretion is the better part of valour, and you try to fade quietly from the scene. Talking can delay an attacker and allow you time to edge nearer to an escape route or a possible weapon. Screaming or shouting may raise the alarm and could discourage your attacker. Try to avoid getting within the grasp of an attacker, but if you do then anything goes. Use any sharp object you have, kick, bite, pull hair, etc. Go for the face, genitals and other tender parts of the body. As soon as you can, break away and run, remembering to kick your shoes off if you are wearing high heels. With a bunch of hijackers in the confined space of an aircraft things are more serious. They are likely to believe in a cause and be less concerned about ultimate death than the average cowardly attacker. The key thing is to keep cool, calm and not to draw attention to yourself. Slump in your seat and remind yourself where the escape hatches are should you need them. Make no sudden movements. Quietly get rid of any documents or literature which might antagonize the hijackers. Currently this is anything American or Israeli, but could change in the future according to the political views of the hijackers. Demand nothing, offer nothing. Reasoning or discussion of their alleged cause is unlikely to assist the situation. Rest, sleep and generally husband your physical and mental resources for the time when they may be needed which will come, inevitably, sooner or later.

PART TWO: TAKE THE SURVIVAL CHALLENGE

CONTENTS

INTRODUCTION

So, you want to challenge your ability to survive in difficult conditions? Although to do so is not unusual – in fact you are already a part of a large and growing hobby leisure group – it is not by definition a standard activity among the human race. Accordingly you should ask yourself a series of questions before you give any further thought to pursuing your idea. Let us start with why.

WHY TAKE THE SURVIVAL CHALLENGE?

If you are contemplating survival seriously because it will make you fit and strong and some kind of hero you will probably end up by failing the challenge! By putting yourself into a survival situation you are likely to make yourself less fit and strong by virtue of denying yourself the very things that enhance those qualities. At the end of any survival test you are more likely to be dirty, smelly and thoroughly unkempt, than attractive to others.

Perhaps you want to test yourself in conditions of stress because you are happier in circumstances which find you alone with your thoughts and away from your fellow men. For you, survival may be the answer, but only because a few days truly alone and entirely without the goodwill and comradeship of others may suggest to you that you are not the loner you

thought you were. You may want to get yourself into a strong circle of supportive friends before you 'Take the Survival Challenge'.

Many turn to survival as a hobby pursuit because their daily life is one of routine, boring, uninspiring and lacking in variety; perhaps they think that there will be satisfaction in a situation where they control their own destiny. From such a rut the drama and diversity of survival against the elements can seem extremely attractive and the urge to undertake such efforts of self-cure is commendable. Do not be surprised, however, if after such an exercise the drudgery and mechanics of daily chores seem sweeter than before.

If like many readers of this book, you have 'worked' up to the individual survival challenge by means of group activities with Venture Scouts, Forces Cadets, YHA, YMCA, Ramblers/Trekking Groups, and Outward Bound activities or by courses and weekends run by Survival Clubs, you will be familiar with the nature of many of the hazards involved. Now, for reasons of finance or changing circumstances, you are considering devising your own survival course, and your main hurdle is likely to be the stress of loneliness and the absence of support and advice from companions. You must abandon all normal ideas of comfort and well-being and be prepared to accept hardship and discomfort, factors completely alien to the majority of 'civilized' people.

Whatever the answer to the question – why? – you should not be put off by minor doubts. Your intention is a worthy one; success, if you accomplish the challenge set, is hugely satisfying and the ability to survive in uncomfortable, unfamiliar and unwelcoming conditions can bring out many fine human qualities and a host of other benefits including a greater knowledge of the world you live in and deeper respect for it. Survival means becoming part of the countryside, not fighting it. It means using nature's resources, not abusing them. It means you will feel at home in the great outdoors, not an intruder, or at best a visitor.

WHEN?

If you have satisfied yourself with the answers to Why you would Take the Survival Challenge? you should now decide when you will undertake it. The basic advice is – not yet! Unless you are very well trained in survival techniques and have consistently kept in training in all seasons and various conditions, you will need to prepare until you believe you are ready, then do the exercises again to be sure. For survival is not a holiday, it is not a novel weekend activity; survival means placing yourself in extraordinary situations without even ordinary facilities. At best it is uncomfortable and, if improperly handled, unhealthy; at worst, it is likely to pose considerable physical and mental stress, and danger. So

prepare, and prepare again. For the more impatient among us this is the first 'challenge' to be overcome.

You should read as much as you can on the subject. Apart from various magazines on the market, there are some excellent books, both basic tuitional titles for the layman and others based on service manuals for the UK and USA. Then you can begin to collect a full set of survival kit. As with most manufactured items, quality costs money and here the cheaper purchase will probably rebound on you by either a malfunction or sub-standard results at a later stage. Take care though, because high cost does not always mean greater effectiveness, and in the equipment jungle, knowledge can only come with experience. The range of survival items is growing all the time and can confuse the newcomer. The lists provided later in the book take account of various preferences and purposes. If you are attracted to creating your own Survival Challenge, you will have the benefit of selecting your own climate and geographical location, so determining the range of kit you need to have.

HOW?

With great responsibility. If you Take the Survival Challenge in an irresponsible manner – by having inadequate skills, preparation, equipment or determination, you will be a danger to yourself and others. If you show the necessary diligence and conduct your exercise with good sense, you can achieve the satisfaction you seek without harming other people's property, without infringing their privacy and without calling upon their goodwill to come to your aid.

In devising your own Survival Challenge you will have first to undertake an honest personal assessment of your own skills and experience. Throughout this book we shall normally be assuming that an intermediate type of challenge is required, while at the same time commenting on situations and remedies which should be called upon were the course more severe in terms of climate, terrain, personal injury or unforeseen danger.

Your first course will probably be set in a region of your country that can be reached without too much difficulty and which, while sparsely inhabited and poorly suited for easy living, offers no life-threatening danger to the well-equipped outdoorsman. You will probably choose a month of the year when you will not suffer low extremes of temperature and will certainly not plan your first course to last beyond four or five days and nights. A checklist of preparation is provided elsewhere in the book. The objective of the challenge is to test yourself and learn while achieving, not simply to endure. Endurance may be required, but it should not be because you lack the basic skills or are unwilling to modify techniques to suit circumstances.

WHERE?

Survival in the urban jungle has been the subject of many books and is not our topic here. So you will move beyond your own environment and seek the less populated areas. Most readers will have to travel a considerable distance to reach a suitable location and, in view of the likely international readership of this book, we will provide some key elements of the best sites for your course rather than list specific parts of any country. This topic will be dealt with more fully later, but suffice to say that most areas offer a location which, within 48 hours' walking distance, can offer substantial vegetation, running water, some ruggedness of terrain and, of course, a good chance of complete seclusion.

This book is intended to help those who wish to devise their own survival test. It gives advice and cautionary comment to the reader preparing a challenge, and recounts the undertaking of such a Challenge during which many of the possible problems of survival were encountered and remedied. It is designed to be read in its entirety before Taking the Survival Challenge, with much instruction appearing within the Challenge section, as well as in the preparation chapters. We suggest that you consider the one aspect of public behaviour that causes you personally most annoyance – loud transistor radios in public places, litter, or whatever – and then realize the problems the irresponsible survivalist can cause before resolving that you will set about your Survival Challenge with good sense and preparation.

Within the Challenge, therefore, must be the aim to complete it with minimum environmental impact.

PREPARATION

We have already accepted that the first priority of survival is to be prepared. In respect of equipment, this can mean the novice survivalist ensuring that the kit he buys is suitable for the use expected of it; for the experienced hiker or camper this means realizing that the gear taken on a seaside holiday or a ramble through lowland countryside is not likely to be adequate for the severities which genuine survival living can bring about. Bear in mind that highly trained military personnel have been known to suffer injury or even perish because they were ill-equipped for the unforeseen accident or bad weather

CLOTHING

Anyone practising survival skills should have appropriate clothing. Nowadays there is a bewildering array of outdoor clothing available. Manufacturers produce clothing for every conceivable outdoor activity, using a variety of high-tech and traditional materials. There is also a proliferation of suppliers of military surplus clothing and equipment – more of this later.

It is not possible to detail all the varieties of clothing available from different manufacturers; that could fill a book in itself. There are many magazines in which manufacturers advertise, and reputable manufac-turers are quite happy to respond to a written request for product details.

There are certain principles to be considered when buying clothing to provide protection against the weather. Remember your clothing will be the main factor in protecting you against the danger of hypothermia caused by cold, wet and wind, and must therefore be up to the task. It is generally accepted that the **layer principle** offers the maximum flexibility and protection. Dead air is the best form of insulation and one of the best ways of creating dead air is to trap it between layers of clothing. The greater the numbers of layers the greater the insulating effect. This means that a number of layers of thinner clothing is much more effective insulation than a single thick layer. In addition, temperature control is achieved by removing or replacing layers as necessary. This adjustment is important because overheating is as much of a problem as overcooling. Avoidance of overheating is very important in cold/freezing weather as well as in warm because it leads to sweating and in cold weather this rapidly chills the body as soon as sweating stops; for example, resting after a period of activity. Clothing wet with sweat acts as a pipeline for body heat to be drawn away into the air.

In summer, during the day, only a single layer such as a tee shirt may be necessary, and the main point to be made regarding summer is that protection against sunburn may be as important as insulation. In open country it is not always possible to get out of the sun and clothing must provide adequate protection.

In winter, or colder weather, the layer principle comes into its own. Starting at skin level, thermal underwear, including long johns, provide warmth out of all proportion to their weight. Also, most modern thermal underwear has the ability to 'wick' away sweat from the skin, thus considerably increasing comfort and reducing chilling. A woollen or wool mixture shirt comes next, and finally on top of the shirt a woollen or fibre-pile sweater or jacket. I prefer a good quality fibre-pile sweater because it is warmer and more windproof than wool, lighter and packs smaller in my pack. If it does get wet, and this happens sooner or later, it retains its insulating qualities and dries quickly. For cold conditions all of this can be topped with a fibre-pile, down or holofil vest or jacket. Down is not really suitable for cold/wet conditions; when it gets wet it clumps together and loses its insulating properties. Once wet it is difficult to get dry again and finally it is extremely expensive.

The final layer must be wind and waterproof; a jacket is better than a parka which pulls over the head, because the zip can be opened or closed for ventilation purposes, and the layers underneath the waterproof shell need not be specially purchased as most people have suitable shirts and sweaters. It is worth while spending a bit of money on the outer water-

proofs. The zip should be covered with a storm flap which also has an independent means of fastening. This fulfils two purposes – it prevents the wind and water entering through the zip and provides an extra means of fastening should the zip fail. The flap may be fastened by buttons, stud or Velcro. Buttons are easy to replace, but difficult to fasten when wearing gloves; studs are easy to fasten but difficult to replace; Velcro is easy to fasten and easy to replace, but sometimes fastens itself, inconveniently, to other clothing and it is noisy. My own preference is for button fastening.

A deep hood, big enough to accommodate a hat and which comes up to cover the lower part of the face and has a wire stiffener, is essential. Hood draw-cords which close with cord locks rather than tying are useful when wearing gloves. Sleeves should be long enough to cover the hands and have a wrist fastening of some sort, and in general the jacket should be a size bigger than normal to accommodate several layers of clothing in cold weather and allow a free flow of air in warmer weather. It should reach to the knees and be fitted with draw-cords at the waist and hem. Some jackets have a host of pockets, but all that is really needed are two outside pockets with waterproof flaps and an inside pocket big enough to hold a map. I personally prefer and advocate colours that blend with the countryside to avoid colour pollution in the wilderness areas. For safety's sake it is easy to carry a brightly coloured bivi-bag with you.

Material may range from PU proofed nylon (cheap) to the latest breathable fabrics such as Cyclone, Sympatex, Entrant and Goretex (expensive), depending on the depth of your pocket. I have been using a jacket made of Entrant for about two years now and find it quite satisfactory. Although it is vapour permeable, it is less expensive than some other materials of this type.

A further possible addition, preferred by myself, is to use a close-weave cotton windproof for its comfort and breathable qualities in all but persistent rain.

The lower extremities are easier to accommodate with clothing. The thermal underwear can be topped with a pair of windproof and, if necessary, a pair of waterproof trousers. Good quality windproof trousers are available from a number of manufacturers and cost no more than the best quality military windproofs. They tend to be lighter and quicker drying, but perhaps not so hard wearing.

Waterproof trousers should have either a side zip to allow them to be put on while wearing boots, or be wide enough in the leg to allow this. Materials is the same as for jackets with the same provisos. To my knowledge there is no waterproof material that is as comfortable to wear as cotton-based windproofs. Synthetic materials tend to be noisy and I find this a bit of an irritation, especially with trousers, but that is a small price to pay for staying dry and safe.

Footwear is every bit as important as the waterproofs. Trying to keep dry is a major pre-occupation for the survivor, but the feet may be the means of extricating him from his situation.

It is generally accepted that boots are the best type of footwear, but it is important to choose the right kind of boot. Walking across rugged terrain calls for a boot that is flexible and as waterproof as possible. Therefore, avoid boots specifically designed for climbing, either the heavy rigid sole type or the lightweight style with smooth soles and suede or canvas uppers. A walking boot should have a flexible sole with a deep tread, and the tongue sewn in high up the ankle. A soft or padded cuff greatly adds to comfort. High-leg boots are now generally available, but tend to be more expensive, and although they are more waterproof as the tongue is sewn higher up the leg, if they get wet they take a long time to dry.

Nylon gaiters go a long way to enhancing the waterproof capabilities of standard boots, which in my opinion are more comfortable to wear. The performance of any boots will be enhanced if they are treated with a good waterproofing compound. Boots must be clean and dry before applying the compound, and it should be rubbed well in, particularly along the seams and where the tongue joins the upper. Do not neglect the bootlaces either; at the first sign of wear, replace them immediately. This is a piece of common sense that is often neglected.

Good boots must be partnered with good socks. Two pairs of socks are more effective for preventing blisters. It could be two pairs of thick or one pair of thick and one pair of thin. I find the latter most comfortable, the thin socks being the thermal type – Merkalon or similar, and the thick pair loop stitch. The main thing is to find a combination that suits you, and stick to it. I must say that for much survival training, wellington boots are fine. I have used them at various times over the years. They are completely waterproof and have a good gripping sole. If worn with thick socks they are warm enough. However they are not very suitable for cross-country journeys, and if they are worn for any length of time cause the feet to sweat a lot and soften the skin.

In cold weather the head and hands also need protection. This applies in particular to the head. Various figures are quoted for heat loss from the head and neck area. I believe that a figure of 40–50 per cent heat loss can occur in some conditions and that is serious. A woollen or similar watch cap or balaclava is a lightweight and versatile solution to the problem of heat retention, particularly if worn under a waterproof jacket hood. As far as the hands are concerned, mitts are far superior to gloves for heat retention as well as being easier to put on and take off. With a little practise, a surprising number of tasks can be accomplished without having to remove them. The layer system can also be applied by wearing thin gloves inside mitts if the weather warrants it.

SURVIVAL KITS

There are a host of survival kits available on the market. They vary in content and quality and therefore in value and purpose. Some are based on military-issue sets while others are the survival equivalent of the free sewing kits in hotel rooms; the latter are seldom of any use to the typical traveller and the cheap, gimmicky survival kit is the same.

The items carried will become a matter of personal choice to the seasoned outdoorsman with pieces added or subtracted to suit his own preferences, locations or techniques. The prerequisities of a survival kit are compactness and lightness of weight combined with contents that represent items not readily available from natural sources, in true or substitute form, in the survival situation.

The services your survival kit will provide consist of the provisions of shelter, the means of producing fire and pure water, the wherewithal to cut a variety of substances, and a facility to apply personal first aid. Let us consider these aspects individually.

Shelter A survival bag or blanket is an essential item, particularly in open terrain. A bag is better than a blanket. An injured survivor will find it easier to crawl into a bag than trying to wrap himself in a blanket, and more importantly, stay wrapped. Two bags which can fit inside one another are very good; the gap between them can be filled with grass, ferns or similar insulating material. A little nylon cord will make shelter construction that much easier.

Fire Wind and waterproof matches are the easiest way to light a fire, but do not forget the striker. Flint and steel or 'Permanent Match' will act as a back-up to matches and will provide many lights. The 'Permanent Match' consists of a small plastic

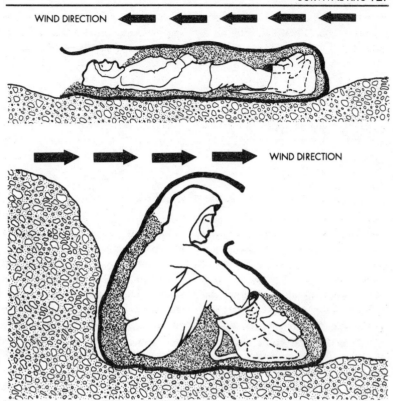

WIND DIRECTION

WIND DIRECTION

FIG. 1. USE OF SURVIVAL BAG

container filled with petrol-soaked cotton wool. A metal rod with a wick is screwed in through the base to allow the wick to soak up the petrol from the cotton wool. When it is unscrewed it is ignited by striking it along the flint embedded in the side of the casing. Even after the petrol is exhausted metal match and flint can still be used to ignite cotton wool tinder. The cotton wool can be obtained by breaking open the casing. Candles or solid fuel tablets are useful firelighters, although they need to be lit themselves; a burning or magnifying glass is very useful provided that there is an adequate source of sunlight.

Pure Water. Twenty water purification tablets take up no space at all. Use them unless you are 100 per cent sure that the water is pure. You should also take a water carrier – plastic bag, balloon, condom – all of these will do, but will last longer if carried in something, like a sock, when full.

Cutting Edge. A hacksaw blade, with the plain edge sharpened and brought to a point, makes a good knife cum saw. Tape wrapped around it provides a handle, and it is useful

CUT ON PULL STROKE ⟶

FIG. 2. USE OF WIRE SAW

for other purposes. A scalpel blade, such as a razor blade or craft knife blade, would do as an alternative but should be kept for fine work. A high-quality wire saw will complement these items nicely. Apart from the blades carried in your survival kit, any long-term survival situation or test demands a survival knife. Competence in the selection, use and care of the various types of knife is a prerequisite which should be fulfilled as part of your preparation.

More than any other items of kit, survival knives seem to exercise a fascination for the potential purchaser, and I am giving some personal observations and ideas as to what constitutes a good survival knife. Knives range from the cheap and useless to the very expensive and those of doubtful value for money. I have used a variety of knives over the years and have formed some very definite opinions as to what works best. There are two main uses for a knife in survival – cutting and chopping. Under the heading of cutting comes skinning, gutting, fine shaping of wood and similar work where a sharp, narrow blade is desirable.

Chopping, on the other hand, includes splitting, prying, hammering and digging. These tasks require a long, thick, heavy blade with the centre of gravity forward of the handle, about halfway up the blade.

While endeavouring to conform to the popular notion of a survival knife, most commercially available knives are actually a compromise between these two requirements, cutting and chopping. Like most compromises they do not excel at the extremes of the requirements. Many knives are designed to look the part rather than to give good service or value for money.

A hollow handle means that the handle has to be fixed into the blade in some way. Hollow handles and saw-tooth blades look good in the store or in the brochures, but there are disadvantages associated with them. A hollow handle has to be fixed to the blade and that creates a potential zone of weakness. To eliminate this is not easy and only the better manufacturers can afford the investment necessary to ensure the quality of the final product. This makes it a more expensive article. A tang that is part of the handle is easier and cheaper to make and is potentially stronger. A saw back is only useful if it actually saws – many of them do not. It also makes it hazardous to hold the back of the blade, and this is sometimes necessary when doing delicate cutting. It adds to the cost for little benefit, and so is of dubious value. My conclusions is that two knives are called for: a large one for chopping and similar work and a small one for finer work.

The larger knife should be at least the size of the MOD survival knife, or, better still, a Golok or a Parang. A suitable alternative would be a small metal-shafted hand axe. While not as versatile, it is a good substitute.

At the other end of the scale the Swiss Army Knife is most suitable. It must be the genuine article, not an imitation. It also has the advantage that it includes other tools. I have used the basic model with two blades, screwdrivers, can- and bottle-openers for many years and found it to be perfectly satisfactory. This type of knife is small enough to be carried at all times but it does have one disadvantage – the blade does not lock in the open position, and in some circumstances when using the point of the knife the blade can close on your finger, giving a nasty cut. There are other similar size knives with locking blades, and these are certainly safer, especially when equipped with a positive gripping handle.

For any survival knife, a stainless steel blade is desirable; for a folding knife it is essential because any rusting is detrimental to the blade and the pivot. It is impossible to remove rust entirely.

Beware of copies of military survival knives. They may not be copies of survival knives, but rather of fighting knives. Also they may be of inferior material and construction. The quality is of course generally reflected in the price. While of suitable design, they may well be made of soft steel which does not hold an edge. A slender tang will be a definite weakness.

Hunting knives with their thick strong blade, straight-through tang and slab handle, is perfectly suitable

FIG. 3. GOLOK/SURVIVAL KNIFE

FIG. 4. HUNTING KNIFE

FIG. 5. LOCK KNIVE

FIG. 6. SWISS ARMY KNIFE

FIG. 7. MILITARY KNIFE

FIG. 8. MOD SURVIVAL KNIFE

DIRECTION OF STROKE

DIRECTION OF STROKE

FIG. 9. KNIFE SHARPENING

for survival purposes. This type of handle prevents the knife from turning in the hand when chopping and the blade is hard enough to retain a good edge.

A typically well-made survival knife should have a good join where the blade and handle meet. Some have a saw back, which I do not like, but the blade will probably be stainless and thus takes a good edge. The knife I possess originally came with a compass in the screwed butt cap, but I have replaced this with a solid cap. I would not like to rely on a compass after the knife had been heavily used a few times. As regards the hollow handle, I keep only some windproof matches and cotton wool in it; a hollow handle is NOT a substitute for a survival kit.

The Golok, which I mentioned earlier, is the preferred knife for chopping, splitting, prising, digging and other similar tasks. The handle is riveted to the tang and, being the slab type, gives a good grip. The steel is perhaps a little bit soft, but a sharpening stone should be carried, and in the worst case the blade can be sharpened using natural stone.

All cutting tools should be kept sharp. This greatly reduces the effort in using them, and makes it less likely that they will glance off the target. A knife blunt enough to slip is still sharp enough to cause a nasty gash. A small sharpening stone is an important item of kit. A great deal has been written about sharpening to a razor edge but this is not necessary. While a good sharp edge must be maintained, it must not be so delicate that it gets damaged when used for a bit of rough work. Whatever is being used as a sharpening stone, must be held at such an angle that it bears on the bevel that leads to the edge. The sharpening stroke is made from the edge towards the back of the blade. Make several strokes covering the blade from the heel to the tip on one side, and then repeat on the other side. The motion is as if shaving the stone.

As the blade approaches its final edge, the number of strokes per side is reduced to one per side alternatively, making sure that the entire length of the blade is covered. The angle to maintain is about 15 – 20° on each side. Strictly speaking, oil should be used on the stone to float away the particles, but at a pinch, water or even saliva will do. Sharpening should be carried out regularly, and particularly after the knife has had heavy use, so that the edge can be maintained with minimum effort. It is useless to wait until the blade is blunt because it takes much longer to achieve a sharp edge. A professional woodsman, for example, would sharpen the edge of his axe at least seven or eight times during his working day.

Medical. The list of possible medical items would be extensive, but some basic first aid items should be carried. Bear in mind though, that these items are the minimum and additional kit may be required depending upon the particular situation or location: painkilling tablets; waterproof plasters; antiseptic cream; cotton wool; potassium permanganate crystals. The latter are truly multi-purpose, their use including water purification, disinfectant, antiseptic, a marker dye in snow or water, a firelighter when combined with sugar.

When training or testing yourself it is best to carry a more extensive first-aid kit. Although there are many natural remedies, your health is not something you should be casual about. Splinters, itches, infections, stomach upsets, nausea and headaches are all problems which can be coped with by a basic kit. These can be purchased complete from pharmacists or outdoor stores. In addition to the items above I would consider the following desirable: two large wound dressings; needle; scalpel blade; micropore tape; tweezers; small roll of adhesive tape; foot powder; one bandage; two safety pins; anti-diarrhoea treatment; and some wound closures.

Naturally, everybody has his own idea of what should be in a first-aid kit. A more compact kit, my personal preference, might consist of: antiseptic wipes and cream; plasters; needle and thread; medicated wound dressing; safety-pins; painkilling tablets; scalpel and razor blade. When wrapped in a couple of plastic bags and secured by elastic bands it makes a very small package.

Sundry items can find a place in most kits, for instance: a plastic whistle which, unlike metal, won't stick to your lips in cold weather; a mirror for signalling; fish hooks, line and weights; sugar cubes; beef stock; a small button-type compass; brass snare wire; aluminium foil; and a pencil and paper. These, combined with the medical items, can be stored in a 50 gram tobacco tin sealed with potentially useful electrical tape. It is a shame that the compactness of this tin limits its usefulness as a cooking pot. It can, however, be packed into a small metal cup, such as those used on Meta-type stoves, which can still be carried in your pocket.

It may be obvious, but one of the best tests of the value of your equipment is the number of different tasks for which it can be used. One item that fulfils several functions takes up less space and is easier to carry. It is not enough simply to have the best kit; you must be proficient in the use of all the items in it and you must have some knowledge of first aid. The survivalist will rue the day that he or she undertakes a challenge without first having worked with and mastered each piece of equipment carried, preferrably in a range of conditions. Although you may feel a little foolish trying to light a fire in the middle of the night, or perhaps during a downpour in your back garden, it is better to learn that way rather than fumble and panic to complete the task in some unknown forest because you have not tried it before.

The ardent survivalist will not want to carry large amounts of kit unless it is considered absolutely vital. The novice is well advised to gain a great deal of experience before forsaking the following: cooking utensils; tent; basic food ration; and a sleeping-bag. It is as well to remember that you are choosing to test yourself and that undue risk and self-imposed hardship of extreme proportions are both unwise and unwarranted.

A TRAINING GROUND

In testing your equipment you can use a nearby field or coastline, or your garden if it is large enough, but you should keep in mind the intended location in which you will undertake your Challenge. You will need to establish its suitability, in respect of the severity of the test you plan; its accessability and the cost and time to reach the starting-point; and you need to check whether you require permission from landowners or preservation bodies in order to avoid trespassing.

When you commence your Survival Challenge an important part of your kit will be a large-scale Ordnance Survey Map. Time spent learning to 'read' such a map is essential for the ability to translate the flat plane of the map into a three-dimensional panorama which gives a real picture of the ease or difficulty of potential routes and, in the early planning stages, indications of suitable areas for your Challenge.

The basic requirements for an area in which to conduct your test will depend on the actual content you decide to put into it, but as the major objective on a physical level will be to make as much use of natural resources as possible, your area should have at least some of these resources present: Shelter, fire and water are the major needs when conducting your test so a location or locations where these are available is what to look for. A steep-sided, wooded river valley, for example, would be ideal and is unlikely to be of much agricultural use. Two or more such locations separated by rugged moorland terrain would be desirable because this also introduces the element of travel between sites. A site such as has been suggested will also provide an appropriate habitat for the other elements of survival such as plant and animal food and medicinal herbs.

The situation nowadays is that most land belongs to individuals or has an official or semi-official body looking after it and permission will have to be sought to conduct the kind of activities related to the Survival Challenge. This permission should be obtained in advance by writing, or better still by going to the appropriate responsible authority in person. This gives you both an opportunity to demonstrate that you are a responsible individual and to offer any assurances required by the owner. It will be of great assistance at this stage if you have made arrangements for Public Liability Insurance. This is very cheap for the short period of time your Challenge will take and is a further demonstration of your earnest intent.

In many instances, if simply travelling across an area, permission is not so important; theoretically it is still required, but many areas now have open access to the public without specific permission being necessary. It will help your case in seeking permission in future and generally creating a good impression if you leave absolutely no trace of your activities. Not only should you leave no litter, but you should also remove all traces of your shelter, if you build one, all signs of your fire if you light one and in general aim at minimum impact on the environment.

The coast offers many opportunities for a survival test. There are few problems of access to most sea-shores. Even in holiday seasons it is relatively easy to find a quiet area by checking the map and looking for an area of coast that does not have ready access for vehicles. Most people do not want to venture too far from their car. It also helps that the best type of sea-shore, in survival terms, is a rocky coast as opposed to a sandy beach. Rocks offer the best chances of fishing and other types of food gathering such as shellfish and seaweed. Firelighting and cooking on the shore is safe and beachcombing will provide a ready supply of firewood as well as other items that can be used to aid survival; tin cans, plastic floats, fish boxes, rope, nets – all can be put to good use.

The terrain of suitable areas for the Challenge poses a great potential for danger in terms of injury and extremes of weather. To go without adequate preparation or equipment is foolhardy, particularly if you are going alone. You must not undertake this type of venture unless you have the experience and equipment to cope with the worst conditions that can be expected. The terrain that is available will also influence the type and content of the Challenge. That to which the latter part of this book is devoted embraced as many different types as possible, within the constraints of time and distance that could be covered on foot between locations, while leaving time to try out and perfect various survival skills. I was fortunate to have access to a variety of ground and I therefore set the Challenge accordingly. It would be over moorland, open and wooded terrain and last for five days and four nights. The time-scale would be fairly flexible, but there would be travel between areas, requiring survival navigation skills on two of the days and the rest of the time would be spent on the day-to-day business of survival – keeping warm and dry, gathering and cooking food, practising various techniques and seeking out natural alternatives to manufactured items of survival kit. A major objective would be to make maximum use of nature's survival kit, bearing in mind that the countryside cannot be plundered indiscriminately.

When setting your own Challenge do not try to organize a detailed timetable; only set major objectives related to the locations and movement. It is correct to have an idea of what skills you may be required to use or wish to practise, but these should only be applied when appropriate, not to a rigid agenda. A flexible response to the actual situation is a cornerstone of survival and that will not be enhanced by pursuing a minutely detailed programme.

TECHNIQUES

SHELTER

It is a commonly held myth that the warmer and dryer the weather the less shelter is required. The truth is that in most countries and in most seasons the night temperature is sufficiently lower than the daytime temperature to warrant a good body cover for outdoor sleeping and this is before taking into account the ability of the weather to change quickly, for unforeseen threats to occur and for certain forms of wildlife to choose to share your unprotected warmth! During your Challenge you will need to create a variety of shelter and you should be aware of the types that can be constructed and the materials used.

Protection from the elements is normally the first priority after first aid. In a temperate climate, as stated earlier, this means protection from cold, wet and wind, but occasionally it may also mean protection from the sun. There are countless variations of shelter, using equipment and natural materials, with varieties of protection. This can range from a simple windbreak to a well-constructed shelter that will be wind and waterproof, constructed entirely from natural materials. They are all variations of a few basic types.

All shelter construction benefits from the selection of a site that maximises any advantages the terrain may offer. A good site will considerably reduce the time, material, and effort required in construction. There are some natural sites which need little or no additions to be waterproof. Natural caves are a good example, but caves come in all shapes and sizes and even an unpromising looking area can, with a little work, yield good shelter.

In mountain or open moorland terrain, caves will provide the only possible waterproof shelter to the survivor who has absolutely no equipment. No one should be caught like this, but it does happen and even if you have equipment a cave will provide a good starting-point. The normal understanding of a cave is a hollow, small or large, in a cliff face. Boulder fields where large rocks are piled up on one another can also create cavelike structures. These caves tend to be draughty and need to have the holes plugged up with stones and earth. The material used for blocking the holes is easily available in a rock field. In using this type of shelter great care must be taken to ensure that the cave is not a channel for water in the event of heavy rain. As boulder fields are often found in valleys, it is better and safer to stay away from the lower part of the valley when looking for shelter so as to avoid the possibility of flooding.

A less obvious form of rock shelter can sometimes be found where large

FIG. 10. ROCK SHELTER

FIG. 11. STONE SHELTER

rocks are scattered and embedded in softer ground. This situation is often located at the bottom of rocky outcrops and crags. A large rock with a space underneath is suitable. This space may need some excavation to make it habitable or even large enough to crawl into, but when done, this type can provide one of the snuggest shelters possible.

These types of natural shelter require improvement to increase their water or windproofing, and the addition of ground insulation. Cliff face caves can be improved by building a windbreak wall across the front. The building material may be stones or rocks, built dry stone dike fashion; turfs built like bricks; or ferns, reeds, long grass and heather, piled up and weighted down with a few stones. If you are lucky enough to find fuel for a fire, light it at the back of the cave. If you light it at the front, the smoke will eddy about inside, choking the occupant. Ground insulation is an essential requirement for all types of shelter. In moorland terrain this will be ferns, reeds, grass, heather or any other plant material you can find. The thicker the insulation the warmer you will be. Aim for 18 inches (45 cm) thickness below and the same thickness above to allow you to burrow into the middle. In extreme circumstances, on flat, featureless terrain, a windbreak or even an enclosure of turfs can be built. It takes a lot of turfs and is very difficult to construct without some means of cutting the turfs, e.g., a survival knife.

Finding a suitable natural shelter may not be easy and making it habitable can be time-consuming. A survival situation is often associated with adverse weather and searching for a nice cave in the mist or when the wind is blowing hard and it is raining is not to be recommended. Finding such a place to augment the survival kit carried is a bonus, but to go into the wilderness in the expectation that you will find a natural shelter is foolhardy and dangerous; *never* go without adequate survival kit. (An essential item of kit in this terrain is a bivi-bag and instruction in its use will appear later in the book. A polythene sheet eight feet (2.5 metres) square, or a poncho is a useful addition to your kit as a variety of shelters can be constructed from it).

Mountain and moorland terrain

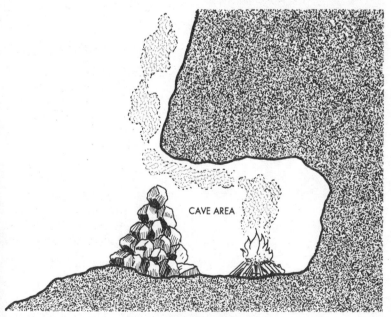

FIG. 12. CLIFF CAVE AND FIRE

offer the least assistance for survival in terms of natural resources. Thin ground cover and exposed areas, combined with weather that is usually more severe than lowland weather, makes this terrain inhospitable and the survivor should get out of this terrain and into an area where there are more natural resources. This applies in particular to shelter-building as the construction of a shelter from scratch is much easier if you have access to the kind of natural material available in wooded terrain.

A natural shelter is much more time-consuming to build than a poncho or plastic sheet shelter, and requires a great deal more skill, but the principle types remain the same. The shape may be influenced by the availability of the necessary natural material and can be classified as shown below.

Shelter covering should aim to be as windproof and waterproof as possible and covering materials can be:

Shelter Type	Advantages	Disadvantages
'A' Frame	1. Weatherproof, particularly with doors added. 2. Self-contained; can be built in an open area. 3. Warm if made compact.	1. Time-consuming construction. 2. Much material needed. 3. Difficult to heat with a fire.
Low Profile	1. Quick and simple to build. 2. Low profile. 3. Uses little material. 4. Warm, with a door. 5. Sturdy.	1. Little room inside. 2. Difficult to heat.
Open Front	1. Roomy. 2. Can be heated by a fire. 3. Provides storage for kindling, fuel, etc.	1. Must be quite large and thus time-consuming to construct. 2. Must be carefully sited with regard to the prevailing wind. 3. Change in wind direction causes problems.
Hasty or Overnight	1. Very quick and easy to build. 2. Uses natural assets: fallen trees, rocks, etc. 3. Easily heated.	1. Problems with shifting winds. 2. Very temporary.

FIG. 13. POLYTHENE SHEET LEAN-TO

branches, with or without leaves; grass, ferns, reeds and leaves; survival blanket, poncho or plastic sheeting; turf; bark, or perhaps large leaves such as those of wild rhubarb or butterburr, used as tiling. A shelter that is proof against rain takes quite some time to construct, even given the ready availability of sufficient materials – allow about three hours for a good job. Details of construction techniques are given in the Challenge section.

WEATHER

We have seen that various types of shelter can protect the outdoorsman in certain weather conditions. In preparing to challenge our survival skills we need also to be aware of the physical problems which unpleasant weather can cause, and how you should combat them. Remember that survival – be it voluntary or enforced – may not entail always remaining under cover so one cannot expect to cocoon oneself from bad weather all the time. In a temperate climate, weather hazards range from merely inconvenient, to deadly. Every year people die because of the weather; most deaths are due to cold weather, but some are due to heat problems. Hot weather hazards are less common, but they do occur in the warmer latitudes of the temperate zone.

In a survival context, **cold weather** problems start at a temperature of about +10° Centigrade. This temperature, combined with other adverse factors such as wet and wind, can be the starting-point for hypothermia, a condition which occurs when the body's heat loss rate is greater than its ability to generate heat. This results in a reduction in the core temperature. Even a small reduction has major effects detrimental to survival. If you are alone this is especially dangerous.

The body produces or conserves heat energy in various ways:

1. Conversion of food;
2. Muscular activity;
3. Closing down blood flow to peripheral parts of the body;
4. Shivering – another form of muscular energy.

On the other side of the scale, heat is lost by:

1. Conduction – direct heat transfer between a warm surface and a colder surface, e.g., sitting on snow;
2. Convection – cold air passing over a warm surface takes the heat away, e.g., wind chill;
3. Radiation – direct heat loss from a warm body to still air;
4. Evaporation – evaporation of sweat or loss through expired air.

The factors that exacerbate the various heat loss conditions are:

1. Cold – as already stated, temperatures of less than +10° Centigrade can be the starting-point for hypothermia;
2. Wet – wet clothing loses much of its insulating properties as water conducts heat at a far greater rate than air;
3. Wind – causes heat loss by convection and may render insulation layers ineffective, unless they are covered by a windproof shell;
4. Fatigue – reduces the body's ability to generate heat by muscular activity.

Any combination of the above conditions increases the danger greatly. Even if well equipped, the danger of fatigue must not be underestimated. I have seen it reported that after five or six hours' strenuous walking, fatigue risk is at its highest. Problems can arise much quicker than that. Cases have been reported of death occurring as little as one hour after the first symptoms of hypothermia. The lone traveller or survivor must be aware of the dangers and symptoms of hypo-thermia and be particularly scrupulous in applying immediate remedy, because after the first stage, assistance is required to effect a recovery. The symptoms associated with the first stage are:

1. Cold extremities;
2. Violent shivering;
3. Lethargy;
4. Nausea and dizziness.

An immediate response is essential to prevent progress to the next stage where you may be incapable of helping yourself. Reduce the heat loss by finding or creating shelter. Get out of the wind and/or rain. Use your survival bag and a sleeping-bag if you have one. Similarly, change from wet clothing to dry if possible. Brew up a warm drink and eat some high-energy carbohydrate food like chocolate or Kendal Mint Cake.

The next stage is characterized by:

1. Cessation of shivering;
2. Lack of co-ordination;
3. Stumbling and weaving;
4. Mental confusion;
5. Irrational behaviour.

Assistance at this stage probably needs to come from someone else. The remedy is the same as before, but with the added capability of skin to skin contact inside a sleeping-bag. This is the best way of warming a casualty. Even with assistance, helping a casualty is not necessarily straightforward as he may be behaving irrationally and be not at all willing to co-operate in the life-saving measures.

As with most problems, **prevention** is better than cure, all the more so because of the speed at which hypo-thermia passes beyond the stage of self-help. Appropriate clothing is the first line of defence. The layer system should be employed and a water-proof top layer must always be avail-able. Use the system properly and be prepared to remove layers to prevent sweating as well as adding to combat cold. High-energy foods taken in

---

Windchill is when the wind draws the heat away from the body to create the equivalent of a much lower temperature. This situation is much worse if you are wearing wet clothing. On the chart it can be seen that even a moderate breeze reduces the equivalent temperature quite dramatically. The lower the temperature, the worse the effect.

Still air temper-ature	Calm	Wind felt on face; leaves rustle	Small branches move	Larger branches move	Small trees sway	Large trees sway	Difficult to walk against the wind	
	0mph 0kph	5mph 8kph	10mph 16kph	15mph 24kph	20mph 32kph	30mph 48kph	40mph 64kph	
10°	10°	9°	4°	1°	−1°	−3°	−4°	Very cold
0°	0°	−4°	−10°	−12°	−15°	−18°	−21°	Bitterly cold
−10°	−10°	−12°	−18°	−23°	−26°	−32°	−35°	Flesh freezes in 1 min; travel is disagree-able
−20°	−20°	−23°	−31°	−40°	−42°	−48°	−51°	
−30°	−30°	−35°	−45°	−54°	−60°	−65°	−70°	Flesh freezes in ½ min; travel is dangerous
−40°	−40°	−43°	−57°	−65°	−70°	−79°	−82°	

This chart gives a lot of interesting information and is a little difficult to remember. The simplified version here can be remembered easily and shows the borderlines. Keep very much in mind, however, that wet clothing and fatigue raise the hypothermia danger level well above the frostbite danger levels.

Frostbite danger conditions

Wind speed	Still air temperature
0 to 5mph	−20° and −40°C
5 to 20mph	−10° and −30°C
20 to 40mph	0° and −20°C

small amounts at regular intervals and hot, rather than cold, drinks provide the best defence against energy deficiency. No alcohol should be taken; never give alcohol to a hypothermia victim as it has the effect of dilating blood vessels and thus drawing warm blood away from the body's core, and returning cooled blood.

Tied to food requirements is the need to avoid over-exertion, which might lead to fatigue in potential hypothermia conditions. Taking into account the terrain and time of year, appropriate survival equipment must always be adequate to cope with the worst conditions likely to be encountered. A sleeping-bag, survival bag, and emergency high-energy food, together with a means of preparing a hot drink, is the basic survival kit in wilderness areas, irrespective of the time of the year. Old people are particularly susceptible to hypothermia, but so are youngsters and thin people. I have seen people affected by the early stages of hypothermia in wet and windy conditions in spring.

The accompanying chart shows the effect of windchill on apparent temperature. This effect is known as the windchill factor, and refers to the phenomenon that winds of various speeds reduce the temperature to a much lower equivalent still air temperature.

In most countries it is possible to suffer from **hot weather** hazards. The most common is sunburn, but heat cramps, heat exhaustion and heatstroke are also potential problems. *Sunburn* is a problem that is eminently preventable. Trying to obtain that sun-bronzed look will often only result in red, blistered and painful skin. Once that stage has been reached there is little that you can do about it, as there is really no cure as such; you can only apply ointments or salves to reduce the pain/itching/discomfort while the body is healing itself.

During hot weather *heat cramps* occur in muscles which are being used, e.g., arms or legs. They are caused by depletion of the body's salt reserves, allied to muscular effort. The remedy is to make sure of adequate salt and liquid intake. If necessary fifteen grams of salt can be consumed in one litre of water. *Heat Exhaustion* can be caused by prolonged intensive efforts in high temperatures. The symptoms are: clammy skin, headaches, nausea which may lead to vomiting. Immediately cease all activity, rest in the shade if possible, bathe the body with cool water and drink copious amounts of water with a little salt added.

Heatstroke is caused by *very* intensive activity in high temperatures. It may come on suddenly, and can be very serious indeed. The skin is hot and dry, there is no sweat and the pulse is rapid. As for other heat hazards, stop all activity, get into any available shade and bathe skin with cool water, or immerse in it. Apart from sunburn, heat problems are caused by the fact that the body is unable to dissipate heat as fast as it is producing it. The main mechanism for heat dissipation is sweating. This, in turn is affected by muscular activity and, particularly, fluid intake.

Dehydration is the beginning of heat problems. Set a water intake schedule and stick to it. Only drinking when you are thirsty is an unreliable way of ensuring a sufficient fluid intake. An absolute minimum fluid intake to maintain water balance in a temperature of 18° Centigrade is two litres per day. That amount is on the basis of resting in shade. Any activity requires that this minimum be doubled or trebled. Higher temperatures require higher intakes. A normal outdoor diet will provide enough salt usually, but in hot weather a little additional salt can be carried for adding to meals. For survival training salt tablets or electrolyte drinks should be carried in very hot weather.

Weather hazards can be coped with by use of proper clothing and equipment and a sensible approach. It is not sensible to walk to exhaustion in either cold or hot weather. This is particularly important if you are on your own, as is immediate action when the symptoms of a problem appear. It is not easy to prepare oneself for weather hazards. It is always an intriguing test of one's 'gameness' for the survival hobby by choosing to take a brisk walk on a particularly wet or cold day and there is much to be said for learning more about natural forms of shelter from wind and rain at any time you find yourself in such conditions; what rain shadow is formed by certain overhangs of buildings or trees, which wall of a square building affords the best shelter to a certain wind, and which sort of daily clothing provides the most effective barrier to cold.

FIRE

Fire is often associated with protection. It is much more than just a means of warding off the cold. It is a most important survival skill to be mastered. Competence in this skill means being able to light a fire under the most adverse conditions with absolute certainty and with the minimum use of survival kit items. While it is simple to write down the benefits a fire gives, it is impossible to describe the fantastic boost to morale in getting a good fire going. A fire will:

1. Protect from the cold;
2. Cook food and purify water;
3. Dry clothes;
4. Signal rescuers, both by day (smoke) and night (flames);
5. Provide protection against insects (smoke and wood ash);
6. Improve tools, e.g., hardening fishing spears, digging sticks, soften wood and metal for easier bending;
7. Preserve food for future consumption.

In short, it provides a great deal of assistance to the survivor. It can also provide a great amount of danger. Minor burns are to be expected, but the danger goes far beyond that. Sparks can ignite a shelter, particularly if it has been up for a few days and the thatching has dried out. Worse still, it has the potential to cause a major woodland fire. Either of these dangers can cause severe injury, or kill. In extinguishing a fire always take the precautions listed and *never* leave a fire unattended for any length of time. In a real survival situation you may not have this option for various reasons, but the fire should be banked as for an overnight fire, by laying the logs parallel and covering it with turf.

Firelighting. The site for the fire will normally be associated with the shelter site. The area around the fireplace should be cleared of inflammable material for six feet (two metres) around. Be careful of overhanging branches, especially in coniferous woods; a high flame can set them alight with dire consequences. First of all remove a turf about two feet (0.6 metres) square and place it to one side, upside down. The turf is replaced when you leave and within a few days it will be difficult to see where the fire has been. The turf should be kept in good condition by an occasional watering, if you have plenty of water. The next stage is to gather the ingredients for a successful fire: tinder, kindling, and fuel.

Tinder converts match flame, or spark, into a flame hot enough and sufficiently long-lasting to ignite the next stage in the fire chain. Dry tinder is something to be sought out at every opportunity, and once found, kept dry and secure. You can never have enough dry tinder. I classify tinder into two groups: spark ignitable tinders and flame ignitable tinders. The spark ignitable might consist of cotton wool; paper handkerchiefs; thistledown or similar seed types such as dandelion or willowherb; teased-out cloth; very dry grass or similar vegetation crumpled into separate fibres, including birds nests and dry leaves. The flame ignitable items include paper; fine wood shavings; very thin twigs; dry bark; resin lumps from coniferous trees; dead spruce or pine needles; and birch bark which will ignite even when damp. Dry tinder can be found even after heavy rain, under logs and overhanging rocks. Dead lower branches are likely to be dry and can be shaved to give fine dry wood shavings or fuzz sticks. The smart survivor collects his tinder when it is dry and keeps it dry until needed. Once the fire is alight, additional tinder can be dried for future use.

Kindling bridges the gap between the tinder and the smallest size of fuel. There may be little difference between thin twigs used as tinder and the twigs used for kindling. The kindling must also be dry enough to ignite from the fairly brief flame the tinder gives, and in turn provide enough heat to ignite the fuel. The best kindling is to be found still attached to the trees. Any on the ground is likely to be damp. It must be dead and matchstick to pencil thickness. Dead wood snaps cleanly when grasped in the hand.

Fuel ranges from wood of pencil thickness to substantial logs and should be fed to the fire in graduated thicknesses, gradually increasing as the fire gets stronger. The first amount of fuel should be dry and may need to be shaved to expose a dry area if wet. Softwood from coniferous trees contains resins which greatly assist ignition and burning. Spruce, pine and fir are all coniferous trees. Hardwoods are a bit more difficult to ignite, but burn with less smoke, last longer and provide good embers for cooking. Ash, beech, oak, birch,

DIRECTION
OF FALL

2ND KERF

1ST KERF

FIG. 14. TREE FELLING

hawthorn, sycamore, willow are examples of hardwood which provide good firewood. Learn to recognize these and the softwoods mentioned above. An ample supply of all three ingredients is necessary before taking even the first steps to lighting the fire. It always takes far more tinder and kindling than you think necessary, and make sure you have an ample supply of suitable fuel. I have seen many fires fizzle out after the initial amount of fuel burned up because the student had not gathered enough.

If a fire is to be put out, it must be done properly. Any unburnt wood is removed and the embers spread out, trampled down and thoroughly doused with water. There should be no trace of smoke from them at all. If an area of turf has been removed, it is now replaced, trampled down, and watered, if you have water to spare.

This procedure eliminates any risk of fire spreading and causes minimum impact to the environment. There are obvious military situations where leaving as little evidence as possible may be desirable, but minimum impact is an end in itself and should be pursued whenever possible. Remembering the advice about being prepared for actual conditions likely to be encountered, you should practise all firelighting procedures in as many types of weather and light conditions before having to tackle them in earnest in the survival situation.

WATER

No matter how extensive your survival kit is, and no matter how experienced in survival skills you may be, you cannot manufacture water. It is possible for the knowledgeable survivor to obtain water from very unlikely sources, but it must be there to start with in some form. No matter how fit and strong you are, and no matter how determined you may be, without water, you will die. Only the time-scale is variable. Survival times of ten days without water are sometimes quoted. This is possible, but the condition of the survivor by then would be desperate. Three days is a more realistic figure in a temperate climate. By that time the survivor will be so desperate he will be inclined to drink liquid that is unfit for consumption thus causing illness and further dehydration. Water is therefore high up the priority scale, even in a temperate climate. If it is practicable the shelter should be sited close to a water supply.

Symptoms of dehydration start with thirst and go through headaches, loss of appetite, flushed skin, nausea, and dizziness. Anyone suffering this range of symptoms is dehydrated to the extent of being ineffective. Further dehydration leads through various other symptoms such as delirium, inability to walk, deafness and thus to death. To maintain efficiency in a temperate climate 2.5 litres of water a day is considered to be the minimum. It is possible to survive on less, but to operate effectively 2.5 litres at least is necessary. If possible, drink more than that. Drinking more than necessary will cause no problems.

If water is scarce, steps should be taken to reduce fluid loss. That applies whether it is hot or cold. In hot weather keep to the shade and keep the skin covered to slow down sweat evaporation. Avoid heavy exercise. Activity should take place during the cooler parts of the day – early morning, late afternoon and evening. In cold weather, prevent sweating by removing excess clothing when exercising. Drink only pure or purified water. Some tree saps are temporary substitutes, but there are many liquids which should not be drunk: sea water – the salt in sea water will draw fluid from the body's reserves speeding up the dehydration process; water containing anti-freeze solution; urine, which has the same effect as sea water; and more obvious fluids such as petrol, oil, paraffin or any similar liquids.

Much of this advice is only common sense, but extreme thirst can lead to taking chances and drinking unfit liquids. The penalty for drinking impure water may be only slightly less severe. Ninety per cent of illness in survival situations, either in training, or real, comes from drinking impure water. Even the most basic reaction of an upset stomach, sickness and/or diarrhoea, has a dehydrating and debilitating effect on the survivor, and as there is likely to be a shortage of medicine and food the recovery time is likely to be long rather than short. During the time the survivor is ill he will be unable or find it difficult to obtain water, food, firewood and generally look after himself. Remember once the liquid has been swallowed, the damage is done and it is almost impossible to undo. It takes very little to make someone sick. On a more general note many of the major epidemic diseases are caused by infected water. On a world-wide basis these diseases include amoebic and bacillary dysentery, cholera and typhoid.

In a temperate climate there is normally no problem in finding water. Making sure it is pure or purifying it is a different matter. The obvious **water sources**, streams, ponds and rivers, hardly need mentioning. Water from these sources should always be purified. In using ground water it is advisable to try and find the source and use the water from there. This is not always practicable, but the further water travels the greater the chance of pollution. Pollution mainly comes from animal matter in the water or from animal faeces. A dead sheep lying in a mountain stream can pollute it, no matter how crystal clear and inviting it may look further downstream. Rather than take water direct from such sources as rivers, ponds and streams, it is best to try and find a spring which feeds into them. A spring may not be too obvious, but can often be found by looking for particularly green and lush vegetation. It may need to be dug out a little to allow access to fill a water-bottle, but this effort is very worthwhile. Even water drawn from a spring should be purified.

Rainwater collected in a clean container, can be used without purification. The container may be a cooking utensil, a plastic sheet, a waterproof jacket, or even absorbent material which can be wrung out into a container or straight into the mouth. To collect water in a plastic sheet, the sheet is laid down in a hollow so that the sides are slightly higher than the rest of the sheet. If a convenient hollow is not available the sides can be raised by logs, stones or propped up with sticks.

Snow and Ice. Ice is much better than snow because it produces more water for the same volume. In melting either snow or ice, it is important to start off with some water in the utensil. If you only put snow or ice into a pot the bottom of the pot will burn before the snow or ice starts to melt. Enough can be melted by holding it at the side of the fire to drip into the pot until it covers the bottom. The pot can then be put on to heat and more snow and ice added gradually until the required amount of water is obtained. Avoid, if possible, sucking snow or ice to melt it in your mouth. As you swallow the very cold water chills the body's core and can cause

FIG. 15. RAINWATER COLLECTION

stomach cramps and vomiting, thereby losing valuable fluid and/or food.

Dew can be collected early in the morning before it evaporates from grass, bushes and tree foliage. Collect it by wiping absorbent material over the dew-laden surface and wringing it out into a container. Grass probably yields the most liquid per square metre, but may also have contaminants, so purification is desirable.

Solar still. This is easily constructed and will produce drinkable quantities of water as a result of condensation. Place a container in the centre of a one metre square hole and cover it with a plastic sheet firmly and evenly secured with soil around the edges, but not touching any part of the interior of the hole. A stone in the centre will weight the plastic down so that as condensation builds up, due

FIG. 16. SOLAR SURVIVAL STILL

THE AIR UNDER THE PLASTIC SHEET HEATS UP AND BECOMES SATURATED WITH MOISTURE FROM SOIL AND/OR VEGETATION IN THE PIT. WHEN SATURATED AIR CONTACTS PLASTIC SHEET IT CONDENSES AND WATER DROPLETS RUN DOWN AND DRIP INTO CONTAINER.

FIG. 17. RIVERBANK FILTER

AS THE WATER FROM THE STREAM OR POND SEEPS INTO THE PIT DUG ABOUT 1.5 METRES FROM THE EDGE, THE INTERVENING EARTH ACTS AS A FILTER.

to sun-to-ground water evaporation, the water drips into the container below. To avoid removing and replacing the sheet a tube could have been inserted at the outset which allows the user to drink at leisure from the collection point without upsetting the delicate conditions under the sheet. A variation on this is achieved by placing a plastic bag around vegetation and sealing it; when the plant transpires, water vapour is emitted which condenses and collects on the plastic.

Filtration and Purification. Sometimes, but only occasionally, water may be drinkable just as it comes, but usually it will need to be filtered and/or purified. If the water is clear filtration will not be necessary. Some water may be dark – if it has travelled through peat, for example – but this is all right; in any event, filtering will not remove the dark colour because it only removes small solid particles. Water that needs to be filtered should always be purified as well. The absolute importance of pure water cannot be overstressed; contaminated water is likely to be the biggest danger you will face in survival or during the Challenge.

FOOD AND COOKING

Finding sufficient food in a survival situation is extremely difficult. Forget any notion of 'living off the land'. Think instead of 'surviving off the land'. At best only enough food for basic survival can be expected. If operating on or near the coast the food situation is easier, but in general, getting enough food from the countryside is very difficult. Obtaining food can be considered as a simple equation. The food gathered *must* produce more calories than you use in obtaining it. Add to this equation the fact that fairly large quantities of natural food are required, and you begin to see the size of the problem. The environment and the time of year may be additional complications.

In short-term survival and survival training, food is not a priority. Survival times in excess of three weeks without food can be expected, and a few days or even a week without food is no real problem. The exception would be where high carbohydrate food is used to generate body heat in a situation where there is a potential risk of hyperthermia. That circumstance is why survival rations are carried.

Normal food requirements average out at about 1,700 calories per day to keep the body supplied in a mainly resting state – sleeping, sitting, standing, etc. Even non-energetic activity requires a further 450–500 calories. Heavy physical effort may easily increase the energy expenditure to 3,500 calories. To try to achieve this amount of calorie intake in survival would be extremely difficult indeed. The required calorie intake can be reduced by conserving energy. Rest as much as possible; do not chop firewood if it can be put on the fire and burnt through into manageable lengths; do not wander about to no purpose. If gathering food, try to gather as much on each trip as possible. Improvise a means of carrying plant foods. You will need a lot, and a bag is very useful. Never return to the shelter empty-handed; bring back food, water, firewood, even fresh bedding.

Compare the energy value of survival rations with that of the most commonly available natural foods. There is a very big difference between them. A selection of wild foods is quoted here to illustrate this. The values are given for quantities of 100 grams or about four ounces:

Green-leaf wild foods (dandelion, nettle, plantain, etc.)	140 calories
Bramble	28 calories
Bilberry	64 calories
Trout	100 calories
Rabbit (there is no fat in rabbit meat).	100 calories

A much higher food value can be obtained from:

Hazlenuts	432 calories
Beechnuts	640 calories
Duck egg (each)	170 calories

Unfortunately, these higher calorie foods are seasonal and for a short period at that. Chocolate has approximately 650 calories per 100 grams. To come close to the minimum normal requirement of 1,700 calories takes a large volume of wild food, and a lot of energy to gather it. Conservation of energy is therefore as important as the gathering of food.

Studies conducted for the Canadian Air Force suggest that a man can survive for a long time on 500 calories a day without any permanent ill effects. Obtaining this amount of food is a much more practical proposition. Ideally the diet should contain a balance between protein, carbohydrate and fat, that is, between animal and vegetable foods. In reality, however, the survivor would need to make do with whatever he could get and the same applies in survival training. A plentiful supply of easily obtained food is more valuable than a nice variety of food that is difficult to obtain. A supply of water is essential before any food is eaten. The digestion process uses up the body's liquid reserves, particularly the digestion of protein and fat. The same warning applies to food as to water. Apart from the elements, the biggest danger to a survivor's health will come from what he eats and drinks.

As **vegetable foods** (and fishing) feature in the Challenge section, suffice to say here that the idea is to be able to identify those edible plants that are plentiful and therefore easy to obtain. A good field guide is an invaluable asset for this. It will not only show the plant in colour, but will give details of size, habitat, and distribution of the plants. The aspiring survivalist is in the position of learning which plants are edible and then trying to familiarize himself with them as opposed to finding plants in the wild and then trying to establish their edibility or otherwise. Vegetable foods are likely to upset the stomach if eaten in large quantities. Eat little and often to minimize the upsetting effect, and allow the stomach time to adjust to a new diet. The volume of food can then be increased gradually. You should remember that many common plants are poisonous. Plants such as Deadly Nightshade, Buttercup, Foxglove, Giant Hogweed and trees such as Yew, Laurel and Laburnum can make you very ill indeed.

I do not recommend that fungi be experimented with at all. Fungi recognition is best learned from an expert in the subject. For that reason there is no reference to edible fungi in this book. Even with a good field guide it is quite easy to make a mistake, particularly when the fungi are in the 'button' stage. Temperate climates produce some very dangerous fungi, and some are *deadly poisonous*. The most deadly of all – the Death Cap – can kill even if only a small amount is consumed. The first symptoms may not show for 48 hours and there is no known antidote. Identifying and trying out wild plant food is an important part of preparation. Avoid picking plants from the roadside, where they might be contaminated with exhaust fumes, or from field edges where they may have been sprayed with insecticide.

Pound for pound **animal food** provides the greatest amount of nourishment. It is especially rich in protein and fat. Rabbit is an exception to this as it contains little or no fat. It is however the most readily available form of animal food in a survival situation. Animal food is not as easy to come by as plant food, despite what you may read in some survival books. The techniques of trapping should be studied and the principles understood by any serious student of survival, but they need not and should not be used in survival training. Some of the methods can cause pain and suffering to the animals and their use can only be justified in extreme circumstances. They cannot be justified for training purposes. In any event, survival trapping techniques are illegal in most countries and their use would only be condoned in a real survival situation. Trap construction and setting can be practised as a separate skill and to that purpose I detail some different types of traps that are suitable for catching small game. Even in a survival situation small game is the best type to go for. Larger animals can be trapped, but they may not be killed in the trap, and personally I would not want to catch anything that is bigger than I am.

Apart from the simple snare, the most important element of the trap is the trigger mechanism. The illustrations show a variety of triggers and the different principles shown can be used with a variety of traps, limited only by your imagination. Experiment with the different types of triggers to discover how to set them light and heavy. A reliable trigger is

FIG. 18. STANDARD SNARE

ATTACHED TO SECURE PEG AND SITUATED ON ANIMAL RUN.

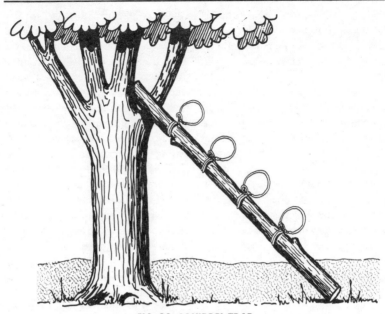

FIG. 19. SQUIRREL TRAP

A SERIES OF STANDARD SNARES ON A POLE.

FIG. 20. ROOST SNARE

A SERIES OF STANDARD SNARES PLACED TO CATCH ROOSTING BIRDS.

FIG. 21. SNARE-PULL TRIGGER (1)

MADE TO CATCH AROUND THE NECK: AS THE ANIMAL CATCHES THE NOOSE IT PULLS THE TRIGGER OFF THE PEG.

NATURAL TRIGGER STICKS

CARVED TRIGGER STICKS

FIG. 22. SNARE-PULL TRIGGER (2)

the best guarantee of a successful trap.

Under the heading of animal foods I should also like to consider fish and birds. With animals and birds there is no point in setting traps unless there is some indication that they are about. They may be seen of course,

but the more usual signs will be evidence of droppings, feeding, and tracks.

There are many varieties of traps, but it is better to understand the principles and adapt them to suit the actual situation. The traps shown in the illustrations are a representative

FIG. 23. STEP-ON TRIGGER (1)

AS ANIMAL'S FOOT HITS AND DISLODGES TRIGGER STICK, BENT SAPLING TIGHTENS SNARE AROUND LEG. USED FOR LARGE ANIMALS.

FIG. 24. STEP-ON TRIGGER (2)

AS ANIMAL STEPS ON TRIGGER PLATFORM, ITS WEIGHT PUSHES TRIGGER BAR DOWN RELEASING TRIGGER, AND BENT SAPLING TIGHTENS SNARE AROUND LEG. USED FOR LARGE ANIMALS.

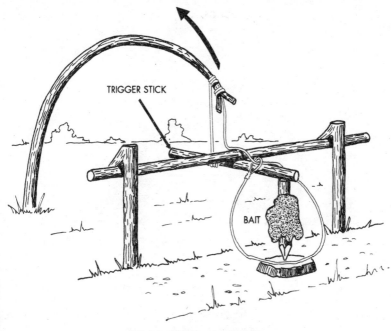

TRIGGER STICK

BAIT

FIG. 25. BAIT-PULL TRIGGER

AS ANIMAL TAKES THE BAIT IT RELEASES THE TRIGGER ALLOWING BENT SAPLING TO CLOSE SNARE LOOP AROUND ITS NECK.

selection showing various trigger mechanisms, and are divided into snares and deadfall traps. When using a twitch stick with a trap, keep the head and face well away from the area above the trap when setting. The trap may spring when adjusting the trigger setting and if the twitch stick hits the face it could cause injury. With baited traps it is essential that they be fenced with stakes or brushwood to guide the animal to enter from the correct direction that will ensure its capture. Even with runway traps it helps if obstructions are placed to make it difficult for the animal to avoid the trap. Animals are very wary of anything contaminated with human scent. Do not cut the

various items to be used in the trap construction at the trap site. Cut them elsewhere and bring them to the site. Human scent can be disguised in a variety of ways – smoke or flame destroys it and does not alarm the animals. Animal urine or droppings rubbed on also disguises the scent. If this is not possible the trap may need to be left for several days for the scent to 'weather' away.

Trap manufacture is an art which can be learnt quite easily, as it is a simple mechanical skill. What is difficult is knowing where to set the trap and what type to set under various circumstances. Time spent in the countryside in survival training gives a unique opportunity to observe

GUIDE STEADY POSTS
IF NECESSARY

FIG. 26. ROLL TRIGGER (1)

FIG. 27. ROLL TRIGGER (2)

the habits of animals and birds and become familiar with their habitats and feeding habits. It is the detailed knowledge of his quarry that makes for a successful trapper.

The importance of effective **cooking** when living in rough and tough conditions cannot be overstated. Hunger can reduce physical and mental strength and with every moment the feeling grows worse, yet satisfying the need for food not only repairs the body, but if done by dint of your own initiative and survival techniques, is psychologically rewarding. Going without food may not be a problem in survival training, or even in the short-term in a real survival situation. Procuring and preparing food is an important skill in the survivalist's repertoire, and should not be neglected just because some of the foods are 'weeds' or are life forms normally stamped on rather than eaten. If you

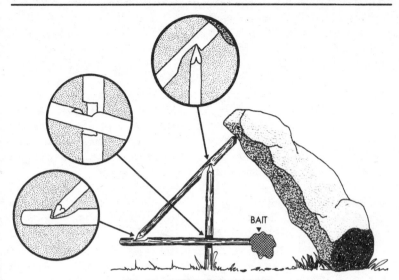

FIG. 28. FIGURE FOUR TRIGGER

NOTE:
ALL SNARES MUST BE CHECKED MORNING AND EVENING AND LEG SNARES MUST BE CHECKED FOUR TIMES PER DAY.

have eaten something unusual once you will give little thought to eating it again and gradually you will extend your 'palate'. Basic survival cooking is exactly that – basic. It can be appetizing and even very tasty, but the limited choice of food and/or cooking utensils means that variety is unlikely. In survival or survival training, the point is to eat to live rather than living to eat, as is perhaps more normal in everyday life. Abandon any thoughts of normal eating, and what is acceptable. If it is edible, eat it. Nourishment will be hard to come by.

The maximum nourishment is obtained from a soup or a stew, eating the meat and/or vegetables and drinking the liquid. The ingredients are the same. If you have a lot of ingredients and a little water, you are making a stew. If you have few ingredients and a lot of water you are making soup. In both cases the meat ingredients should be cut into small pieces and brought to the boil and then allowed to simmer for two to three hours. Soups and stews are the best way of cooking some of the less appetizing foods such as, worms, grubs and insects. It is best to cook all foods if possible, especially animal foods which may contain parasites harmful to man and need cooking to destroy them. Fish should be cooked as soon as possible after being caught as they can go off very quickly indeed if the weather is warm. If you have a plentiful supply of fish, they can be preserved by smoking them.

NAVIGATION

As hunger can dispirit the most ardent survivalist, so the feeling of disorientation is one of the most frightening senses known to man. It is most unlikely that those taking part in the Survival Challenge will, in early tests at least, place themselves in a situation where minor errors in route-finding cannot be easily corrected. Again, as with hunger, the confidence and satisfaction that comes from efficient navigation has immense benefit, apart from the certainty of knowing where you are. The element of energy saving is crucially helped by avoiding strenuous or time-consuming routes through skilled navigation and map-reading.

A map and compass open up avenues of understanding to anyone who takes their recreation in the hills or moorlands. The map gives a picture of the terrain and can be used to provide a picture of an area without actually seeing it. The compass allows routes to be plotted and followed with the certainty that your destination will be reached. It allows you to find your position if lost, and is an essential item in misty conditions to enable you to maintain your correct course. The best map to use is the Ordnance Survey type, which shows height by means of contour lines. These are available in a variety of scales; for walkers, the scale of 1:50000 is the smallest scale that is useful. The 1:25000 scale map gives more detail, but there may not be a sheet to cover the area you want. The phrase 'reading the map like a book' is often quoted but this only comes with a lot of practice. The most important skill in map reading is the ability to translate the lines on the map into the actual shape of the terrain. It is for this reason that a map such as an Ordnance Survey one is desirable as the contour lines are the most accurate method of doing this.

Gradients, hills, valleys, spurs, rivers, intervisibility, are all important to understand for route planning. Understanding these physical features means understanding contour lines and what the patterns of the contours represent. Contour lines are shown in brown on the map and represent points of the same height. The distance between the lines shows increase or decrease in height. The height interval and the distance between the lines gives an accurate representation of the steepness of the terrain and good interpretation of these lines is the major skill for the outdoorsman to master. In survival travelling it is best to avoid gaining or losing too much height unless forced to do so by the terrain or weather. If you have a map available, intelligent route planning can save a great deal of effort. This is a skill that can best be mastered on the ground with a map in your hand; contour lines on the map take on a real meaning when the legs have walked up them in reality.

A reliable and accurate **compass** is an essential companion to the map. Most times, in clear visibility, the compass will not be needed, but in poor visibility the compass, and the ability to use it, can become a lifesaver. As with other outdoor gear, quality is the key and to this add absolute reliability because when a compass becomes essential, you are in a potentially dangerous situation.

The best type of compass for cross-country work is one which incor-

FIG. 29. TYPICAL PROTRACTOR COMPASS

porates a baseplate. This is generally known as the 'Silva type', and has the dual purpose of compass and protractor. The protractor is the means of laying off the course on the map. Other manufacturers make this type of compass apart from Silva – Recta and Suunto being the best known. Only buy a compass made by a reliable manufacturer, and check that it has these necessary features for accurate navigation:

1. The capsule should be filled with liquid to dampen the needle's oscillations as it settles to magnetic north.

2. The graduations on the rotating housing should be no more than two-degree intervals.

3. The housing should be easy to turn when wearing gloves.

4. There should be a linear scale on the baseplate for measuring distances on the map. These are the basic requirements, but additional capabilities might be:

(a) Luminous reading marks, needle point.

(b) Sighting mirror or prism.

(c) Adjustment capability for magnetic variation.

(d) Clinometer needle for measuring slope angle.

As the sophistication increases so does the price; as long as the basic features are there the rest are optional extras.

A **route card** is a most useful aid to navigation. It is filled in when route planning at base, and a copy left with someone giving instructions what to do if you fail to turn up by your latest check-in time. If it is left with Police or Rescue Post they will automatically go into action if you fail to check-in. This is very important if you are going alone, and it is essential that you stick to the check-in arrangements otherwise rescue services may be called out unnecessarily. The route card is also very handy when travelling on a series of compass bearings. It shows the bearings and distances between way points. It is much easier to plan the route and establish bearings in comfort at base. The card is kept in a pocket and referred to *en route*. It is very difficult to lay out a route and work out bearings during bad weather in the field. A sample card is shown illustrating the kind of information that may be included.

Before **survival navigation** can be learned, an understanding of conventional navigation using map and compass is essential. It should not be assumed, however, that survival navigation is as precise as navigation

OBJECTIVE						TERRAIN	REMARKS
DATE:-							
O.S. SHEET No.		COMPASS BEARING	DISTANCE KMS.	ASCENTS METRES	TIME		
FROM	TO						
GRID REF	GRID REF						
TIME IN:		DATE:					
TIME OUT:		DATE:					
NAME:							

▲ **FIG. 30. ROUTE CARD**

▲ STEP 1   **FIG. 31. NAVIGATION**   STEP 2 ▲

1. LAY COMPASS ON MAP, STRAIGHT EDGE JOINING START-POSITION AND DESTINATION, WITH DIRECTION OR TRAVEL ARROW TOWARDS DESTINATION.

2. TURN HOUSING UNTIL ORIENTING LINES ARE PARALLEL WITH N–S GRID LINES, WITH ORIENTING ARROW TOWARDS THE TOP OF THE MAP

using map and compass. The basis of survival navigation is to establish one or more cardinal points of the compass (north, south, east, west) and using this information to estimate or crudely measure the bearing of the desired direction of travel.

There are refined methods of survival navigation, but all require the use of tables and/or the drawing of

ADJUST FOR DECLINATION

▲ STEP 3   ▼ STEP 4   STEP 5 ▶

SIGHT TO LANDMARK

3. READ BEARING AND ADJUST FOR DECLINATION (MAGNETIC VARIATION) USING DATA ON MAP MARGIN. IF DECLINATION IS WEST – ADD TO GRID BEARING. IF DECLINATION IS EAST – SUBTRACT FROM GRID BEARING.

4. USING ADJUSTED BEARING, HOLD COMPASS WITH DIRECTION OF TRAVEL ARROW POINTING AWAY FROM BODY AND TURN UNTIL MAGNETIC NEEDLE LINES UP WITH ORIENTING ARROW.

5. SIGHT ALONG THE DIRECTION OF TRAVEL ARROW AND SELECT A CONVENIENT LANDMARK.

6. WALK TO LANDMARK AND REPEAT PROCEDURE UNTIL DESTINATION IS REACHED.

very accurate diagrams, and need procedures that can in no way be described as simple or easy to remember. The main purpose of the techniques, when combined with cross-country movement methods, will allow the survivor to make progress in the desired direction and, more importantly, prevent him getting lost and wandering in circles.

It is essential that navigation can be carried out using only natural phenomena, as our forefathers did centuries ago during the eras of the great explorations. Many of the techniques used then are still perfectly valid today and to these have been added methods learned due to contact with primitive peoples all over the world. Many of the more sophisticated navigation methods in use today measure precisely the position of various heavenly bodies. The survivor does not have the instruments, but he can

estimate the positions of the same heavenly bodies to come up with a cruder navigational plan that will still be perfectly valid. The heavenly bodies have to be split up into specific star constellations at night, and the sun during the day. The most useful constellations are: **The Pole Star.** This is the best direction indicator of all as it never deviates more than one degree from true north, and is at its best height in the temperate latitudes. Further south it is very low in the sky, often reducing its visibility, and further north it is too high to be easily used as a direction indicator. In the southern hemisphere it is not visible at all and the best direction indicator is the **Southern Cross**, which is not as easy to find as the Pole Star. It is situated to the right of a dark area of sky, which has virtually no stars in it. The datum point for south is measured along the longest axis four-

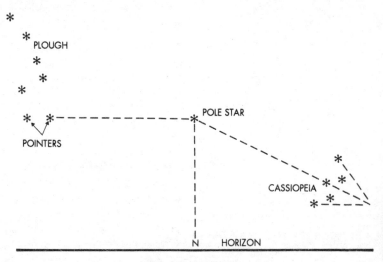

FIG. 32. POLE STAR

USES 'POINTERS' ON THE PLOUGH OR BISECT THE ANGLE ON CASSIOPEIA TO FIND THE POLE STAR.

and-a-half times the length of the constellation from the bottom star. **Orion** is a useful constellation, but it is not always visible. When it can be seen it is on the other side of the sky from the Pole Star and is used when clouds obscure the Pole Star.

Star movement can only be taken as a rough guide. Because the stars apparently rotate around the Pole Star, if a star is observed over two fixed points for about fifteen minutes, it will be seen to move:

1. If the star is rising, you will be facing East.
2. If the star is falling, you will be facing West.
3. If the star is looping to the right, you will be facing South.
4. If the star is looping to the left, you will be facing North.

When using this method choose a star low down in the sky, both for easy sighting and for maximum movement.

Navigation by **the sun** is the method of most use to the survivor when travelling during the day. If you have a watch, you can establish direction from the sun with a good degree of accuracy, or failing that, several varities of sun compass can be constructed, which give various degrees of accuracy.

The moon reflects the light from the sun, and if the moon rises before the sun sets, the illuminated side will be on the west. If the moon rises some time after the sun sets, the illuminated side will be on the east. If the moon rises at the same time as the sun sets, it will be full and its position in the sky is as follows:

Time	Direction of full moon
1800	East
2100	South-East
2359	South
0300	South-West
0600	West

There will be times when none of the celestial bodies are visible due to weather conditions and it is then that **natural signposts** come into their own. They are not as precise as the celestial bodies and their use needs to be treated with caution and double checking. Tree and plant growth as affected by the sun and prevailing wind are the most reliable way of

FIG. 33. ORION

PROJECT LINE UP OVERHEAD AND DOWN TO HORIZON TO FIND NORTH (APPROXIMATELY).

using natural signposts, and some means of averaging should be used to avoid being fooled by a 'rogue' sign. The Challenge is an ideal way of trying survival navigation against map and compass.

It is worth remembering that trees will normally grow the most foliage on their sunny side, which is the southern side in the northern hemisphere. Conifers will be bushier there, and willows and poplars will lean towards that side. Trees can also provide clues if they have been felled; most people know that you can tell a tree's age by the number of rings but most people don't know that where those rings are widest apart indicates the northern side. Such pointers may well prove very useful in a survival situation. Obviously, if these facts fit for the northern hemisphere then the opposite is the case for the southern hemisphere. Conversely mosses will favour the dark and damp side of host objects; if you therefore combine both elements a general direction indicator is available in most situations. Another useful tip, for coastal areas only though, is the fact that winds blow offshore in the morning and onshore in the evening. Being armed with these 'nuggets' will improve your confidence but they are not foolproof methods. They do make a test scenario that much more interesting though.

MENTAL ASPECTS OF SURVIVAL

It is impossible to create a totally realistic survival situation during a survival test. The test or challenge must be covered by adequate safety precautions and this, by definition, means that it cannot be a true survival situation. Physical challenges can be set closely to approximate the physical problems likely to arise during a survival situation, and these will to some extent create some of the mental stresses that arise in survival. Although in the Challenge you will not be exposed to the same extremes of mental stress that you should be prepared to encounter, all the stresses will definitely be there to a lesser degree. It is important not to try to ignore these problems, but to tackle them head on and recognize that understanding the problems goes a long way to reducing them and making that knowledge work for you. **Fear** is probably the major emotion to begin with, and how it is handled influences the chances of survival. If it is allowed free rein it will lead to

FIG. 34.

DIRECTION BY TREE GROWTH (SUN)

SOUTHERN ASPECT

panic. It comes in a variety of forms: fear of the unknown, fear of being lost, fear of open spaces, fear of being unable to cope, and probably many others. Physical conditions of climate and terrain may exacerbate that fear. Lack of knowledge will certainly increase it.

This lack of knowledge in turn leads to lack of confidence in your ability to cope and thus a possible reluctance to try anything that might improve your situation. Appropriate preparation in mastering the skills and an honest evaluation of your own personality will do much to minimize many of these fears, but there will always be some present. Much of the preparation should be aimed at ways of combating the enemies of survival: pain, cold (or heat), thirst, fatigue, hunger, boredom and loneliness. Everyone has experienced these at some time or other, but it is unlikely that they will have experienced them all together in the compressed time-scale likely to occur in a survival situation. The physical problems can be prepared for by virtue of adequate preparation in the form of a mastery of skills, and/or the use of appropriate equipment or natural resources; knowledge of edible plants, likely places to obtain water, which types of woods are good for lighting a fire and which are better for keeping it going. Information of this nature augments the skills, but still on a somewhat physical level.

In addition to the physical problems the enemies of survival might present, there is also a mental dimension which must be addressed. The fear of these enemies can be a powerful emotion and it can in turn lead to panic and irrational action or in some cases complete inaction. It is impossible to specify a procedure that will apply in detail to every possible survival situation that could arise. A set of guidelines for tackling the mental shock that would inevitably accompany the transition into a survival scenario can be set down. The immediate action plan is largely a mental exercise and will help to push the fear and panic out of the mind. This plan will change you from a victim into a survivor. It is built around the mnemonic **RIPE** – Remove, Inspect, Protect, Evaluate:

Remove
From immediate danger, e.g., flooding river, landslide area, weather hazard.

Inspect
1. For injury and treat if necessary.
2. Any available survival equipment.
3. Other items that may be of use in survival, e.g., clothing, contents of pockets, part of vehicles.

Protect
1. Organize temporary shelter from weather if necessary.
2. Decide if some movement is necessary to achieve temporary protection, e.g., move to the lee side of a hill.
3. Decide on other survival priorities.

Evaluate
1. Your current location. How close does it come to meeting your survival priorities?
2. Whether to stay in close proximity or try to travel out, and how a

decision affects the chances of rescue.

3. When to organize some means of signalling possible rescuers.

Possible reasons for staying where you are:

(a) The possibility of rescue is high.
(b) Travel would be dangerous due to terrain or weather.
(c) Injury or poor physical condition.
(d) The probability of ending up in a worse condition, through inability to navigate adequately.
(e) There is access to items to assist survival.

Possible reasons for moving:

(a) Your current location is dangerous.
(b) Your current location lacks vital survival needs, e.g., water or material for shelter building.
(c) Your whereabouts are unknown and rescue is unlikely.
(d) You have information that will enable you to navigate to safety.
(e) You have suitable equipment for travel, particularly footwear and food supplies.

Under the heading 'Protect' I mentioned priorities. The accepted order of priorities is generally:

(1) First Aid   (4) Water
(2) Protection   (5) Signalling
(3) Fire   (6) Food.

Conditions can change the order of these priorities. Weather conditions could easily render Protection and Fire more important than minor First Aid. Signalling could also move up the list if there is a possibility that a search will be imminent. A way of establishing the priorities order in a particular situation is by considering them in the light of the Neglect Factor which ranks the priorities in the order that they might kill: *First Aid* – serious bleeding can kill in minutes, minor injuries can be ignored; *Protection and Fire* – exposure to cold, wet and wind can kill in as little as one hour; *Water* – lack of water can kill in days; *Food* – lack of food can kill in weeks; *Signalling* – if a rescue is expected, signalling may be at the top of the list of priorities. These time-scales are on the extreme side and will be affected by climate (hot/

SERIOUS INJURY
NEED DOCTOR

NEED MEDICINE

UNABLE
TO PROCEED

ALL WELL

NO   YES   NOT UNDERSTOOD

FIG. 35. GROUND TO AIR SYMBOLS (MARKERS)

ALL OK   PICK ME UP   NEED MEDICAL HELP   WILL PROCEED
DON'T WAIT   WAIT IF POSSIBLE

FIG. 36. GROUND TO AIR SIGNALS (BODY)

cold) and terrain (high/low), but will assist in setting appropriate survival priorities as part of the survival plan.

Many of the mental problems that arise can be reduced or even eliminated by appropriate training and the availability of survival equipment. Individual fitness also plays a part inasmuch as it affects the survivor's ability to handle the physical challenge and his ability to travel. Additionally, there are personal attributes which will greatly improve the survivor's chances:

Knowledge and Training. Take every opportunity to increase knowledge and to prove it by practise.

Adaptability. Make the best of the situation and adapt to cope with those things that cannot be changed, e.g., terrain, weather.

Ability to Improvise. Real situations are never as neat and tidy as are shown in books. Knowledge is used as a basis from which to improvise to suit actual circumstances.

Willingness to Try. Do not be put off because something is difficult, will take a long time, or you do not know for certain if it will work. While caution is necessary sometimes, do not succumb to over-caution.

Patience. There are few instant solutions in survival. Most activities take time. Have the patience to see them through.

Persistence. Do not be put off by failure, keep trying. Activities such as food-gathering, particularly trapping and fishing, require a great deal of persistence.

Mental stresses, I am sure, play as big a part in survival as physical challenges. Indeed they may play a bigger part, as anyone who is unable to cope with survival on a mental plane is unlikely to last long enough to meet many physical challenges. On the other hand there are many documented cases of people, who for various reasons of ignorance, handicap or injury, were unable to respond to physical challenges, but survived by sheer will and determination to live. People have died in circumstances where they had equipment and the theoretical knowledge to survive, because they made wrong or stupid decisions when faced with the mental stress of a survival situation.

The combating of mental stress does

not easily lend itself to a formula approach, but the antidote can surely be only mental or physical activity. Use the stress as a guide to the remedy. If you are afraid of being cold, use this as the spur to get a fire going, or collect more firewood or improve your shelter. If you are lonely or bored, occupy yourself with mental or physical activity. If you are worried or afraid because you do not feel well, do something about it, even if it is only keeping warm and drinking plenty of water. If you do not think you can cope, set yourself a simple task you know you can complete to build your confidence. If you are injured or in pain, treat yourself somehow, even if it is only bathing the injury with sterilized water and applying some medicinal plant.

It is not possible to make a complete list of appropriate responses to the variety of possible situations, personalities and characteristics, but as part of your preparation for your Challenge that is something you can do. The principles are easily stated – *DO NOT GIVE IN – MAKE A PLAN – DO SOMETHING* that will improve your situation, will make you feel better and will clear your mind for the important business of Survival. It will require a strong will and a lot of determination and you may not feel like trying. But if you do not try, you will fail the Challenge. If you do try, and meet the Challenge, you will attain a measure of satisfaction, sense of achievement and self-confidence in having succeeded in this, man's first and most important ability, which most people have now sadly lost, and which is difficult to duplicate in any other endeavour.

THE CHALLENGE

When the basic skills have been mastered there comes a time to challenge your ability to apply these skills, which may have been learned gradually over a period of time, in a situation that resembles a true survival situation as closely as possible. Although we have already accepted that there will be some artificiality in any challenge, it is possible to devise a scenario where, unless you apply and perfect appropriate techniques, you will pay the penalty of being cold, hungry, wet, miserable, lonely, fed-up, and prey to the temptation to give in and get back to normality. This type of scenario probably comes as close as is possible in a test situation, particularly if you tackle the Challenge alone.

A realistic length of time for such a Challenge would be four or five days and certainly not less than three, otherwise it could just become an exercise in endurance and not an opportunity to hone your survival skills and learn from experience what really works, and more importantly, what does not. A word of warning, however, should be given. With this type of test, which can be extreme and has the potential for accidents, it is **essential** that safety measures be taken to allow for anything that might go wrong. Appropriate precautions are:

1. Someone must know roughly where you will be at any time and when and where you will turn up on completion.
2. An agreed method of signalling if anything goes wrong. This method must be guaranteed to work.

To pre-empt the need to implement these safety measures there is a requirement to carry some safety gear with you which it is to be hoped you will never use.

The safety gear needed depends on the terrain and the time of year. A sleeping-bag and bivi-bag would be normal safety equipment, with perhaps a mini-flare kit if the safety check is to be by signalling. If you feel this amount of precaution seems excessive, you have not got the correct mental attitude. Survival is dependent on taking the necessary safeguards and avoiding unnecessary risks; and in any event think of the embarrassment in needing to be rescued while testing yourself in survival. It is important not to neglect these precautions. The scenario I devised was mainly dependent on the availability of suitable terrain to try to encompass as many survival skills as possible. I am fortunate to have access to areas that offer a variety of terrain and are separated by enough distance to make travelling on foot between them a challenge in itself. These areas are used by arrangement with the farmers who own some of the ground and by courtesy of the Forestry Commission. The terrain is a mix of high moorland and different forest types, and thus presents a wide variety of problems and requires a host of different skills.

The Challenge began on high moorland; Day two was spent in moving to a more suitable location with an overnight stop to try to obtain food; Day three completed the move to the final location and the construction of a more permanent survival camp; finally, Day four established the routine for obtaining food and refining the camp site. Most of day five was spent in dismantling the camp and returning the environment to its natural state and then walking out. The season was early spring.

The amount and variety of kit taken on such a test is, of necessity, a bit more elaborate than a survival kit in a tin. One of the objectives of the exercise was to gain expertise in the use of various items of kit and to evaluate their usefulness. In addition to my normal survival tin, I took: a double survival bag; three hexamine blocks; a Poncho; a Golok; a lock knife; a magnesium firelighter; a Small first aid kit; waterproof matches; emergency rations (chocolate and Brix); and safety gear consisting of a light-weight sleeping-bag and a torch. One of the bivi-bags was orange in case it was required for signalling. A little paracord and a couple of plastic bags completed the outfit, and this, together with wet weather gear of waterproof jacket and trousers, was carried in a small daypack rucksack. A belt with the survival kit, lock knife, and magnesium firelighter was worn. Clothing was generally in line with that stated in the section on preparation: boots; socks – one pair thick, one pair thin; thermal vest; shirt; wind shirt; woollen hat.

An additional item was a prototype survival knife which I had designed and was intending to test thoroughly. I designed this knife because although for practical use I emphatically favour a large knife such as a Golok, its very size does not make it convenient to carry on every occasion. I therefore wanted to experiment with a smaller design that could, in the main, be as effective as the larger knife and in some circumstances an improvement to the Golok by using a better quality steel and by making the blade shape different to create a sharp point. There are already knives of this size and type on the market, but the cheaper models do not use a very high-quality steel and the more expensive models are exactly that – more expensive!

I also wanted to see if I could devise a strong method of attaching a hollow handle to the blade without the inherent weakness of this type of design. The blade shape was of a modified Bowie design with a very short false edge to improve the strength at the point. The blade thickness was 'beefed up' for the same reason. The materials I chose for the prototype were medium carbon steel for the blade and aluminium for the handle. The blade material would not necessarily be the final type, but it was good enough to test the design, was fairly easy to work with and would still hold an edge for a reasonable length of time. An appropriate grade of stainless steel would be used for the final blade material once the design and construction was thoroughly tested. As to the manufacture, I shaped the blade myself using a variety of files and emery paper. A friend with a small lathe machined the handle and I had the cross-guard and handle support brazed in position. The handle was retained in position using a socket head screw which can be bought at any good ironmongers.

Fully equipped and brim full of confidence, I was ready for the Challenge itself.

DAY ONE

I began at the edge of some high moorland terrain at 1930 hours. I would travel up into this area and try to find a place to spend the night, thus simulating a situation of being trapped overnight in open ground. I would find somewhere in the next two or three hours as it got dark at about 2200 or 2230 hours in that part of the country. It was cold when I started out and the short-term weather forecast was for rain. I put on the belt which held my survival kit, knife and firelighter. The larger Golok was carefully packed in my rucksack as there would be no need for it in the immediate future. It is best not to go about festooned with a variety of knives even in remote areas. I also carried my waterproofs in my pack, because although it was threatening to rain I do not like to put on waterproofs until I actually need them. The first stage of my trek was uphill and even with a lightweight pack weighing only about twelve pounds (six kilograms) it would be warm work. My heading would be approximately due east. At this stage I had no specific route planned, but I intended to climb the hill to the top of an escarpment to see what I could find by way of a shelter site. The first stage was over a field which was being grazed by sheep; this makes for very easy walking and broke me in nicely as I like to start off slowly and gradually work up to full pace. I could see, where the field ended, that the next phase would be over heather, but could not tell from this distance how dense it was. The hill was becoming steeper and I had to shorten my stride; the idea is to maintain a steady rhythm and to lengthen or shorten the stride according to the terrain. Careful foot placement was not too essential at this stage, as the ground was fairly flat, but I was still trying to make sure of my footing by placing the whole of the foot down as opposed to the normal heel first method of town walking.

The field was bordered by a dry-stone wall that would be a good windbreak, but I was heading higher up into a wilder area before looking for a place to settle down for the night. As I came up to the wall I looked for a solid place to climb over; some walls of this type are only loosely built and climbing on them can easily cause them to collapse. Having found a suitable place, I climbed over carefully. There was a sheep track on the other side, but it was at right angles to my intended route and was of no use at all; my worst fears about the heather were confirmed as it was thick and deep, the most difficult kind to walk through. Travelling over this kind of ground is very tiring because each foot has to be lifted high with every step and the contours of the ground are hidden so you have to take a great deal of care when stepping forward. It is essential to watch precisely where you step, and while doing this it is all too easy to wander from the desired course. I got out my compass and took a rough bearing by setting the compass dial to 90 degrees and turning to align the needle with the orienting lines, then looking along the line of travel arrow to find a landmark to walk to. As the ground was still sloping upward I could see only about 200 metres in front, but there was a boulder on the line of my route which would do as a marker. I started through the heather and every twenty paces or so I stopped to look up to make sure that I was still on course. The slope had steepened to the extent that it was becoming extremely difficult to ascend. I was glad to reach the boulder, stop and take another bearing.

The top of the escarpment was now in sight, about another 400 metres ahead and the slope to the top was easier. The next landmark was the right-hand side of a small mound at the top and I set off again to complete the ascent and have a well-earned rest. At the top the ground ahead was fairly level, but still covered with heather. Over to my left a small stream had cut a valley and along the side of the valley the heather had given way to short moorland grass. As this was aligned along my intended route, I chose to walk along the side of the valley rather than through the heather. On flat plateaux such as this the sides of streams are often the driest areas because they are better drained; the flat, level areas can be boggy with water which tends to lie there. By now I had been travelling for about an hour and wanted to go on for another thirty minutes before looking for a shelter site. A bearing of about 45° from where I stood would take me to the northern edge of the escarpment where I would find the best terrain on which to shelter. The threatened rain had now started and I decided to put on my waterproofs. I did not want to get wet; it would be cold enough sleeping out without resorting to my sleeping-bag, which was only carried for safety reasons. I did not want to have wet clothing to contend with as well. The stream petered out after ten minutes or so and it was back to tramping through the heather again until I reached the northern edge of the escarpment, and started my descent of the slope.

It was not too steep and going down was fairly simple. Halfway down the slope was an area of boulders and undercuts that had been made by sheep. I was sure I would find a suitable place to shelter in without too much trouble. It is important to try to get out of the wind in this type of terrain and if caught on open ground it is necessary to find a fold in the ground or a valley that runs at right angles to the wind. If neither of these options is available the only thing left is to build a windbreak using turf or any other material you can find, e.g., rocks, or bundles of whatever vegetation is available. Man-made materials such as the ubiquitous plastic fertilizer sack should not be disdained in this situation.

It is worthwhile bearing in mind that the construction of a turf windbreak will need a decent-sized survival knife and if you are carrying one you should also be able to find space for a survival bivi-bag as well.

However, to get back to my shelter construction. The north side of the escarpment would give shelter from the prevailing wind and careful selection of an actual site among the rocks would provide additional protection. After a quick reconnaissance I found an area where a bank had fallen away from a boulder and decided to settle for this as the site for my shelter. It was by no means ideal since the level area in front was fairly narrow and the ground fell away steeply into a hollow. Ideal sites are rare and with time moving on it was imperative to proceed with the arrangements for spending the night out in the open. It was still raining, so the first stage was to erect my poncho thus preventing the ground from getting any wetter and to provide a sheltered area in which to put my pack. As the ledge was long and narrow and I would be lying along the face of the boulder I stretched the longest length of the poncho along

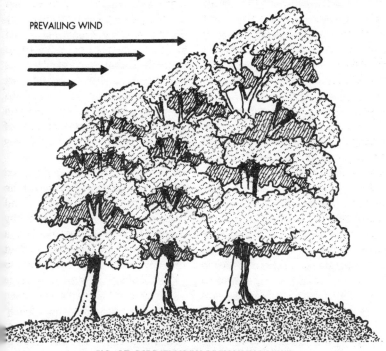

PREVAILING WIND

FIG. 37. DIRECTION BY PREVAILING WIND

the ground and the top of the boulder. The top of the shelter was secured to some tough heather stems with paracord and the bottom held in place by some heavy rocks. With a waterproof material, the angle of the roof is not very important; it can be built to suit the actual site, and only takes a few minutes to erect.

I next collected some insulating material to stuff between the inner and outer polythene survival-bags to create a do-it-yourself sleeping-bag. Although the immediate area did not look too promising, a closer examination revealed moss which, although now quite wet, was suitable. Last year's growth of tussock grass was also plentiful and fairly simple, if rather time-consuming, to collect, being dead growth and pulling off easily. It was beginning to get dark and I had to stop collecting before I had gathered as much as I would have liked, but I did not wish to be stumbling about in the dark, and so I called it a day. While moving over the area collecting material I had the opportunity to see what other natural resources were available to aid survival and found a small stream that would provide a water supply; there were also a few bilberry bushes, but it was far too early in the year for berries, and when there are sheep about the bushes get little chance to produce them.

As I had used one of the bivi-bags to collect grass and moss, getting it ready for sleeping in only required putting the second bag inside, making sure the insulation was equally distributed around the space between the bags. The rain had

stopped and the sky was rapidly clearing which was not as good as it seemed for a clear sky at this time of the year meant low temperatures. I decided to settle down for the night while I was still warm. My first task was to empty my bladder, as once settled for the night I did not want to get up again; I had taken nothing to drink for the same reason. The area I used for this purpose was well away from what was to be my water source. Before getting into the bag I removed my waterproofs, shook the water from them and put them into the shelter; I also removed my socks and spent ten minutes airing and fluffing them up and massaging my feet. This action makes a tremendous difference when the same socks are worn for long periods. I put my socks and boots on again, leaving the laces undone. I wanted to keep my socks dry as there would be condensation inside the bag and wet feet mean cold feet, which in turn means that any chance of getting to sleep has gone, for me at least. Slipping gently into the inner bag, I covered my head and face with my breathable jacket and pulled my bivi-bag tightly around my neck; this meant that my head and face were still protected without putting them inside the bag. Breathing inside the bivi-bag greatly increases the amount of condensation caused by moisture from one's breath.

I find it almost impossible to get to sleep on the first night spent outdoors, even when I have proper camping equipment. In my current situation I knew there was no way was likely to get anything like decent sleep. I resigned myself to dozing off in short spells throughout the night. The insulation between the bags worked quite well, but inevitably condensation occurred inside the bag and made the inner bag uncomfortable. I wriggled about and tensed and relaxed my muscles which seemed to heat me up a little. It was not a comfortable night. My clothes quickly became damp, the effect was more keenly felt on the lower half of my body, which only had trousers for protection. The several layers on my top half kept the dampness from my skin and my wind shirt kept a lot of it out. During the middle of the night it was very cold; the forecast had been that it would reach freezing and I certainly believed that it had. I was well protected from what little wind there was, and even if it had been blowing hard I would still have been fine unless it changed direction to come from the north; if that happened I would have had to rely on the poncho breaking the wind as a first line of defence. Even so, it was cold enough to prevent anything more than short periods of sleep, and it was just a question of relaxing and waiting for sunrise and daylight in order to move to a better location which would provide better shelter opportunities, material for a fire and some food sources. I was uncomfortable, but it was simply a matter of perseverance, knowing it would get better as soon as the sun rose.

It stayed dry through the night and sunrise came at 0430 hours. A welcome sight. The temperature seemed to rise immediately and the bivi-bag somehow became more comfortable.

The temptation was to settle down and try to sleep, but I wanted to move on as quickly as possible as I had a few miles to travel that day. There was time to reflect on what enemies of survival I had encountered and how I had coped.

The problem of Fear had not really arisen because I was confident in my ability and my survival equipment and that is the state of mind you should be in before undertaking the Challenge. There will be a certain amount of trepidation, but there should be no real fear. The physical problems of Cold had been confronted and overcome by knowledge. A good shelter site had been selected, with reference to the prevailing weather, and the survival equipment used well – its capabilities maximised by the selection of the site and the use of natural insulating materials to provide additional protection for the bivi-bag. While even one night spent outdoors in survival conditions dispels most of the trepidation you might feel by increasing your self-confidence, it is as well to remember that Cold will have to be faced again during the Challenge and to overcome it other solutions may have to be found.

DAY TWO

Reflection over, it was time to get up and take some preventive measures against thirst. This was not just because I was feeling a little parched. Thirst should not be confused with the need for water, as it is not a reliable indicator of water requirements. I intended to set a schedule for water intake of a minimum of six pints (2.5 litres) per day. Monitoring the colour of my urine would be a rough and ready guide as to whether I was drinking enough – if it became darker as time progressed I would need to increase my intake. I did not think that was likely as I was sure six pints would be enough and was quite confident that I could procure more than that amount. I made my way to the small stream I had discovered the previous evening and started to follow it uphill until I came to the point where it came out of the ground. I knew that I would find a spring for the stream had to start on or near the top of the escarpment. I had to dig it out a bit to get my water-bottle in and my larger survival knife was useful here.

I had to wait ten minutes or so until the water ran clear again before I could fill my bottle and after I dropped a purification tablet in, I gave it a good shake. The instructions with the tablets indicate that they are effective in ten minutes, but I always allow double this time; I do not take any chances with water purification. The water from the spring was probably pure enough to drink without the tablet and if I had no means of purification this is exactly the type of source I would try to find. As I wandered back down to my shelter I examined the sky to see what the weather might be that day; it looked quite promising with fluffy cumulus clouds blemishing a mainly blue sky. I could not tell from what direction the surface wind was coming because I was sheltered by the escarpment, but the clouds were moving in the direction of the prevailing south-west wind and that was another good sign, at least in the short term.

On returning to the site I packed my kit, first taking the grass and moss out of the bivi-bag and scattering it about; folding up the bags was next and this takes a certain amount of perseverance if there is no flat ground available. The trick is to fold the bag lengthwise first and then to roll it from the bottom upwards to push the air out and make a compact package. The bag was then carefully put into my pack as soon as it was rolled up; it is carelessness to leave items lying about when you have finished using them. For the same reason I packed away my now dry waterproofs in spite of the fact that I would have to unpack them again when I put the poncho away, as I keep my rain gear right on top of my pack. I left the poncho until last as I had some map work to do and although it looked dry I did not want to be caught in a shower of rain.

A 'luxury' item in my pack was a few tea-bags and I set about making myself a refreshing drink while I was deciding my course from the map. A mugful of water on the base of an old Meta stove, half a hexamine tablet, and some rocks around to shelter the stove from any wandering breeze. Lighting the hexamine tablet is not all that easy, but a windproof match does the trick if you hold the tablet in one hand and light the corner.

While the water was heating I turned my attention to navigation. I would be combining conventional and survival navigation on this outing and the first stage was to find

FIG. 38. RESECTION

THREE SEPARATE BEARINGS TAKEN TO PROMINENT FEATURES, AND PLOTTED BACKWARDS ON THE MAP INTERSECT AT CURRENT POSITION.

out exactly where I was. To do this I would use the technique of resection. Although I knew roughly where I was, I wanted to know precisely because I intended to plot a route which would bring me to the south side of a river shown on the map. I already had one river crossing ahead of me and did not want another as a consequence of slipshod navigation.

Bearings were taken on three landmarks, adjusted for magnetic variation (seven degrees west in this part of the country) and the bearings laid on the map by drawing light pencil lines. This located my position within a small triangle and it confirmed my rough estimate. From the position I selected the best course to follow on the map and established bearings for the various legs by:

1. Setting the compass on the map with the long edge along the intended line of travel and the travel arrow pointing towards the destination.

2. Rotating the compass housing until the orienting lines were parallel with the map grid lines and the orienting arrow to the top of the map.

3. Reading the bearings and adjusting for declination.

4. The first bearing was used to sight a landmark farther along the face of the escarpment – a small hummock.

Navigation preparation completed, I found that the water had come to the boil and I dropped in a tea-bag. To complete the meal I ate a small piece of chocolate from my emergency rations. By the time I had finished my tea the stove base was cool enough to pack away and I put the poncho away also. I drank the rest of the water from my bottle and had a last check to see that I had not left anything behind before I set off. I set my route past the spring to replenish my water-bottle (again using a purification tablet) as I was unsure whether I would find quite as good a source again that day. I had decided on a route along the face of the escarpment for various reasons: It was sheltered from the wind; The tussock grass was better to walk on than heather; It saved me a climb back up to the top; It gave me a good view of the route ahead.

Although I was crossing the slope the angle was not too steep for comfortable walking. In crossing a slope it is important to place the foot flat on the ground by flexing the ankle and avoid trying to dig the edge of the sole into the ground unless it is very soft. On reaching my first landmark, the hummock, I could see the ground open up in front of me, therefore it was unnecessary to take out the compass to deviate around the south side of a prominent hill. While descending I made sure that I watched my feet; this is the best way of ensuring that the centre of gravity is kept well forward. It is all too easy to lean back when descending, thus creating a tendency for the feet to slip out from under, and looking down prevents this.

The route took me down to a grassy area between the two stretches of higher ground which was a good place to take a short rest. Five minutes was ample at this stage because I was adequately warm and did not want to cool down and stiffen up. The first stage had been quite hard; I was definitely feeling the effects of lack of sleep. Setting off again took a lot of effort and I was already looking forward to a decent night's sleep. The next uphill stretch was over heather again and turned out to be warm work until I came upon a sheep track going in the right direction. This was much easier to walk on and I followed the track until it began to deviate too far from my chosen course. It took me about an hour to reach the side of the hill and I climbed a short distance to get back on to the grass again. By the aching in my legs I knew it was time for another rest. I rested a little longer this time, taking my boots and socks off, giving them and my feet a good airing. I also took the opportunity to have a few sips from my water-bottle, not gulping it, but letting it trickle down my throat a little at a time.

I decided to put the map and compass away and try out some survival navigation. My intended route was a little north of east and as I was heading for a river, any deviation due to the cruder nature of survival navigation would not matter. I decided to use the sun and watch method – with which some readers might be familiar. In the northern hemisphere the hour hand is pointed to the sun; south is halfway between the hour hand and twelve on the watch (or one in my case with British Summer Time in force). In the southern hemisphere the method is slightly different. The figure twelve is pointed to the sun and halfway between twelve and the hour hand is north, again with allowances to suit any local time modifications. The essence of this method is to establish where the sun would be at noon – this is south (or north) so it is important to make sure that you halve the angle in the right direction – clockwise before noon, anti-clockwise after noon (in the southern hemisphere reverse these instructions).

The next stretch was downhill over grass and the going was easy and unremarkable, and welcome for it. The descent was taking me back down to the treeline and I would certainly find some food and natural survival aids there. The terrain was rough pasture, interspersed with a few stumpy trees and the weather was fine. If I had not been suffering slightly from lack of sleep it would have been a pleasant outing. When I had reached the treeline proper I felt in need of a longer stop and found a place out of the breeze to settle down for a drink, some chocolate and the now regular attention to my socks and feet. I was in no particular hurry. I had estimated that I would reach the river in the early afternoon and that would give me ample time to construct an overnight shelter and forage around for some food. It is important to take an adequate amount of rest when travelling and not to set yourself too strenuous a target; taking care like this is the best precaution against excessive fatigue – one of the enemies of the survivor. Fatigue is exacerbated by low carbohydrate intake and leads to carelessness, bad decision-making and lethargy. You can drive yourself on despite lethargy, but there is little defence against the other two and they can have serious consequences. I rested for about half an hour and could have stayed longer, but I did not want to fall asleep.

Before setting off again I took another bearing on the sun with my watch and set my course accordingly as it had been about one and a half hours since my first bearing and the sun had moved 22.5 degrees in that time. I was now moving into very good survival country with trees and plants growing in abundance and I was keeping a careful watch for anything that might prove useful to me. I expected to find edible plants and hoped to find fish in the river; I was also keeping a keen lookout for some good tinder to start my fire. I came upon some dead grass that was still quite damp, but I collected some anyway, carrying it in my hand to dry it out. Good tinder is something to be prized and collected at every opportunity – you can never have too much. It has become such a habit with me that before I started my Challenge I emptied my pockets and pack of tinder which I had collected on previous outings.

The final part of the day's trek took me to a large coniferous wood. This plantation was fairly mature, but the branches on the trees were still too low for me to walk upright through it. The only thing to do was to detour around it, or continue until I found a firebreak going in the right direction. As it happened I was unlucky and had to walk right around the outside of the wood. Had I been using map and compass navigation I could have plotted a course in advance and entered the wood at a convenient firebreak. The other side of the wood angled down towards the river and it was in the lower edge of this wood that I thought I might spend the night. The river was within easy walking distance and the river bank would be a likely place to find edible plants. After dropping my pack at the edge of the wood I wandered down to the river for a quick reconnaissance; it was rather disappointing, in that the useful plant life was sparse and the river looked quite deep. That might be all right for fishing, but I had to cross it in the morning and that would not be an easy task.

First things first. If this was to be a worthwhile challenge it was important that I test myself on as many survival skills as possible, and not just try out the skills but actually make use of their results to provide solutions to genuine survival problems. I had already successfully employed survival navigation methods, but, as I had reached the river earlier than I had estimated, I wanted to try another technique too. I therefore began to construct an accurate sun compass which would provide me with my initial direction of travel the following day. The best time to do this is during the mid-day period. A stick about three feet (one metre) long was needed and this was easy to find on the river bank. I stuck this into a flat, level piece of ground and marked with a small peg the tip of the shadow cast. This had to be done before the sun reached its zenith. I then drew an arc of the radius of the shadow in the direction the shadow would move; I used a short piece of paracord and a short pointed stick for this but a forked stick would have done just as well. The river bank provided a sandy area

DRAWING THE RADIUS

FIG. 39. SUN COMPASS

that showed the shadow well. When the shadow touched the arc again, a line joining the two points would be a west–east line and joining the mid-point of this line with the stick would give me a north–south line. After fifteen minutes I marked the tip of the shadow again with a small peg; if the sun disappeared in cloud this peg would still allow me to have a sun compass, though a less accurate one.

The method of use is as follows. Draw a line from the first mark through the second mark; stand with the right foot against the first mark and the left foot against the line. In the northern hemisphere you will be facing south, in the southern hemisphere you will be facing north. This method can work during short spells of sun or during rest halts, and is the method I would have used if I had arrived after mid-day. It is only absolutely correct on 21 September and 21 March; this is when the sun is on the Equator. It is least accurate on 21 June and 21 December but even then it provides an approximate east–west line.

While the sun was moving round the compass I walked to the wood to examine the prospects for shelter-building. I still had my poncho with me and could have used that in a variety of ways, but I wanted to use natural materials – if they were available. There were lots of old cut-tops lying around in the wood as a result of previous woodcutting operations and these would be fine for the framework of the shelter, but first, where to build it? A good site should have the following attri-butes:

1. It should be well drained.
2. It should be close to water, but not beside it, as running water can be a distraction when trying to sleep and still water is a breeding ground for insects.
3. It should be well away from any area susceptible to flooding.
4. It should not be close to dead trees.
5. If possible, it should take advantage of natural features – boulders, fallen trees, and tree trunks that could be used as part of the framework of the shelter.
6. It should not be at the bottom of a valley, as during the night the air cools and the cold air sinks to the valley floor.

The situation of the wood some way from the river met most of the requirements and it was just a question of selecting a site in the wood that was not near any dead trees. The wood itself would provide some shelter, but I wanted something that was well protected from the elements as I did not intend to light a fire in the wood, but rather to build it in a safer site down by the river. I decided on a low-profile shelter, and as I was only staying one night it would be easier to build. The cut-tops would provide the framework of the shelter, but the problem would be how to thatch it. There was very little growth of grass or any other material of that type and so I decided to use turf.

The first stage was to find a pole about eight feet (2.5 metres) long; all the cut-tops still had branches on them and these needed to be trimmed

TRANSOM KNOT

FIG. 40. SHELTER FRAMEWORK

FIG. 41. OVERNIGHT BIVOUAC

off. A heavy survival knife is essential for this type of work. When trimming branches the same method is used in every case – always start at the butt end and cut the branches on the opposite side from where you are standing. The use of heavy cutting tools takes a lot of practise and I was fortunate to have worked with a gamekeeper cum woodsman when I was younger and learned the use of the whole range of woodsman's tools and, more importantly, I had a lot of practise. As I trimmed the pole I left little stumps, as these would steady the shorter poles that would support the turf. This type of cutting is mainly done using the elbow and wrist with a full swing and holding the tool as far back as is comfortable. As the turf would be fairly heavy I would need to stack the support poles close together when making the framework for the roof, but a low-profile shelter does not need a lot of wood and short pieces can be used. The ridge pole was stuck into the ground and into the crotch of a tree trunk and branch, about three feet (one metre) up at the top end; the bottom end was pegged to keep it from moving. The most energy-saving way to cut branches for the roof is to hold the branch in the left hand with one end resting on the ground and make four single cuts around it at the selected length; the branch will then break easily at the cuts. This method is far easier than hacking through from one side.

It was soon time to go back down to the riverbank to check my sun compass; the shadow would be getting close to the arc and I did not want to miss it. When I got there I was rather early, but decided just to sit and wait as I needed a rest. When the shadow touched the arc I marked it with a peg. The line between the first and second pegs gave me the west-east line which would be my basis for navigation in the morning. I then went back to finish off my shelter; walking uphill was getting harder and harder, I would need to have a decent rest soon – perhaps even a short sleep? Cutting the sides for my shelter did not take very long as there were plenty of suitable poles available and then it was back out to the edge of the wood to cut some turf for the roof covering. I used my broad-bladed Golok for the turfs; if I had not possessed such a knife I would have cut the outline with whatever knife I had, and levered it up with a stick carved flat at the end, or better still, if I could find one, a flat stone with a sharp edge. I cut the turf quite thin as I wanted it to be flexible and not too heavy. This part of the proceedings was time-consuming and I was glad when I had enough to cover my shelter.

The turfs were laid on the sides of the framework observing the watershed principle – that is, the bottom row laid first and each succeeding row laid so that it overlapped the row beneath. This method makes the roof very waterproof and the use of turfs would also make it windproof. Any turfs that showed a tendency to slide down were held in place with small pegs through them to hold them in position. When I reached the ridgepole the turfs were laid over the top to overlap the top row on each

FIG. 42. ATTACHING GUY–LINE TO POLYTHENE SHEET

side. To complete my sleeping-quarters I needed some ground insulation and some cover for sleeping under. As mentioned earlier, it was rather too early in the year for grass and other suitable plants to have had much growth, but there was a plentiful supply of spruce needles lying on the forest floor that would be ideal. I only wanted the dry top layer and used a dead spruce branch to sweep the needles together until I had a reasonable amount. I used my bivi-bag to carry the needles to the shelter. I filled the bag twice with needles which were placed on the floor of the shelter to give about twelve inches (30cm) of insulation and then filled the bag to give about the same thickness on top as I would sleep under the bag rather than inside it to cut down on condensation.

I felt I had really earned a sleep and after drinking the last of the water from my bottle and eating a little chocolate, settled down even though it was only mid-afternoon. I awoke at 1800 hours feeling much refreshed and set out to get a fire lit down by the river. I wanted a fire, not just for heat but also to purify my water, which I would be taking from the river. The method of purification in this case would be boiling. In my pocket I had tinder in the form of dried grass which I had collected *en route* and had plenty of dead spruce twigs taken from the lower trunks of the trees; all I needed was a supply of fuel and I expected to find that along the riverbank. The side of a river is always a good place to find firewood, swept down when the water is in spate. Sometimes you can find other useful items as well and I came across a decent-sized can which I could use for boiling water and doing some cooking in.

After I had collected several bundles of firewood I was able to set about lighting my fire. First I laid out the log base and put tinder and kindling on it. I was going to light the fire with flint and steel and I gave the dead grass a good rub between my hands to break up the fibres and then put it on to the base in a tight bundle with a hollow in the centre to catch the sparks. It took quite a few attempts before the tinder was alight, but eventually, after some gentle blowing, it was well alight. I gradually added the kindling, a little at a time; it is important not to smother the fire with too much kindling at this stage. The lightest of the fuel was placed on wigwam-style when the kindling was well alight. The fire was contained by putting a log on each side and these also made a base for building up the heavier fuel in log-cabin style, and then it was just a question of sitting back and letting it burn up. While this was going on I decided to sterilize my can by boiling water in it and collected a full can of water from the river and set it upon the fire.

The murky nature of the river presented me with a further test of my survival skills. Although I had purification tablets, I had no specific item of kit for filtering murky water. I would have to improvise something to remove the solids from the river water. My preferred method is the riverside filter and I decided to try this. It needed no equipment other than a means of digging a hole. Other methods consist of using grass or natural fibrous material twisted into a cone to make a filter, or if you have something made of close-weave material, this can be used as a very effective filter by simply letting the water seep through; a handkerchief, shirt, or, best of all, a pair of trousers with one leg inside the other and tied at the bottom. The riverside filter has the advantage that it works without needing continual attention, neither does it necessitate going about half-clothed.

The ground at the side of the river

SATURATED CLOTH

FIG. 43. DISTILLATION BY BOILING

STEAM FROM THE BOILING WATER CONDENSES ON CLOTH, SATURATING IT WITH WATER. CLOTH IS WRUNG OUT INTO A CONTAINER.

was quite sandy and that was good as it would have a good filtering action and, just as important in my current state, it would be easy to dig. I used a digging stick – that is simply a stick about two inches (five cm) in diameter with one end sharpened. The ground is loosened with the stick and the loose soil or sand scooped out. I kept digging until the water seeped into the bottom of the hole, and then dug down another six inches (fifteen cm). The water was muddy of course, but after it had been scooped out a few times it would be clear. I would just need to be careful not to stir up the mud when scooping out the water.

During the time I had been digging, the fire had burned down quite a bit and my can was looking rather precarious. I lifted it off by gripping the top, which I had hoped would not be too hot – it was and I burned my fingers very badly. I plunged my hands into the river; that is the best remedy for burns – cold water. I kept them there for five minutes or so, but they still stung very badly when I took them out. I was more concerned that I had done something as stupid as burning my fingers; you cannot afford to be careless when on your own. I decided then to fix up a fire crane, something I should have done to begin with. The material was at hand and all I needed was some wire from my survival tin to make a handle for my can. I punched the holes for the wire with my knife; the whole job took only ten minutes. A little laziness had caused me to burn my fingers – not good at all.

I pushed the fire together to bring the water to the boil and went along the riverbank to collect some firewood – when you have a fire you need to spend a lot of time collecting fuel for it. On the way I found a patch of nettles which would provide me with a meal that evening. I did not intend to eat a lot of vegetation as it can have a laxative effect. It has been my experience that when I am out like this I tend to become constipated, but I was not taking any chances as I would be travelling the next day. I would also be putting out some night fishing lines in the hope of catching some fish which would provide me with something to eat in the morning. When I returned to the fire the water was boiling and I put some more logs on, laying them all parallel; this way the fire would keep the water boiling briskly but would not consume the fuel so quickly. It was time to collect the nettles; the best way to do this is to cut the whole stem rather than pick the leaves. You are liable to get stung that way. Some grass wrapped around the stem simplified carrying them back to the fire. I had about a dozen stems and that would provide enough for a meal and, more importantly, a drink as I still needed another two pints of fluid to keep up my intake.

My riverside filter had filled up and I took a few minutes to bale it out; the next time it filled up, the water would probably be clear enough to use. The water in the can had been boiling for about 45 minutes and that was long enough to sterilize the can. I took it off the fire, without burning myself, and poured the water out on to the ground downstream from my filter.

Time was moving on and I wanted to get some night fishing lines set, but first I needed to find some bait. A rotten log, hacked open, provided a selection of beetles and grubs; whether they would make good bait or not I had no idea, but I would try them anyway. To augment the bait I caught some minnows; I did this by tying the corners of my handkerchief to the forks of a branch and used it as a scoop net. The trick is not to scoop but gently to ease the net up to the minnows and herd them into the shallow water next to the edge until some minnows have swum over the net then lift the net out. Using this method eventually produced half a dozen minnows and I put them into my can with some water to keep them alive. I had six hooks in my kit and I set them all. Two were simply put into the river from the bank and the other four hung from a couple of poles extended over the river. I had cut the poles from the riverbank – with a decent knife, one cut on each side did the job with the minimum of effort. The hooks and lines were prepared so that they would hang at different depths. I used a couple of split shot on each line to sink the hooks and a twig float on the two lines that were tied to the bank. The area I intended to fish was a pool out of the main current where the water was fairly still. The hooks were baited with a variety of the beetles, grubs and minnows and dropped into the water. I scattered the extra bait I had collected on top of the water to encourage the fish – if there were any.

I felt I had done well so far and was now looking forward to resting beside the fire and having something to eat and drink. I made my way back to the fire, collecting the inevitable firewood as I went. The fire had burned down and needed stirring up and some more wood added. The water in my filter was ready and I put about one pint on the fire to boil for the nettles. While it was heating I stripped the leaves off the nettles, holding the bottom of the stem and cutting the leaves off with my knife. The amount needed was about two handfuls – or rather what would constitute two handfuls if you held them in your hand. I like to wait until the water is actually boiling before I put the leaves in; this applies to other vegetable food as well – although they need to be in boiling water long enough to kill any bacteria – say about five minutes. They taste better with the minimum of cooking, at least I think so. Some roots need a lot of cooking to remove the earthy taste, but this is best done by boiling them in several changes of water rather than keeping them boiling for a long time in the same water.

It was late evening now and I could easily have dropped off to sleep sitting there in front of the fire. I was pleasantly warm, the fire was burning well and soon I would have something to eat and drink. All in all a very satisfactory day, if I ignored the burnt fingers. There is always something else to do though. I would take the opportunity to air and dry the perspiration from my socks at the fire and bathe my feet in the river, again well downstream from my water-collection point. This is important in order to protect the water supply, even if you are boiling the water. All washing activities must be further downstream from the collection-point – any pot washing first, then personal ablutions last of all.

When drying socks, or indeed any clothes, at the fire it is best not to put them any closer than you can hold your hand; this will guarantee that they do not get burned. I have lost quite a few pairs of socks by ignoring that piece of advice. While my socks, propped up on a couple of sticks, were airing at the side of the fire, I dried and warmed my feet. The water had come to the boil and I tipped in my nettle leaves; I was really looking forward to my meal. It may not seem very much, but the satisfaction of having created it from virtually nothing was almost as good as eating it. I get that satisfaction no matter how many times I do it; that to me is one of the attractions of the survival hobby. In five minutes the meal was ready and I lifted it down to the side of the fire to cool a little before I ate it. It is difficult to describe the taste of nettles. There is nothing that I know of in normal cuisine that tastes quite like them. They have a bitter tang which I find quite refreshing and the strength of the liquid can be altered by changing the proportions of plant to water. Cooking the leaves destroys the sting of course, and a shaved stick is a substitute for a fork to lift the nettles out of the pot.

The inner man was satisfied, for this evening at least. It was now time to make preparations for the night. I had gathered a few stones about the size of a small melon and put them into the side of the fire. These stones were taken from well above the high-water mark to make sure that they were perfectly dry inside. Stones that are porous and have water in them will explode if put in the fire and the flying fragments are very dangerous. While the stones were heating I made my way back up to my shelter, collecting some kindling and small to medium-sized fuel which I put inside the shelter. The weather had been kind, that is dry, so far, but clouds were building up and thickening, and there was a distinct possibility of rain. If it came, the little preparation of keeping some fuel dry would make firelighting much easier. I went back down to the fire to check on how the stones were doing. I did not want them to be too hot to touch as I would be using them as hot-water bottles. While waiting for them to reach the right temperature I boiled some water. This would be dual-function water – it would be purified for drinking and, put into my bottle hot, would augment the stones as a source of heat.

Almost ready to settle down for the night, I put a few more logs on the fire and covered it with a turf in the hope of keeping it burning overnight. The stones were gathered up in my jacket and carried to the shelter. The last thing to do before settling down was to empty my bladder, but I knew that with the amount of liquid I had drunk I would almost certainly need to get up in the middle of the night. Ideally, nothing should be drunk for two hours prior to going to bed, but circumstances made that impossible. My priorities had been clear: shelter, fire, water, food – in that order.

However, accepting that I most probably would have to get up in the middle of the night, I picked a suitable area and cleared a path to it, making sure there were no branches that would catch my face.

Settling down in the shelter took a lot of manoeuvring. Lying on my side under the needle-filled bivi-bag with my jacket as a blanket between me and the bag to cut down on the amount of condensation, two stones at my feet, one behind my knees, one at the small of my back and my water-bottle clasped to my stomach, I felt at peace with the world and knew that it would not be long before I fell asleep. The only fly in the ointment was that now that I had nothing to do my burnt fingers seemed to be throbbing a lot more than they had been.

DAY THREE

Morning, and it was raining. It had been raining most of the night. I had slept soundly for about five hours and then had to get up at three o'clock. It was raining then, but very little rain had penetrated down to my shelter. It was dripping quite steadily now, but none had come through the shelter covering, and I was still dry. I had been warm enough through the night and felt much better for having slept. I did have a headache, but that is normal when not eating properly and it would go away as soon as I got on the move again. First of all though I had to check my fishing lines.

I am not a fisherman and I did not have any great expectations, so I was highly delighted to find not one, but two fish on my lines. The lines with the minnows as bait had worked best. To be honest the fish were quite small, but because I fail at fishing as often as I succeed I was very pleased. I was not pleased though to discover that my fire had gone out during the night. I had dry kindling and fuel in my shelter to start another fire, and a little dry tinder, but I decided to save that. The dry kindling and the candle from my kit would soon get the fire alight again. I brought the wood down from the shelter and propped the kindling against a log to leave some space underneath for the candle. It took less than a minute to set the thin twigs alight and I was able to remove the candle with hardly any of it used. I built the fire up with the dry wood. The wood I had collected at the river the night before was wet and I stacked it beside the fire hoping it would dry out.

I decided to cook one of the fish in mud and dry the other, which I would take with me, by planking it. That way the fish would need little attention as I wanted to clear away my shelter while they were cooking. Fish are best gutted right away and it is simply done. The fish is cut from the vent to the gills along the belly, taking care not to cut into the internal organs; these organs can then be pulled out. I threw them in the fire. In other circumstances I might have used them to bait hooks or other traps. They should not be left lying about because they stink and attract flies and other vermin.

Some stones, about the size of tennis balls, were put into the fire to heat while I got on with digging a pit at the side of it. Soil, when mixed

FIG. 44. COOKING IN MUD

with water would provide mud. I wrapped the fish in grass, soaked the grass with water and covered it with the mud, making sure it was completely covered. While the stones were heating I took the time to cut a flat face on a piece of wood – that would be for the other fish. The stones took about half an hour to heat and I spent the time extending the fire. When they were ready I pushed them into the pit and placed the prepared bundle in. Part of the fire was then moved over on top of the meal; that was the reason for extending the fire as I would actually need two fires. Both of the fires were then built up. To prepare the second fish I removed the head and tail and opened it out to expose the inside to the heat. I pinned it to the prepared piece of wood with a couple of wooden pegs and propped it up be-

side the fire.

Other methods of cooking fish, or any animal food for that matter, would be to do it on a griddle of green sticks, hanging it at the side of the fire on a string so that it rotates and is cooked all round, or steaming it. Steaming is another pit cooking technique using hot stones. They need to be really hot and this is best done by lining the pit with the stones and having the fire in the pit. When the stones are ready the fire is cleared out and a thick stick pushed in vertically; next comes a layer of grass, the food, another layer of grass, and finally a layer of soil to seal it all. The stick is pulled out and water poured in the hole to create the steam. Finally the hole is sealed. It takes a minimum of three hours to cook a fish or a small animal this way, but the food cannot burn.

FIG. 45. SUSPENSION ON STRING

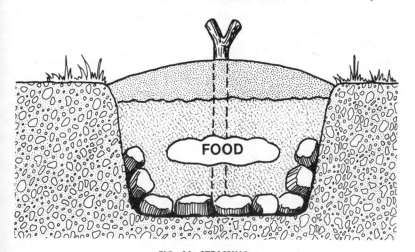

FOOD

FIG. 46. STEAMING

The rain had hardly let up since I awoke and although it was not heavy, it was steady and did not look as if it would stop. That did not bode well for being able to use the sun for navigation and I would have to try to navigate by natural signs if I did not want to resort to the map and compass. It was a good test to try to do without these navigational aids, if this proved practicable. Survival navigation needs good visibility and although there are a variety of techniques that can be applied most of the time, there are occasions of poor visibility where movement without a compass would be inadvisable at best, or in some circumstances, dangerous – when travelling over terrain which has sheer drops, for example. My east-west line from the previous afternoon was still there and would give me a good start.

I reckoned it would take an hour to cook the fish and that would give me ample time to dismantle the shelter. I consider this to be essential as it is bad practice not to tidy up after you. A word here about the shelter – it was built completely from natural materials and the only aid was a knife; no string or cord was used. The structure was self-supporting and sturdy enough for my needs. It was also simple to dismantle. The turfs were replaced and the pieces of wood from the frame stood upright against the trees. If I ever used this site again I would be able to re-use the pieces of wood. I scattered the spruce needles about as well. It would have been fine to remain where I was, sheltered from the rain, but I had to go and see how the fish were doing.

The fish on the plank seemed to be all right; I was not sure whether I was drying it or cooking it. I did not know how successful drying would be in the rain. It would keep until that evening and that was all I needed. I filled my can with water and put it on the fire to boil for more nettle tea to have with the fish. I still had the purified water in my bottle from the night before, but I wanted to keep that for drinking during the day. There seemed to be a slight break in the cloud and the rain had eased off a little but I was sure that it was only temporary. Both fish were ready by this time; I wrapped the planked one in a small plastic bag and put it away

in my pack. I dug up the other and cracked open the mud. It lay on its bed of grass cooked to perfection. Cooking this way retains all the natural juices and the flesh is succulent. It was hot and tasty and I ate every piece of flesh. It went very well indeed with the cooked nettles and nettle tea. The hot food was a tremendous boost and I was ready to resume my travels, even to facing the fact that I would have to cross the river before I could proceed any further on my chosen course. I carefully accounted for all my kit. I could not afford to lose anything and it is very easy to leave something behind if care is not taken. I also took along the can I had found – it had already proved an asset. The last thing to do was to put out the fire and scatter the embers, a simple task with the river near at hand.

I checked my direction from the sun compass to establish a datum for using the natural signs – the signs in question would be the effect of the prevailing wind on the trees. The prevailing wind was from the south-west and its effects were evident on small clumps of trees and on individual trees by the slope of the foliage. Using the sun compass as a datum I was able to confirm that the trees I could see did show the signs of the effect of a south-westerly prevailing wind. It pays to check the natural signs whenever possible.

At this stage it is wise to re-affirm the purpose of the Challenge. The intention is to set out a test of abilities and to try to stay the course, and to practise and perfect as many different techniques as possible. These techniques should, of course, be appropriate to the situation; the objective being to string the skills together in a realistic survival scenario. In fulfilling the Challenge the survivalist must still be aware that in a real situation his decisions might be different. The decision to stay or move, will normally be made before the Challenge is started, and cross-country movement, in a real situation, will be planned to take advantage of any benefits the terrain may offer.

Although I was setting out to cross the river, there were other options which could have been considered. One would have been to simply remain where I was to rest and recuperate; the site had a lot going for it. There was good shelter potential – water, various food sources (fish and plant) and enough fuel to keep a fire going. The other would be to travel, but rather than cross the river, follow it. Rivers usually lead to civilization, provide a ready supply of water, contain fish, attract animal life, have an abundance of plant growth on the banks, and all in all the survivor who comes across a river would do well to follow it.

My Challenge had been set out, however, and crossing the river was part of it. I was not sure how deep it was and set off upstream to look for a better place to cross. What I was looking for was a place where I could see the bottom or at least have an indication of it by the way the water ran over it. Reading a river takes a lot of practise, but if it is slow moving it tends to be deeper, and where it is faster flowing, shallower, particularly if it is wide. Where there is a series of bends there is often an area of shallower water between the apex of consecutive bends. If a river has a rocky bed it is not good practice to jump from rock to rock; a slip could be very dangerous. Even stepping from stone to stone can have serious consequences if a slip results in a sprained ankle. Even falling in fully clothed would lay the survivor open to hypothermia in many circumstances. River crossing needs a lot of care in the selection of the place and method of crossing.

Although my intended route was directly across the river, I was prepared to walk upstream for some distance to find a better place to cross. The prospects did not look too good; the terrain was fairly flat and the river was running slow and deep. I decided that I would walk for half an hour and then cross at the best place I found. The going was easy on the riverbank, but the rain was heavier and the prospects were pretty miserable. I was heading more or less north, the wind was blowing the rain against my back on the left side, but during the morning some rain had got down inside my jacket at the neck and the top of my windproof shirt was decidedly damp. My trousers, under my nylon waterproofs, were damp with condensation and I was feeling uncomfortable. I was warm enough as long as I kept walking. I would cool down rapidly if I stopped walking and in view of this decided not to stop for long periods as the body combating cold uses up calories and I hadn't any to spare.

During the half-hour I had set myself I did not find what I would term a good crossing-place. I retraced my steps to the least unsuitable place which was an area where the river turned at a fairly sharp angle and I could see that it was shallower towards the other bank. It was deeper on my side and I cut a sapling to test the depth. It was better than I thought – about three feet (one metre). I would have to take all my clothes off, but I would not need to swim. If swimming had been necessary I would have had to organize something in which to carry my pack. A large plastic bag tied at the neck would have been ideal or I could have built a small raft on which to push my kit. Its main purpose would have been to carry the kit, not to support the swimmer. Non-swimmers would need a much bigger raft, although anyone taking a serious interest in survival should learn to swim.

Not knowing just how deep the river would be, I removed all my

FIG. 47. CUTTING SAPLINGS

clothes, wrapped them in my waterproof jacket and strapped them to the top of my pack – everything except my boots that is – they went back on my feet as I had no idea what the riverbed was like, but from experience I suspected that it would be muddy with waterlogged bits of wood embedded in it. The survivor must protect his feet at all times. He needs them not just for getting to safety, but, for gathering firewood and hunting for food. Other camp chores will be severely restricted if the feet are injured in any way by cuts, blisters or even such a mundane thing as a stubbed toe. Athlete's foot or immersion foot (trench foot) are also problems that may be encountered if the feet are not given attention in hot or wet weather. Athlete's foot is exacerbated by excessive perspiration, and trench foot is caused by prolonged wetness, but the preventive measures are the same. The feet should be washed regularly and dried carefully, particularly between the toes. Wet socks should be replaced by a dry pair. If you do not have any spare socks, as was my case, every opportunity must be taken to dry them, and they need to be washed every three or four days. Foot powder should be applied liberally not just to the feet, but also to the crutch and armpits – in fact any part of the body subject to perspiration.

The river was bitterly cold. I edged in gradually to get used to the temperature. I had loosened the straps of my pack so that if I fell I could easily slip it off. I have seen it suggested that one strap should be left off, but I cannot operate that way as the pack always slips off my shoulder and down my arm leaving me to try to catch it in the crook of the elbow. I was glad there was no one about as I waded in clad only in boots and backpack. Using the stick to probe in front, I moved cautiously across, facing upstream; this is important particularly if the current is strong as it tends to lock the knees straight. Facing downstream, however, allows the current to act on the back of the knees to collapse the legs. Facing upstream also enables the survivor to see anything which may be coming down on the current.

The movement in crossing is a sort of sideways shuffle, never crossing the feet but sidestepping with the leading foot feeling for a secure place while the body is balanced on the other leg with additional support from the stick. This is slow and laborious, and discipline is needed to restrain the urge to hurry on, but it is absolutely the safest way if you are alone. When the water is cold, as it was in this instance, it takes even more self-control, but I was very conscious that all my clothes would be wet if I stumbled and dropped my pack, so I had reason to be careful. The area in the middle was deeper and the water was above my waist before the riverbed started to slope upwards again, and I was glad to get into shallower water, then across and out at the other side.

I took my boots off. They were filthy with the mud and ooze from the river bottom. I gave them a good wash, being careful to get all the mud out from the insides and hung them upside down over a couple of branches to drain off. Using my shirt as a towel I had a brisk rub down. I put the wet shirt on top of my pack; I would be warm enough wearing my waterproofs. In these circumstances dryness is a relative term; it is impossible to undertake an exercise like this and be dry at the end of it. By the time I had got my clothes back on I had to settle for being damp all over and cold. Very cold indeed. Moving on, protected by my waterproofs, would eliminate any danger that might exist of hypothermia so I started out as soon as I had my clothes and boots on. I was still heading north of east and took my direction from the trees shaped by the prevailing wind; this brought the wind round to blowing on my back, slightly to my right. This would be useful as a direction indicator. The method of using natural indicators for navigation is the same as using a compass – once the direction has been established a landmark is selected and you then walk to it by the easiest route. The process is then repeated. If you can position yourself on a line between your last landmark and your next, it is sometimes possible to select another landmark farther on past the one you are walking to. My travelling was a combination of these methods and by reference to the wind direction.

The terrain was open rough pasture with small clumps of trees and the walking was on an uphill slope. I found it hard to get going again; I did not know whether it was because of my exertions the previous day or lack of food, but I had to force myself onward. Motivation is different for different people. I try to eliminate all non-essential elements and concentrate on where I am going and where I am putting my feet. I stop to rest every hour and sometimes more frequently if travelling over steep ground. There is no point in walking to exhaustion, but it helps if the mind can be detached from the nagging pains in the muscles, the heaving of the lungs, and all the other discomforts. It may help to set an easy target, say another 50 paces, and when that has been achieved, do the same again and so on. It is amazing the ground that can be covered using this technique.

Another way to take your mind off the current situation is to think of something more pleasant or in my case reviewing the situation so far, given that it would end up in manuscript. My main thought so far was that the equipment required had been minimal. A bivi-bag for the moorland phase and a decent knife after that; the other items coming from my small survival kit. One thing was crystal clear though, a good set of waterproofs and a good pair of well broken-in boots had been essential items and were the means of allowing me to carry on. Without the boots I could not have covered the ground and without the waterproofs the weather would have forced me to give up the test, or at least to shelter until it improved. That would have been the same as having to give up because I did not have unlimited time to complete the test and nor would the majority of people.

Most of the morning was taken up with the trek to the fringe of the moor, through intermittent rain, with stops for a rest and a drink. It was a pleasant relief to be heading downwards again, going towards my last stopping-place. The next obstacle was another wood, but one I could walk through and practise another survival navigation technique. Moving through woodland is tricky and offers a great potential for walking in circles as there are no distant reference points to keep you on course. A compass is the only sure way of accurate navigation and even that needs to be used in the knowledge of its limitations. To move through a forest alone without a compass is a slow process and needs a reliable method.

As I approached the edge of the wood I made sure I was heading in the right direction. At the edge I visually lined up two trees on my line of travel. As I came up to the first tree I lined up a farther tree with the first two so that when I passed the first tree I still had two in line on the desired direction of travel, and so on, always keeping two trees in line. This is a primitive method of navigation, but I have seen it used in this country to maintain a straight line when planting trees by hand and it does work. It is, however, not as easy as it sounds because it is not always possible to get three trees in line and even when it is, getting to the target tree oftens means a detour round impenetrable areas. If it proves impossible to reach it at all, the only thing to do is to get the line as closely as you can and pick another target tree. Sometimes, looking back to the last target tree can help. It is a laborious way to travel, but in a forest it is necessary to maintain a reference to the intended direction of travel otherwise you will become hopelessly confused. Walking through close country such as woodland or forest calls for a different method from that used for walking in open country. Not only is there the need to watch foot placement, but it is necessary to keep an eye open for branches at face level – that is if you want to keep an eye! Lower branches catch your clothing and force you off line and all the time you have to try and maintain a steady course.

The trick is to restrain the rate of progress to a speed where you are in control. A leisurely stroll might be the best definition. Trying to go faster than this will result in stumbling, being struck by branches and generally getting into trouble. As you gain experience the rate of travel will increase, but that comes in its own good time. It is pointless trying to go through an area of dense undergrowth or an area where trees have been blown down; it is quicker and easier to go round and there is less chance of becoming lost. A forest is a treasure house for the survivor. Identifying different tree types and their potential use, the varieties of plants that are beneficial, animal sign, and how all of these relate to one another are all part of the survivalist's continuing education. This is part of living in harmony with nature instead of fighting it. If you fight it, you will lose. The great outdoors is bountiful to those who understand it and become part of it, but it is cruel to the ignorant and ill-prepared. One of the best

FIG. 48. AIMING OFF

ACTUAL LINE OF TRAVEL IS OFFSET FROM THE THEORETICAL LINE TO ENSURE ARRIVAL AT RIVER AT A POSITION WHERE THE REQUIRED DIRECTION TO REACH THE RIVER FORK WAY–POINT IS OBVIOUS. SIMILARLY THE LAST LEG ON THE ROUTE USES THE LAKE TO TAKE UP ANY NAVIGATIONAL ERRORS.

things about the survival hobby is that there is no end to the learning; you can never say you know it all.

I had now been travelling for five hours – six counting rests, and another hour would bring me into the area where I would look for a site for my next camp. I knew roughly where I was, having remembered the forest from the map. Due to the need to end up in a specific area and the inherent inaccuracy of survival navigation, I had set the course using the 'aiming off' technique. This is done by deliberately heading to one side of the actual destination to strike a linear feature such as a stream, a track, the edge of a wood, and then following the feature to a known point. By aiming off I would know which way to turn when I came to the feature. In my case I had a small stream as the feature and when I came to it I would turn north until I reached a junction. At this point I should see the wooded area which was to be my destination.

After I emerged from the forest it was only a mile to the stream and I was pleased to see that the rain had ceased. When it rains steadily during the day it often clears by late afternoon, and I had high hopes for a dry evening. It took longer to reach the stream junction which meant that I must have deviated further to the south than I thought. This did not surprise me; most people have a tendency to veer to one side or the other and I know that my tendency is to go to the right. I was, however, becoming anxious by the time I reached my way-point at the stream junction.

It took almost another half-hour to reach the area of mixed woodland where I intended to make my next camp. The first thing I did was carefully to reconnoitre the area to see what it offered and accordingly I set off to find a good shelter site and water supply. The area featured a mix of coniferous woodland, a small strip of deciduous wood and a stretch of ground where the trees had suffered from storm damage and had been subsequently cleared. The water supply was a drainage ditch and although it was not the best-looking water I have seen, I had a can to boil it in and was quite happy that it would suffice. The ditch had a lot of insect life in it and that is always a good sign of reasonable purity.

The best site for a shelter was in the deciduous wood because there was plenty of deadfall there for shelter construction and fuel for a fire. The trees themselves would provide additional shelter from the wind and rain, if it started again. Deciduous wood is longer burning than coniferous and that is an important feature when relying on a fire to supply heat and minimize the calories needed for keeping warm. The main problem was that there was no normal thatching material. The text book solution of using long grass, ferns, or similar material did not apply; what little there was within easy reach was still too short to be ideal. This was the same problem I had had the previous night, but this time I would try a different solution. I decided to build my shelter in an area of beech trees; this part of the wood contained deep ground cover of dead leaves, which had accumulated over a number of years and would provide a sufficient

FIG. 49. OPEN FRONT SHELTER

FIG. 50. LOW PROFILE SHELTER

amount of material to 'thatch' the shelter; all I needed to do was devise a method whereby the leaves could be used as thatch without them sliding or blowing away.

I intended to build an open-front shelter which I could heat with a fire. I wanted to try the lightweight space blanket from my survival kit on the inside of the shelter to reflect the heat from the fire down into the sleeping area. This seemed a good way of using the blanket to take advantage of its reflective properties without the condensation problems that wrapping oneself up in it would bring. I still needed some means of keeping the leaves on the roof and decided the best way would be to pile them on a lattice of dead spruce branches on top of a solid framework. The site was selected to take advantage of a couple of trees that would serve as uprights; these, with a crossbar lashed across,

FIG. 51. 'A' FRAME SHELTER

BATTENS

HORIZONTAL STRUTS

**FIG. 52.
BATTEN THATCHING**

VERTICAL STRUT

HORIZONTAL STRUTS

WATERSHED PRINCIPLE

WOVEN THATCHING

BENT THATCHING

**FIG. 53. WATERSHED PRINCIPLE/
BENT AND WOVEN THATCHING**

would provide a solid base for the rest of the framework. There was an ample supply of dead wood lying about and there was no need to cut saplings for the framework. A lot of wood would be needed to stop the leaves falling through gaps and I set about collecting that first. Although I had cord in my survival kit, I intended to stretch my survival ability further in procuring as many aids as possible from natural sources. It is no real test of anything, except perhaps knot-tying ability, to use string or cord from a survival kit. There is a limit to how much cord the survivor would have and when natural alternatives can be obtained they should be used.

I would use bramble stems for tying the frame together, and collected these from a patch at the edge of the wood. The best type to use are the green fresh growth and this was the time of the year for it; later on the stems become woody and less flexible and, while they can still be used, are not so good. In any event the stems need to be made a little more flexible and this is done by pounding them gently between two rounded stones to break up the fibres. Bramble leaves are a valuable food source and the berries which form in late summer are tasty and nutritious. The bramble was used to tie the top and inter-

mediate crossbars, the five main uprights and, later, a side crossbar, using a transom knot. The main struts were pegged in position at ground level. The spaces between were filled by simply placing other branches between the main struts against the lower crossbar. The space blanket was put in position inside the roof area. The next stage was to put the spruce branches on to the framework, lacing them in to retain them if necessary, with the tips facing upwards so that they would catch and retain the leaves. When one layer of leaves was in position they in turn held subsequent layers and I carried on until I had a thickness of about nine inches (23 cm) built up. I thought that would be sufficient to give good wind and waterproofing. I collected more leaves to provide ground insulation and cover for the sleeping area. I had to build a low

FIG. 54. TRANSOM KNOT

A QUICK AND SIMPLE WAY OF ATTACHING POLES AT RIGHT ANGLES, BUT NOT AS STRONG AS SQUARE LASHING.

retaining wall of logs to prevent the leaves in the sleeping area from spreading, but as it was only twelve inches (30 cm) high it did not take long. The depth of ground insulation was eighteen inches (45cm), with more spruce branches and yet more insulation piled on to act as a top cover.

Getting into this bed would require a lot of manoeuvring and keeping covered during the night would be a problem, but I would be up several times anyway to tend to the fire. It took about three hours to build the shelter to my satisfaction and when it was completed I decided to have a short rest after which I would light a fire. There was plenty of wood, but it was all very wet and I would need to find some suitable tinder and dry kindling if possible. I had tinder in my kit but I wanted to practise some wet weather firelighting using the magnesium firelighter. I set out to see what tinder I could find. On the fringe of the beech wood were other varieties of trees: sycamore, rowan, willow and, of immediate interest, birch. The paper-like bark of the birch would provide the tinder I needed, but I still had to create a flame to ignite it. Birch bark will light when it is wet and that was just what I needed. Having secured my tinder, the next stage was to gather some kindling; dead, matchstick-size twigs from the trunks of the conifers were damp, but by scraping the bark off I exposed the dry surface of the wood underneath. I did the same with the larger size of kindling (pencil size) and the smallest sizes of the fuel. All the material taken was dead standing

START WITH CLOVE HITCH

FINISH WITH CLOVE HITCH

FIG. 55. SQUARE LASHING

USE WHEN A STRONG 'PERMANENT' MEANS OF TYING TWO PIECES OF WOOD IS REQUIRED.

wood, that is wood that is still attached to the trunk. Any firewood lying on the ground would be damp at the best of times and absolutely sodden under the current conditions.

The magnesium firelighter is simple to use – scrapings are taken from the magnesium block and these are ignited by a spark from a flint embedded in the block, providing a very hot flame which will ignite tinder or even very thin kindling. The shavings tend to fly off all over the place so I shaved them on to a handkerchief to make sure I caught them all. Shaving them on to the ground, which was covered with forest litter, would be a sure way of losing them. A heaped bundle about one inch (2.5cm) diameter would be enough to light my tinder and when I had this amount I wound it up in my handkerchief which I put in my pocket. I had other preparations to make. An area of about four feet (1.2m) in front of the shelter was cleared down to the soil; then the base logs were laid down with the dryer side up, the dryer side being the underside of the branch as it grew on the tree. The kindling and small fuel was broken into small lengths and stacked at one side on the base logs ready to hand. Finally the magnesium shavings were placed on a flat piece of bark in the middle of the base. This type of preparation is the best guarantee of a successful fire. The shavings lit easily with the flint and I immediately started feeding narrow pieces of bark on to the flame, gradually putting more and more on as the flame took hold until I had a good-going little fire of bark. At this stage I started putting on the thinnest kindling, building it up into wigwam shape. This is the proper method when using birch bark; if the kindling is put on before the bark is lit it will be scattered as the bark twists and curls with the heat. Once the kindling was alight it was simply a matter of slowly adding fuel, taking care not to smother the flames until I could put on some heavier fuel that would keep the fire alight for some time. I put one

log on each side to contain the fire and searched for a couple of forked branches to make a crossbar for cooking.

The crossbar material gathered, I decided to prepare something to eat. The small fish left over from the morning would be ideal and I would look for some plant food to eat with it, but first I needed to collect some water to boil. The water from the ditch was clear enough and provided that I did not disturb the mud lying at the bottom it would not require filtering. I collected about a pint and put it on the fire to boil. I kept the fire going to bring the water to the boil as quickly as possible. I wanted to look for some other food, but did not want to leave the fire unattended. It was now 1900 hours, the rain was threatening again and I wanted to be more or less settled for the night before it came on. I was pleased with the day's work and something to eat would round it off nicely. Sitting, waiting for the water to boil I realized just how tired I was, and decided that I would turn in as soon as I had eaten and collected wood to keep the fire going throughout the night. When the water had boiled, I let it bubble briskly for ten minutes; by this time the fire had burnt down to embers and I felt it was safe enough to leave for a short period while I looked for additional food.

What I had in mind was some willowherb which I had seen on my first recce of the area. There was plenty of plant food in the area, and I would be trying various other kinds the following day as I intended to use the time to practise some skills in a realistic situation. The willowherb was still in the early stages of growth and I picked the top two inches (5cm) from about two dozen plants. The small plastic bag from my kit was useful for carrying plants, but a pocket would have done just as well. I always like to wash plant food, and used some of the boiled water in my metal cup to do so. I built up the fire and put the rest of the water, with the dried fish in it, back on to boil. I let it simmer for about half an hour and dropped the willowherb in for the last five minutes. When it was done, I lifted the fish out and carefully stripped all the flesh from it into the pot; the bones I put in the fire – no scraps lying about the camp. The meal was superb. The fish was tasty and the willowherb, being young shoots, was tender and had a pleasant vegetable taste. It turns a pale yellow when cooked and the stems and leaves of young plants are edible. The flowers, when they appear later on, are also edible and the seeds, formed in a cotton-wool like matrix, make superb tinder. I also made sure that I drank every drop of the liquid in the pot to help keep up my fluid intake and to ensure that I derived the benefit of all the nutrition from the food.

I now set about the major task of gathering enough firewood to last through the night. This takes a lot of wood. The amount can be reduced if you can find some logs of decent thickness, and that is what I was looking for. In addition, I wanted to gather some kindling and small fuel which I would dry at the fire and store in the shelter overnight; it was

starting to rain again. My site was sheltered within the wood, but if it rained heavily everything would be wet in the morning, and if the fire went out it would be much more difficult to start again. I stacked the fire-starting wood at the side of the fire, to be put into the shelter before I turned in. I had been unable to find any long logs, but had managed to get some of reasonable length and I put these on to make a star fire. This is simply done by putting the ends into the fire and feeding the wood in as the ends burn away. In conjunction with this I also built some logs up at the back to make a reflector to throw the heat into the shelter.

After a final trip to collect water and empty my bladder, it was time to turn in. It was still an hour or so till dark but I was ready for some sleep. First, though, the ritual of airing and drying my socks at the fire and massaging and warming my feet. In the circumstances, warm dry feet and warm socks are what could be termed a luxury. I would sleep with my boots off as they were quite wet. I suppose I could have dried them at the fire, but I was wary of this as they would be difficult to replace if they got burnt so I settled for putting them into the back of the shelter to make sure they did not get any wetter. I also accounted for all the other items of kit I had been using and put them into my pack, the pack in turn going to the back of the shelter. Finally I gently eased myself between the layers of leaves and laid my jacket on top for additional cover. I heard the rain pattering on the trees above, but little if any was penetrating down to ground level. I was dry and snug in my shelter. The fire was casting a warm glow into the shelter and would last for some time. I was pleasantly drowsy and it seemed to me that I fell asleep almost immediately.

It was dark when I awoke the first time. The fire had burned down to embers, but when I pushed the logs in and put some additional small fuel on it started to burn up again. Checking my watch, I noticed that it was 0100 hours, which meant the fire had lasted about three hours and that was quite good. I could feel the chill and welcomed the heat from the fire as the flames took hold. The little extra heat soon made me drowsy again and although I felt a bit stiff, because I was trying to avoid moving too much and scattering the leaves, I was quite comfortable. The next time I awoke it was almost daylight. The fire was very low and I had to get up to pull it together again. There were still glowing embers which some gentle blowing and a little fuel transformed into a flame. Additional fuel soon created a more respectable fire and although water was dripping from the trees I sat close in to the fire to get the benefit of its heat. It had been the chill of the night air that wakened me and I sat by the fire for a while to get warm. Eventually I did crawl back into my bed. It was very pleasant lying there watching the fire and it was some time before I dropped off to sleep.

I did not sleep so soundly this time, perhaps because it was almost light, but when I next looked at my watch it was 0700 hours. I did not get up right away, but kept the fire going while I lay and relaxed for an hour or so. During this time I reviewed the adequacy or otherwise of the sleeping arrangements – shelter, fire, etc. The shelter had been sound and dry enough and the firewood had been adequate, but only just. I would make sure I collected more to last through the following night. The main problem had been not enough insulation to cover me and thus I had felt rather cold during the night. I would remedy that before the coming evening.

DAY FOUR

My plan for the coming day was to search for food and practise some skills that are more associated with longer-term survival as opposed to travelling to safety. Although I had some emergency rations, these were only for a real emergency, and I was determined to procure as much natural food as possible. Indeed I would eat only what I could procure or nothing at all. The reasons for going or staying were discussed in an earlier part of the book, but this was a Challenge and it was important to allocate some time to the practising of skills appropriate to the terrain and weather, while still finding time to carry out the repetitive tasks that need to be done to maintain a high level of comfort.

I intended to keep the fire going all the time if possible. In a real survival situation this would be desirable to boil water, dry clothes, provide heat, cook and not least, to boost morale and create the impression that the camp was home, a place where I could be safe and comfortable. It is also very therapeutic in that it requires activity to collect enough fuel and that in itself is an antidote to boredom. Additionally a warm fire to sit beside goes a long way to dispelling feelings of loneliness. Keeping the fire going reduces the demand on firelighting kit which should be carefully husbanded for as long as possible. Wood collection therefore was my first task, and every time I left the camp I would collect fuel on the way back.

I decided that it was time I paid some attention to personal hygiene because I was feeling extremely grubby and in need of a wash. I do not carry soap, so water and some grass to rub the worst of the grime from my hands would have to do. It was quite amazing how much better I felt after washing my face, hands and feet. It brought to my attention however, various cuts and scratches on my hands and I would have to look for some medicinal herbs to clean

them thoroughly. It is most important to keep any breaks in the skin as clean as possible to prevent them from becoming infected. A quick foray produced some nettles for breakfast, supplying both something to eat and drink, after which I set out to explore the surrounding area to see what other resources it might provide. I would be looking for plants that would provide nourishment and medicinal aid, a better water supply, fuel, and – in a real survival situation – examining the prospects for catching some animal food.

This type of reconnaissance of an area needs to be done with some method, particularly in wooded terrain. Getting lost at this juncture was not a good idea. I decided to combine the use of a baseline with a grid pattern of reconnaissance and the first stage was to explore along the side of the baseline in both directions just to make sure it did not take a dramatic change in direction. Initially I covered a distance equivalent to about only fifteen minutes' walking

FIG. 56. MOVEMENT PATTERNS (FOR EXPLORATION)

CROSS–COUNTRY MOVEMENT USING ANY OF THESE PATTERNS ENABLES THE SURVIVOR TO RETURN TO HIS STARTING–POINT, OR KNOW WHERE HE IS IN RELATION TO THE STARTING–POINT AT ANY TIME.

FIG. 57. CAMP LAYOUT

because I wanted to check the immediate area around the camp. I did not mind travelling to find food, but I was averse to carrying firewood for long distances. Having explored the baseline I used a grid method for a more detailed examination of the area around the camp on my side of the ditch. Later, if necessary, I would use the same technique on the other side.

The terrain was mixed woodland, predominantly beech but with a scattering of other deciduous trees in the immediate vicinity of the camp. This natural wood blended into an area planted with spruce in various stages of growth, from about ten years old to some more mature trees. The other varieties of deciduous trees were concentrated at the fringes of the two main varieties. There was a good variety of the common edible

plants and more importantly they were in plentiful supply. It was, in short, a typical area of woodland that might be found almost anywhere. The best place to find plants in a wooded area is in clearings or on the fringes of the wood where there is plenty of light. Tracks or firebreaks through a planted wood are also a good place for plants. On this first reconnaissance I collected some birch bark and leaves, some dock, including the roots, and some dandelion leaves and roots. The birch bark would replenish my supply of tinder. The leaves would be used for medicinal purposes, as an antiseptic to clean my cuts and scratches, and the dock and dandelion would provide food and drink at midday. On returning to the camp, with my various supplies and some firewood, my next move was to attend to the various cuts and scratches. These were on my hands and arms and are inevitable when working with natural materials in shelter building and collecting wood. They may only be minor but a high standard of personal hygiene should be maintained to prevent any infection. On the general subject of cuts and scratches, it is essential that before starting any survival activities you have up-to-date anti-tetanus injections.

The method of preparation of the young birch leaves to relieve my cuts and scratches was as follows. A handful, that is an amount to cover the palm of the hand, was added to a pint of water, which was then brought to the boil, removed from the heat and left to stand for about fifteen minutes. This allowed the water to soak up the properties of the leaves and also cool down enough to allow it to be applied to the skin. I used the leaves themselves to bathe the cuts, taking care to do this thoroughly and making sure all the cuts were absolutely clean. I would repeat this every day until the healing process was well under way.

To prepare the other plants for eating I washed them, particularly the roots. The dandelion roots were put to one side and the dock roots put in a little water to boil. Most roots need at least a couple of boilings to remove the earthy taste they tend to have and I would throw away the water from the first boiling. I prepared the dandelion and dock leaves for cooking by cutting them up into small strips. Dandelion leaves are quite tasty when eaten raw, but I like to cook everything if possible to reduce the possibility of an upset stomach. The two varieties of leaves were added to the second lot of water after it had been boiling for about ten minutes and then removed from the heat after a few minutes. Survival cooking is not the same as ordinary cooking, and because different combinations of plants may be used, some trial and error is inevitable to discover when to add the various ingredients. It must be said though, there is a large margin for error as taste tends to be a secondary consideration.

Having stated that, I have to say the meal was perfectly edible. The leaves had not been cooked too long, which would have made them soggy, and the roots were soft and easily chewed. The taste of this type of meal does tend to be a little bland and a natural flavouring such as mint or wild onion, or curry powder carried in the kit, enhances such dishes. I sipped a little of the liquid, but I intended to make a more palatable drink from the dandelion roots. To start with I put them at the side of the fire to dry out; this would take an hour or so and they would require turning regularly to make sure they would dry properly. Having attended to the necessities it was time to look to my comfort. I wanted to air my clothes at the heat of the fire and to hang them in the smoke for a few minutes as this discourages insects. I used some green spruce needles to make the smoke because spruce and pine seem to have insect-repellant properties. While my clothes were airing I used some warm water to wipe down the sweaty parts of my body – crutch, armpits and feet.

After all this had been done the dandelion roots were dry enough to be crushed into smaller pieces. I used a stone and the side of my knife to crush them, but two stones or logs would have done just as well. The tricky bit is in catching the small pieces as they are crushed and something such as a large piece of bark, aluminium foil, handkerchief or similar item is needed. I used my shirt. Once the small pieces were collected I put them into the bottom of my pot, without water, and heated them gently for five minutes to complete the drying. I was now ready to make coffee. It was made just like ordinary coffee – the water brought to the boil and the dried grounds added, the pot removed from the fire and left to sit until the liquid is cool enough to drink. It does have a proper coffee taste, if a little bitter. Two small roots are enough to make about half a pint of coffee and this can be modified according to taste.

I intended to spend the remainder of the afternoon trying some other firelighting methods – firebow and burning-glass, and set out to collect the necessary materials for this. For the firebow I needed a base log, a bow, a steady stone or block and a drill, and for both methods I wanted to find some really dry tinder. Weatherwise it had been a good day in that it was dry and the sun had come out. The problem with 'natural' firelighting methods is that they require specific conditions which are mainly weather dependent. The

survivalist should practise the skills, but never allow himself to end up in the position where they are his only means of lighting a fire.

The base log for the firebow method was a dead willow branch which was as dry as I was likely to find, and for the drill I used a piece of beech wood, again dead, but still attached to the tree. The willow supplied the springy branch that was to be the bow. The hardest thing to find was a small stone of a size to fit in the palm of my hand to steady the other end of the drill, but eventually I found one. The dimensions of the other items and the method were as follows.

As the base log was round I cut a flat area on the top and bottom. The log was about two inches (5cm) in diameter so it was not a difficult task. The harder drill was one inch (2.5cm) diameter by twelve inches (30cm) long and as straight as possible. I shaped the ends of the drill into a cone of about 45 degrees angle and strung the bow with a piece of paracord from my kit. This is the most difficult item to obtain naturally. I have never found any kind of natural cordage that will stand up to the stress of this sort of use; at a pinch bootlaces would do, but the process is hard on them. The string was attached to the bow at each end with a rolling hitch – that is a clove hitch with an extra turn. I used the point of my knife to gouge a small hollow in the base log close to one side, and to do the same in the middle of the stone; the softer the stone the better for this. A vee cut was made from the outside edge of the log into the hollow and this was flared out on the

FIG. 58. BOW AND DRILL METHOD

underside. The bow string was looped once around the drill, one end of which was placed in the hollow in the base log, and the other in the hollow in the stone or pressure pad. The best way I found was to kneel on the right knee, hold the base log steady under the left foot, hold the pressure block in the left hand, and steady the left forearm on the left shin or knee, with the right hand operating the bow. The fingers of the right hand were held over the string and were used to increase the tension to improve the grip of the string on the drill. Although this sounds complicated it was much easier to do than to explain. The drill was rotated slowly at first with just enough pressure to keep it in the hollow in the base log until it had enlarged and smoothed it. At this stage I tucked some tinder under the vee shape. The tinder has to be bone dry and very fine, and all I had in that category was some cotton wool from my kit. The tinder was placed on a small piece of bark to keep it off the ground. I was now ready to try in earnest and worked the drill at a faster rate. It did not take long to create smoke and some fine brown powder. The idea at this stage is to spin the bow faster and with more pressure on the drill. What should have happened next was that a small glowing coal should have formed on the tinder and I would have been able to blow it gently into

FIG.59. CLOVE HITCH

FIG.60. CONSTRICTION KNOT

CLOVE HITCH
A SIMPLE METHOD OF ATTACHING A CORD TO A BRANCH WHERE THE STRAIN WILL BE STEADY.

CONSTRICTION KNOT
A SELF–LOCKING KNOT, USED FOR TYING THE NECK OF A SACK OR TEMPORARILY LASHING A BUNDLE OF STICKS TOGETHER.

FIG.62.
ROUND TURN AND 2 HALF–HITCHES

FIG.61. NET LINE KNOT

NET LINE KNOT
AN ALTERNATIVE TO THE CLOVE HITCH, IT IS MORE SUITABLE WHERE THE STRAIN IS LIKELY TO BE INTERMITTENT.

FIG.63. TIMBER HITCH

USE FOR NATURAL CORDAGE: COMES EASILY UNDONE AFTER IT HAS BEEN UNDER STRAIN.

FIG.64. TAUTLINE HITCH

USE TO ADJUST THE TENSION ON A GUY–LINE.

flame. Try as I might I could not get a coal. No matter how hard I spun the drill or how much pressure I put on it I could not generate enough heat to produce that glowing coal. I suspected that there was just too much moisture in the air for the wood to be dry enough.

I did have one thing to try – that was to use a mixture of sugar and potassium permanganate to asssist ignition. The proportions are two parts sugar to one of permanganate. When I prepared the mixture and put it into the hollow it ignited with a few turns of the drill, setting light to the tinder. This mixture will work even using a hand drill, that is spinning the drill between the palms of the hands. The amount of flame that comes from it is dependent on the amount of mixture used and you need to be very quick with the tinder to catch it. One final point is that resinous woods are not suitable for any parts of the firebow set, as the resin makes them too sticky. The same resin which collects in blobs on some trees makes superb tinder and is worthwhile looking out for.

I also wanted to try firelighting with a burning-glass. The sun was out, but I was doubtful if it would be strong enough to generate the necessary heat. It was worth a try. For tinder I used some of the dried grass I had collected the previous day. I had been carrying it in my pocket and it was as suitable as I was likely to find. I have found that the magnifying glass on my Silva compass is the best glass for this purpose. Other items that can be used for this purpose are camera or binocular lens, or even the bottom of a glass bottle. If the camera lens cannot be removed, open the back of the camera to allow the sun to shine through with the lens aperture held open. A lens about two inches (5cm) in diameter is a good size and the best time to try it is when the sun is high in the sky, i.e., at about midday.

I crumpled the tinder as finely as I could by rubbing it between my hands and then rolled it into a ball, pressing it flat and concentrating the sun's rays in the middle. The best I could manage was a whiff of smoke, no more than that; the sun was just not hot enough. The best tinder is a strip of cotton or paper handkerchief rolled up like a bandage with the centre depressed to make a trumpet shape. The sun's rays are concentrated on to the centre. This will cause it to glow, then a gentle blow will create a flame. A little charcoal sprinkled on the surface will assist ignition. The alternative methods of firelighting had not been an outstanding success. The effort had not been entirely wasted, however, because I had learned that in this part of the country it is very difficult to light a fire using these methods. If it had not been for the sugar and potassium permanganate I would not have succeeded at all. It reinforced the rule that you must always carry a guaranteed means of firelighting.

This experimenting took up quite a lot of time and I had still to collect something to eat and more firewood. These two activities take up most of the time in a real survival situation and with the additional activities in your Challenge you will find the day packed with activity and be glad to turn in reasonably early at night. There are other reasons for going early to bed, but I will cover these later.

I still had the area on the other side of the ditch to explore and set off using the same technique for covering the ground as before. The ground was a mix of young spruce trees and assorted deciduous trees – birch, willow and ash scattered about some open patches. I hoped that these areas would provide some plant food but I also collected some material from the trees. From the willow I cut some sucker growth from the foot of a larger trunk; from the spruce some fresh growth needles and from the birch some more tinder in the form of paper-thin flakes of bark. The birch is a really useful tree for the survivor, the bark for tinder, and in sheets it can be made into dishes and waterproof vessels. This amount of bark taken from a tree would kill it so it should not be done except in emergencies. The sap is very nutritious and can be obtained without damage to the tree. Using the point of my small knife I bored a small hole in the trunk to a depth of about one and a half inches (3.8cm). It takes a few minutes for the sap to begin flowing so I used the time to make a tube from some ash bark. I did this by taking the end of a branch which had fresh growth and removed a length of unblemished bark by ringing it, then slitting it lengthwise and carefully peeling it off. That way it can be overlapped to fit exactly into the hole in the tree to act as a spout to allow the sap to drip into a container. The container in this case being a

bowl shaped from aluminium foil, which would be left in place overnight. I expected to collect about one pint in that time.

The open grassy areas yielded a variety of edible and otherwise useful plants: plantain, thistle, sorrel, dock and horsetail. The following were collected from the plants:

Thistle (cirsium vulgare)	young shoots and roots
Sorrel (rumex acetosa)	leaves
Dock (rumex crispus)	young leaves and roots
Horsetail (equisetum arvense)	whole plant.

The collection of the plants took a lot longer to achieve than it does to write about, particularly when it entailed digging up the roots. As I made my way back to camp I stopped at the ditch to wash the plants thoroughly, especially the roots, and returned to camp not forgetting to collect some firewood on the way. The plantain, dock and thistle would provide the meal accompanied by some coffee made from dried dandelion roots The sorrel would be used to make a cold drink for the next day and the horsetail used to help scrub my hands, with some left over in case cut myself as it helps to stop bleeding

To prepare the meal I scraped the dock roots, chopped them into smal pieces and put them in some water to boil. The thistle shoots were peeled ready to go into the pot with the plantain leaves when the roots were boiled for the second time. The thistle roots were also scraped and spiked on a few pointed sticks to roast at the side of the fire. Thistle roots can be boiled, but I find them rather stringy and prefer them roasted. They took about ten minutes to cook and I ate them while waiting for the rest of the meal. Roasted they have a pleasant nutty flavour and I find them to be one of the more palatable wild foods. When the roots had been boiling for fifteen minutes the second time round, I added the thistle shoots and plantain leaves to cook for the last ten minutes. It is easy to determine when they are ready by testing the roots with a sharpened twig, the same twig being used as a substitute for a fork when eating.

The meal over, my next task was to gather more wood to last through the night. I intended to settle down early because I was very tired and had been suffering from headaches. These are brought on by a lack of sugar in the diet, and are to be expected after a day or so. From my collection of wood I selected some to go into the shelter in case it rained, and then made an infusion of birch leaves to bathe my cuts and scratches. I also used some of the horsetail to give my hands a really good scrub as the dirt tends to become ingrained. The remaining horsetail I hung in the shelter. These could be used to stop bleeding, either as an infusion or simply pulped to release the juice and pressed on to a wound, if I had the misfortune to cut myself. Plantain can also be used in a similar fashion, but it had value as a food source and I preferred to eat it as it supplies Vitamin C. Sorrel too is a source of this and I prepared it by boiling about two pints of water to sterilize it and adding a handful of sorrel leaves, then gently simmering them at the side of the fire for five minutes. The liquid was then poured into my water-bottle where it would fulfil two functions. It would act as a hot water-bottle during the night and would provide a cool lemonade-type drink the following day. After a day or two drinking only sterilized warm water I began to have a great desire for a cold drink. Boiled water is flat tasting and even pouring back and forth between two containers to aerate it helps only a little. The sorrel leaves give it a sharp, tangy taste which makes it much more palatable.

After collecting some more leaves for a covering, I performed the rituals of airing, washing and drying. These must not be neglected. Once accomplished they provide a feeling of luxury. The final task was to build a star fire before wriggling into my bed of leaves to settle down for the night. It was still early evening, but I needed to sleep, and getting to sleep before the temperature drops is a good method of ensuring that you do not suffer from lack of sleep because of the cold. I had another reason for turning in so early as the following paragraphs will show.

I fell asleep very quickly and woke at about 2200 hours, built up the fire and went back to sleep. The next time I woke it was the early hours of the morning – about 0200 hours. I was very cold and instead of trying to go back to sleep, I built up the fire and put on some water to boil. After it was sterilized I added some spruce needles and let it brew for a few minutes. As I sat sipping it, in the dark, watching the flames dance in the fire, I let myself go to become a part of the forest. This is the time I like best of all. Sitting in the night completely free of any of the sights or sounds of 'civilization', with the fire quietly crackling, sending out its heat into the recesses of my shelter. This would be the time when many people would be liable to feel lonely and some even a little frightened, but for me it was the time to take satisfaction in my accomplishments and to feel that I really belonged. It was also the time to listen to the sounds of the wild, because it is never silent. Listening to the noises and trying to interpret them is an intriguing pastime. It can take a while before the sounds can be heard, but after two days in the wild the ears attune quite quickly and soon I could hear a variety of different noises in the darkness around me. The predominance of noise comes from small ground mammals such as mice or shrews. In a forest, where there is a lot of leaf litter on the ground, the noises they make are greatly magnified and sound as if they are made by a much larger animal. I could hear their movements all round the shelter. The fire did not seem to have frightened them in any way. The noises can be identified by the way they reflect the foraging movements of their makers; a fairly constant movement with only small pauses as the forager finds something to investigate or snap up. The hunting animal such as the stoat or weasel makes a different kind of noise altogether, a much more purposeful sound with movement being steady and stealthy. When it stops it is for a longer period of time while the predator tries to get a bearing on its prey, and sometimes there is the final rush and small squeal of a kill.

Up in the trees there is the occasional crack of branches as a bird, probably a pigeon, seeks a better roosting place. It sounds more like a small aircraft crashing than a bird. It is loud, and as one starts, others follow. Further away are faint noises that might be deer moving through the forest, but sounds can be deceiving and it could be a smaller animal. One sound was heard which was unmistakable. A fox close by out on patrol. The sound of the individual steps was distinct and indicated it was walking or trotting rather than running. It paused occasionally, probably to test the air for scent or listen for anything that might provide a meal, but it was moving quickly and soon went beyond my hearing. Time had slipped past as I listened. Gazing into the fire and the heat from it had made me drowsy again. I put another few logs on the fire and settled down to sleep. If I had nothing else out of the Challenge, the last two hours had made it worthwhile and I was extremely content.

DAY FIVE

In the morning the weather had taken a turn for the worse. It was raining fairly heavily and there was no incentive at all to get up. The fire was reduced to a few glowing embers and I had to get it going again with some small dry kindling from inside the shelter. Once alight it would burn even wet wood from the pile outside the shelter. A morning brew-up seemed a good idea, but I had no water and I had to collect some. I also went to see how much birch sap had been collected in my makeshift bowl and was pleasantly surprised to discover that it was overflowing. There must have been at least two pints in it. Certainly spring is the best time of the year to collect sap, but this was more than I had expected from such a relatively small tree. Instead of collecting water I used my tin to carry the sap back to camp. It is pleasant tasting as it comes or it can be boiled to make a syrup, but I intended simply to warm it a little and drink it. Birch sap contains sugar and I needed that as my carbohydrate intake had been very low, and as I was intending to walk out that day I wanted to boost it if I could. Low carbohydrate intake was probably the cause of my headaches and a general reduction in the speed at which I was working. In a real survival situation everything is done at a deliberately reduced pace to conserve energy, and while this may not be necessary in the Challenge, it will tend to happen anyway if a reduced diet is part of the test.

There were still a few things I wanted to try before leaving and since it was raining I started with something I could do under cover. I gathered the willow branches I had collected the previous day and peeled the bark from them. Willow bark peels in long strips and makes very good natural cordage. The correct way to peel it is to split it into three equal segments and peel each segment down in turn a little at a time. The individual strips can be tied together to make a longer strip or they can be plaited to give increased strength. The simplest method is a three-strand plait. If greater strength is needed three plaits can be plaited together. Starting from any side the outside strand is passed over the new middle strand which has come from the other side and so on to the end of the strands. To join additional strands simply lay the additional strand on and plait it in. Avoid having three joins in the same place by starting off with strands of different lengths. The plait is started and finished with a simple overhand knot. It is important to practise this kind of skill in realistic conditions – cold, wet or whatever. With fingers stiff and tender with scratches and, in my case, burns, it is a different proposition from practising in the comfort of home. The cordage is useful for a variety of purposes – shelter building, trap making, constructing camp furniture, holding first-aid dressings or compresses in position, splints, safety ropes, etc. Making cordage is one of the antidotes to boredom. It should be made before the need for it arises, so if you have no cordage in your kit, making some has a fairly high priority.

On the subject of combating boredom, the preferred method is to undertake some activity that uses minimum energy. Making string or rope, items of furniture to improve camp comfort, manufacturing trap triggers. These are all suitable activities, as is clothes mending and generally keeping whatever kit you have in good condition. So far as loneliness is concerned, I find it somewhat difficult to comment. I have often been alone, but I have never been lonely. This is obviously connected to one's personality and I might only suggest that loneliness will probably strike when you have nothing to do, and therefore similar means used for combating boredom can be used to combat loneliness. Additionally, I suppose that freeing one's mind to think of more pleasant things would be a way of fighting the lonely feeling. If you are affected by loneliness it can have a very depressing effect. I have known people who could not suffer being alone even for one day in survival training to the extent that they just gave up and sat and did nothing. It can have that serious an effect and it might be best to discover how it affects you before taking an extended Challenge.

I had not set any traps because trapping is illegal, but I had noticed some possible sites. Wooded terrain that has thick undergrowth shows up animal trails easily, so trap siting is fairly obvious. In open wooded terrain the trails are not so obvious and may need an experienced eye to spot them. For the less experienced the best way is to look where a tree or other obstruction has fallen and you will likely find animal trails going under it at the easiest place. I had some work to do that morning before I set off and I could not afford to wait until the rain stopped. I put on my rain gear and set myself to work. Food for the day was the main task. I decided to stick to dandelion leaves

and gathered a substantial amount. These are palatable raw and also have a gentle laxative effect. This was something I needed as I had been constipated since the beginning of the Challenge. This state of affairs is not in the least unusual in the circumstances. The dramatic change of diet means that normal bowel movement ceases in the vast majority of cases. Sometimes the bowels react violently in the form of diarrhoea. This is more of a problem than constipation and needs to be attended to right away. The remedy that was generally available in the various locations I had visited was bramble or blackberry. A decoction made from the leaves by adding them to boiling water and simmering for five minutes, drunk three times a day, would I hope, have remedied that inconvenient state of affairs had it arisen. Other well-known remedies might have been bilberry berries, or decoctions of yarrow or camomile. Having gathered the dandelions I was more or less ready to move on, but first I had work to do to bring my camp site back to its natural state.

I may be repeating myself, but I consider it essential that this be done and I make no apologies for it. This even extended to plugging up the small hole in the birch tree (from which I had extracted the sap) with a wooden plug. Before starting to dismantle the camp I carefully accounted for all my kit and equally carefully packed it away in my pack or belt. Restoring the site can easily cover items of kit left lying about. Remember you can not afford to lose anything. I put the fire out by dousing it with water. If had not had water to spare I would have used urine or let it burn to ashes and trampled it until I was sure it was completely extinguished. Dismantling the shelter was simply the reverse of building it and the material used was scattered around to leave the area looking natural. Any natural cordage I had used, such as bramble and willow cordage went into my pack together with a generous amount of birch bark for tinder. This was done despite the fact that I did not expect to need it again. I believe in being prepared. One last check to see that everything was in order and I was ready to go. I had food in the form of dandelion leaves and sorrel-flavoured drinking water and knew that safety was within a few hours' walking distance, which I could accomplish even in my state of reduced energy.

I had come to feel at home in my camp and although I was not exactly reluctant to leave it I did glance back as I walked away. My route was back down to the stream junction and then on down following the stream to where it joined the river. Thereafter I would follow the river. I could have cut across country using map and compass, but I wanted to complete the Challenge in true survival fashion. Following the river would guarantee that the route would be more or less downhill, and that was a consideration in the final stages of the trek. Easy going and no navigational problems should be considered as highly desirable in the final stages of the Challenge when previous efforts and lack of food have taken their toll. You are never safe until you are back. A navigational mistake or an accident at the end of the Challenge can have consequences every bit as serious as one at the beginning. Do not 'switch off' until you are really home and dry. Many accidents in the hills happen when the difficult part has been accomplished.

REFLECTIONS

While the content of the Challenge is obviously a matter of personal choice, it is worth considering some of the different ways in which it may be made more or less difficult. The same Challenge will alter depending on the time of year. The main factors are the availability of food and shelter-building material. Autumn is the time of year when plants for food and other uses are at their most plentiful. The roots of food plants are at their fattest in readiness for winter and there are enough leaves and shoots available for eating. Berries, nuts and fungi (if you are knowledgeable) are all available at this time. The weather can be expected to be fairly cold, but in general it is not usually very wet. Remember that rain is a major enemy of the survivor. Provided that there are no freak weather conditions, autumn is probably the easiest time for the Challenge. Although nuts, and fungi may not be available in the early part of summer, there is still a good selection and amount of plant food and the higher temperatures are a bonus, as are the longer days. Spring, when the Challenge in this book took place, is the most difficult time of the year to try out techniques, perhaps even including winter, because the supply of food plants and other natural materials is restricted by the minimal amount of growth. The temperature is likely to be lower and the weather in general more uncertain, spinning out from winter. Winter is a special case in terms of a Survival Challenge. Under no circumstances should you attempt a Challenge in winter without having enough equipment to ensure your safety even in the worst weather. Food is at its scarcest and the calorific requirements at their highest. Substantial rations must be carried. Extremes of weather mean that some wilderness areas require winter climbing skills and equipment. Such equipment should include warm clothing, appropriate sleeping bag, bivi-bag or tent. There are skills such as snow-holing and shelter building that can be practised, but provision must always be made to survive with the kit carried. Winter survival means keeping out of the weather, staying warm and conserving calories as if they were gold.

The amount of kit carried at other times of the year may make the Challenge easier or harder, but more than that, the amount of equipment used can be a way of modifying the rigours of it. The ultimate is to find an alternative or natural substitute for every item in your kit. In my case, by virtue of knowledge and experience, I had been able to find a great many natural assets to replace or augment kit items. I had of course procured food, but not just any food, it had been a mixture of roots (starch rich) and leaves and stems (vitamin rich).

Additionally, by using birch sap I had procured carbohydrate/sugar; this is hard to come by in a survival environment. I had not even opened my medical pack, although I had suffered minor injuries. These should not be ignored and I had been able to treat them using natural remedies, and the treatment had been adequate. Also adequate was the insect-repellant properties and methods used, although at the time of the year when my Challenge was undertaken it was not a particularly onerous test. I had used natural cordage throughout or devised means of doing without it on one of the shelters I had constructed. Apart from the moorland phase, water purification had been by natural means, i.e., riverbank filter and boiling – both techniques that can be used long term and not dependent on consumable items of kit. the only really indispensible items from the survival kit had been an absolute certain means of firelighting and, to a lesser extent, a knife. At a pinch I could have probably managed without a knife, but I would have been unable to try out many of the techniques. Without the ability to make fire, however, the Challenge would simply have turned into an endurance exercise, if indeed it could have continued at all for any length of time.

Reflecting on how my Challenge had gone, and how my kit had performed, the actual amount of kit I had used had been minimal and had performed well. I had not expected anything different as it had all been tried and tested before I started. Any untried items were additional to kit I already had which I knew would do the job. Some items that I had used could have been substituted from natural sources, but that would have cut down on the time available to try out and practise some of the other survival skills during the Challenge. This question of how much or how little kit to use is a matter of individual choice. There is no one to fool but yourself, but even if you do not intend to use it do not go without it. Exceptional weather conditions, unforeseen emergencies or accident may not give you the luxury of choice.

The finest survival kit of all is to be found between the ears. Imagination and knowledge will allow you to tap into that greatest resource – nature itself. Survival kits that have been purchased or made up to individual requirements will eventually be used up, but there is no end to the natural assets and resources that the experienced survivalist can conjure from the countryside.

The amount of food carried and eaten will also vary the difficulty of the Challenge. This is of course related to the availability of wild foods and therefore the time of year during which the test is taken. A Challenge taken alone is generally a more severe test than one taken in company and while it will be best for honing more of the survival skills it does miss out on the element of teamwork and practise at interpersonal relationships which in themselves can be highly educational in the sense that someone else may more easily identify your strengths and weaknesses. It must be said that to my mind there is more satisfaction to be gained fom the successful completion of a solo challenge.

The Challenge as detailed in the previous pages was by the foregoing definitions a difficult test. Of course the degree of difficulty is related to the skill of the practitioner and I should point out that I have been searching out and practising survival skills for many years. As the Challenge was in the process of being completed it could therefore be considered a success. Some things had gone wrong. I had suffered minor injuries. I had been less than comfortable some of the time. There had been a shortage of food, but I had still been able to practise my skills in a realistic situation. Adapting shelter-building principles to the natural materials at hand, reliable and not so reliable firelighting methods, combinations of different wild foods, not to lift a hot can with bare fingers, the insect-repellant properties of some plants; these things and others were learned or reinforced and added to existing knowledge when related to the weather and the time of the year.

For my part I was grimy, tired, had a headache, and was looking forward to the completion, but the satisfaction that always comes with this achievement was there, and I felt that I could have gone on for a much longer time.

When you complete your first Challenge you will feel on top of the world. Your self-confidence will have increased immensely and you will be viewing the countryside with a completely different outlook. You will be noticing subtle signs that you never noticed before; edible plants will be much more obvious, and animal signs will start to mean a little more in terms of understanding their behaviour and habits. Weather signs will become more relevant and, more importantly, you will remember clearly what kind of weather followed what signs and it is to be hoped that you will be that little more of an outdoorsman than you were when you started.

It is a time to be treasured and in many ways I envy you that first achievement. It has to be earned of course. Earned with knowledge, fitness, the ability to stick it out when the going gets a little bit rough, and finally the understanding that you cannot fight nature and win, that you must be able to adapt and compromise on your expectations of normal comfort. Foolhardy and ill-thought-out actions will have to be paid for. There is no way of cutting corners when it comes to survival. All the skills have a few right ways and many wrong ways of application – no matter how hard you try, if you are doing it wrong it will not work, and all the wishful thinking and even inventive cursing will not alter that.

So good luck in your endeavours to adventure and survive.

SELECTED BIBLIOGRAPHY

The following books contain a variety of realistic survival skills and information. Some were published many years ago – at least one very early in this century – but survival is not a new science; man has been practising it since long before the invention of printing. In addition the world is full of examples of things which were invented, forgotten, and have had to be reinvented years later. Many of the books are now out of print, but should be available by special request from a public library. Some organizations, such as government departments and airlines, publish books for the benefit of their own staff, but these are not available to the general public and have been omitted from the following list which is confined to publications that are or have been available commercially.

Adam, Lieutenant-Colonel J. M. *A Traveller's Guide to Health*. For The Royal Geographical Society, Hodder & Stoughton

Blackshaw, Alan. *Mountaineering*. Penguin

Byrd, Rear-Admiral R. E. *Alone*. Putnam & Sons

Chapman, F. S. *The Jungle is Neutral*. Chatto & Windus

Cherry-Garrard, Apsley. *The Worst Journey in the World*. Chatto & Windus, now a Penguin

Cliff, Peter. *Mountain Navigation*. Cordee

Craighead, F. C. and Craighead, J. J. *How to Survive on Land and Sea*. Naval Institute Press

Edholm, O. G. and Bacharach, A. L. *Exploration Medicine*. Wright & Sons

——. *Physiology of Human Survival*. London, Academic Press

Farrar-Hockley, General Sir Anthony. *Edge of the Sword*. Frederick Muller

Greenbank, Anthony. *The Book of Survival*. Wolfe Publishing Ltd.

Grenfell, Sir Wilfred. *A Labrador Doctor*. Hodder & Stoughton

Kane, E. Kent. *Arctic Explorations*. Nelson & Sons

Kephart, Horace. *Camping and Woodcraft*. New York, Macmillan

Klaben, Helen. *Hey, I'm Alive*. Hodder & Stoughton

Lindsay, Martin. *Sledge*. Cassell

Mabey, Richard. *Food for Free*. Collins

Mawson, Sir Douglas. *The Home of the Blizzard*. Hodder & Stoughton

Mikkalsen, Ejnar. *Two Against the Ice*. Hart Davis

Moran, Lord. *The Anatomy of Courage*. Constable & Co.

Nansen, Fridtjof. *First Crossing of Greenland*. Longmans Green

Nesbit, P. H., Pond, A. W. and Allen, W. H. *The Survival Book*. van Nostrand

Nicholl, G. W. R. *Survival at Sea*. Adlard Coles

Noyce, Wilfred. *They Survived*. Heinemann

Rodahl, Kaare. *North*. New York, Harper

Scott, J. M. *Gino Watkins*. Hodder & Stoughton

Shackleton, Sir Ernest. *South*. Macmillan

Stefansson, Vilhjalmur. *The Friendly Arctic*. New York, Macmillan

Langmuir, Eric. *Mountaincraft and Leadership*. Scottish Sports Council and Mountainwalking Leader Training Board

Mountain Rescue. HMSO

Safety on Mountains. British Mountaineering Council

Survival pamphlets on Arctic, jungle, desert and sea survival, Ministry of Defence, reprint. Survival Aids Ltd.

Troebst, C. C. *The Art of Survival.* W. H. Allen

Wiseman, John. *The SAS Survival Handbook*. Collins Harvill

APPENDIX 1. Survival – Immediate Actions

1. Remove persons from immediate danger. Get them clear of water, avalanche, etc.
2. Render first aid. See below for priority order.
3. Stop, think and plan.
4. Start providing shelter – from wind, wet and cold.
5. Allocate jobs.
6. Put out markers, signalling devices, etc.
7. Find water and fuel.
8. Fix your position as accurately as possible.
9. Decide if, and when, you will send for help.
10. Continue all the above until found.

Remember the keyword – CHASTE.

C – Choking/Cardiac. Get the casualty breathing and his heart beating as quickly as possible.

H – Haemorrhage. Stop major bleeding. Ignore minor cuts.

A – Aid. Get others to help you and, if possible, send for an ambulance.

S – Shock. Treat in the normal way.

T – Treatment. Deal with other injuries, e.g., fractures, burns, etc.

E – Emergency. The situation is one, so deal with it quickly and firmly.

APPENDIX 2. Survival Kits

These are available for various purposes from a number of firms. Their failing is that their contents have to be fairly general in order to cater for a wide market. Survival kits are also to be found on virtually all aircraft, both military and civil and in lifeboats and liferafts. Neither I nor anyone else can decide what you need for the activities you undertake, except by individual discussion with you. I have listed the contents of a very wide range of survival kits. The aim is to jog your memory as to what you might select for yourself. To take all the items listed would require a vehicle just to carry them and there is no suggestion that you should select more than a small number of items. The makeup of any kit is a compromise between what you think you might need and what you can carry or pack. Beware of the kitchen sink attitude and be ruthless in your selection.

Some of the items may appear to duplicate one another or nearly so. Obviously a groundsheet and a poncho could be the same item but they have come from different lists. The items have been grouped under broad headings such as signalling, medical, etc., and a few items appear more than once, e.g., cotton wool has an obvious medical use and can also be used for tinder when lighting a fire. An item like string is so universal that it could appear under most of the headings. Having selected your personal kit you should pack it in a waterproof container and hope that you never have to use it.

Clothing and Shelter
Groundsheet
String
Survival bag
Nylon cord
Space blanket (metalized plastic sheet)
Plastic sheet
Poncho
Half parachute
Sleeping-bag
Woollen hat
Sun hat
Plastic coat and hat
Hammock
Spare socks
Anti-exposure suit
Gloves
Mosquito veil

Signalling
Whistle
Distress flares
Mini flares
Sea marker dye
Torch
Signalling mirror
Distress rockets
Smoke flares
Radio beacon
Ground signals code

Navigation
Compass
Watch
Map

Medical
Chalk
Plasters
Paludrine
Anti-glare shields
Insect repellent
Snakebite kit
Lipsalve
Cotton wool
First-aid kit
Sunglasses
Glacier cream
Shark repellent
Adhesive tape

Firemaking
Matches (waterproof)
Candle
Flint and steel
Lighter
Solid fuel blocks
Cotton wool
Magnifying glass
Firemaking tablets
Small bottle petrol
Liquid fuel stove

Tools
Razor blade
Penknife
Nylon cord
Clasp-knife
Survival knife
Scalpel blade
Wire saw
String
Needle and thread
Oilstone
Pliers
Stout knife
Hacksaw blade
Wire
Nailfile
Sewing kit
Six-inch file
Machete

Obtaining and Preparing Food and Water
Fishing line
Water-purifying tablets
Polythene bag ⎫
Balloon ⎬ for carrying water
Contraceptive ⎭
Spatula
Water-carrier
Solar still
Fishing kit
Tin-opener
Fish-hooks
Potassium permanganate crystals
Gill net

Wire snares
Spoon
Cooking utensil
Weapon and ammunition
Desalting kit
Plastic cup

Sea Survival
Liferaft
Bailer
Bellows
Sea marker dye
Solar still
Leakstoppers
Sponge
Lifejacket
Radio beacon
Desalting kit

Miscellaneous
Candle
Wire
Pencil
Sponge
Toilet paper
Rucksack
Chemical lights
Watch
Notebook
Survival book
Rubber bands

Suggested Items to be Carried in a Car
Blanket
Emergency food (chocolate, nuts, biscuits, etc.)
First-aid kit
Spare clothing
Tools
Torch
Spare bulbs, fanbelt, etc.
Container of water
Shovel
Jump-leads
Tow rope
Sacking

APPENDIX 3. Emergency Foods

Emergency foods must be light in weight, provide energy rather than protein, edible without cooking, have a long shelf life and be reasonably palatable – but not too palatable or the temptation to consume them other than in an emergency will be too great! The range of possible foods is considerable and frequently changing according to the whim of the food trade. A walk round any large food store will provide plenty of ideas. The following items have all been suggested in the past as good for emergency use.

Dextrose tablets
Lemonade powder
Drinking chocolate
Mint cake
Sugar
Porridge oats
Cheese
Nuts
Margarine
Glucose sweets
Salt tablets
Chocolate
Sweet biscuits
Dehydrated meat blocks
Oatmeal blocks
Milk powder
Tea/Coffee
Dried meat and rice
OXO cubes

In addition, specially prepared survival rations are available commercially.

APPENDIX 4. Survival Training Activities

This book should be used as a training guide and manual. For those, especially youth leaders concerned with the training of young people, who want a quick 'ideas list' the following should provide plenty of programme material.

1. Produce a fire with the aid of a lens, e.g., from binoculars.
2. Produce fire with the aid of a natural flint and a metal object such as a knife blade.
3. Waterproof some matches.
4. Produce fire with the aid of a spark from a vehicle's or similar battery.
5. Improvise a Benghazi Burner.
6. Improvise a wick and use paraffin or oil as fuel.
7. Construct a shelter using natural materials, and spend a night in it.
8. Dig a snowhole or snow trench and spend a night in it.
9. Experiment with a solar still.
10. Cook an animal, fish or bird by improvised means.
11. Try some of the natural foods suggested in Chapter Seven.
12. Select the contents of a first-aid kit for a specific type of activity.
13. Select the contents of a survival kit for a specific type of activity.
14. Hold a discussion group on the mental and physical problems of survival.
15. Improvise and use fishhooks.
16. Improvise snares (but do not leave them out as a risk to animals).
17. Compare cooking over a candle enclosed in a tin with one not so enclosed.
18. Improvise a signalling mirror.
19. Produce a survival fishing kit and test it.
20. Make and use a hammock.
21. Improvise a water filter.
22. Test the various methods of finding north and compare the results with a compass.
23. Test dried animal dung as a fuel.
24. Improvise a raft from natural materials.
25. Try making a coat or other garment from sacking or similar material.
26. Practise, and practise again and again your ability to navigate across country in all weathers.
27. Make and use a flinthead axe.
28. Learn to swim if you cannot already do so.
29. Take a first-aid course.
30. Improvise footwear from old tyres, canvas, etc.
31. Practice the use of an improvised lifejacket, e.g., knotted trousers.
32. Learn how to right a capsized canoe, sailing dinghy, etc.
33. Learn how to cross rivers safely.
34. Learn to abseil safely.
35. Learn how a car works and a simple fault-finding procedure.

INDEX

Trigger snare, 75

U
Unconscious casualty, 96, 97
Urine, 64, 107
Using a rope, 57–9

V
Vomiting, 106

W
Walking method, 173
Warmth, 21–4, 106
Watch cap, 126
Water, 63–7, 107, 127, 147
Waterproofs, 24
Water filters, 65, 151, 187
Water purification, 66, 151, 187
Water rationing, 63–4, 107, 148
Water sources, 148
Water substitutes, 64
Water survival, 103–8, 119
Wild animals, 15, 110
Windbreak, 138
Windchill, 23, 24, 143
Windchill chest, 144
Windproofs, 23–4
Wire saw, 128
Women as survivors, 12
Worms, 100
Woodland travel, 199
Wounds, 97

SURVIVAL – IMMEDIATE ACTIONS

1. Remove people from immediate danger, clear of water, avalanche, etc.

2. Render first aid. See below for priority order.

3. Stop, think and plan.

4. Start providing shelter – from wind, wet and cold.

5. Allocate jobs.

6. Put out markers, signalling devices, etc.

7. Find water and fuel.

8. Fix your position as accurately as possible.

9. Decide if, and when, you will send for help.

10. Continue all the above until found.

First Aid Priorities

Remember the key word CHASTE.

C   Choking/Cardiac. Get the casualty breathing and his heart beating as quickly as possible.

H   Haemorrhage. Stop major bleeding. Ignore minor cuts.

A   Aid. Get others to help you and, if possible, send for an ambulance.

S   Shock. Treat in the normal way.

T   Treatment. Deal with other injuries, e.g., fractures, burns, etc.

E   Emergency. The situation is one, so deal with it quickly and firmly.